Green Wars

Green Wars

*Conservation and Decolonization
in the Maya Forest*

———

Megan Ybarra

UNIVERSITY OF CALIFORNIA PRESS

University of California Press, one of the most distinguished university presses in the United States, enriches lives around the world by advancing scholarship in the humanities, social sciences, and natural sciences. Its activities are supported by the UC Press Foundation and by philanthropic contributions from individuals and institutions. For more information, visit www.ucpress.edu.

University of California Press
Oakland, California

Library of Congress Cataloging-in-Publication Data

Names: Ybarra, Megan, author.
Title: Green wars : conservation and decolonization in the Maya forest / Megan Ybarra.
Description: Oakland, California : University of California Press, [2018] | Includes bibliographical references and index. | Description based on print version record and CIP data provided by publisher; resource not viewed.
Identifiers: LCCN 2017031822 (print) | LCCN 2017034385 (ebook) | ISBN 9780520968035 (ebook) | ISBN 9780520295162 (cloth : alk. paper) | ISBN 9780520295186 (pbk. : alk. paper)
Subjects: LCSH: Kekchi Indians—Land tenure—Maya Forest. | Kekchi Indians—Legal status, laws, etc.—Maya Forest. | Q.eqchi. (Community : North)—Government relations—History. | Decolonization—Maya Forest. | Maya Forest—Conservation. | Natural resources—Maya Forest—Management.
Classification: LCC F1465.2.K5 (ebook) | LCC F1465.2.K5 Y33 2018 (print) | DDC 972.82/0049742—dc23
LC record available at https://lccn.loc.gov/2017031822

Manufactured in the United States of America

26 25 24 23 22 21 20 19 18
10 9 8 7 6 5 4 3 2 1

For my father, who taught me to never give up

CONTENTS

ACKNOWLEDGMENTS

When I was evacuated as the army rolled into my field site on my first day of a case study, I immediately called Russell, my *media naranja*. Russell knows enough about rural Guatemala and bureaucracies that he is the first person I ask for advice when I puzzle over the passive-aggressive politics of a meeting or gauge my own safety to ask uncomfortable questions in tense situations. Russell is the person who offers to bail me out of jail if I get arrested in a direct action, who doesn't complain but does carefully stack up the books strewn throughout the house into a towering pile on my desk, and who takes me on sunshine-filled outings to remind me that there is more to life than work. In more ways than I can count, this book is also his achievement.

My intellectual trajectory was shaped by the (then) new Latin American and Caribbean Studies program at New York University, where professors including Ada Ferrer and Mark Healey pushed me beyond Spanish-centric thinking and pointed toward other histories and future revolutions. At UC Berkeley, Keith Gilless was my touchstone who shifted seamlessly from Bayesian analysis to feminist epistemologies. I benefited from the time and intellectual engagement of Louise Fortmann, Jake Kosek, Don Moore, Nancy Peluso, and Isha Ray. Although he had already graduated, Aaron Bobrow-Strain was generous with important advice on job interviews and books proposals as well as reading drafts. I am also grateful to my fellow graduate students, who slogged through drafts that by all rights I should not have inflicted on them and taught me much about their own work along the way: Iván Arenas, Mez Baker, Jennifer Casolo, Catherine Corson, Juan Herrera, Tracey Osborne, Alice Kelly Pennaz (and Chufi), Mark Philbrick, Noer Fauzi Rachman, Jade Sasser, and Bhavna Shamasunder.

At Willamette University, I learned how to teach and how to take care of myself in a context of institutional racism. I learned from Nacho Córdova, although I still think of how much he had left to teach (and I to learn) after his untimely death. A few key colleagues taught me how to teach and how to hold my tongue (even though I still don't do it much!). They held me up when I was falling—my sincere gratitude to Mat Barreiro, Melissa Buis Michaux, and Jonneke Koomen. Above all, students at Willamette were a powerful reminder that the insular intellectual standards of the ivory tower are brittle and will crumble if they do not transform. I laughed, cried, and transformed thanks to Noor Amr, Elizabeth Calixtro, Octaviano Chavarín, Victor García, Genora Givens, María Hernández-Segoviano, Samantha Martinez, Delia Olmos-García, Isa Peña, Juan Ramos, Luz Reyna, Beatriz Sandoval, Martha Sonato, Taylor Wells, and Clarise Young.

There would be no book were it not for the support of colleagues at the University of Washington. Thanks to Eddy Sandoval for taking on the task of being my first graduate advisee and reminding me that transforming geography happens seminar by seminar, paper by paper. You deserve more, and we will forge it together—I promise. I have enjoyed working with folks in Gender, Women, and Sexuality Studies and Latin American and Caribbean Studies departments throughout all three campuses. Among them, I thank Sarah Dowling, Ben Gardner, Maria Elena Garcia, Tony Lucero, Chandan Reddy, and Ileana Rodríguez-Silva for their helpful reads of parts of the manuscript. My greatest thanks go to my "committee of no," who guided me on a path toward professional sanity: Sarah Elwood-Faustino, Lucy Jarosz, and Vicky Lawson. I am grateful for their support when I considered giving up on this book, their helpful read of too many drafts to count, and their advice on navigating the unsteady waters of academia.

I enjoyed institutional assistance and/or particularly helpful interviews from multiple park administrators and the National Council of Protected Areas (Consejo Nacional de Areas Protegidas, CONAP) offices, ADICI-Wakliqoo, APROBA-SANK, and the the National Coordinator of Peasant Organizations (Coordinadora Nacional de Organizaciones Campesinas); ACDIP (formerly COCIP-Petén); CONGCOOP-IDEAR; FONTIERRAS (the Guatemalan Land Fund); Fundación Lachuá; Fundación Talita Kumi; Mercy Corps; the Registro de Información Catastral; Procuraduría de Derechos Humanos in Alta Verapaz and Petén; ProPetén; Secretaría de Asuntos Agrarios in Guatemala City; Universidad de Rafael Landívar in Alta Verapaz; and Veterinarios Sin Fronteras. Within these institutions, a few people were particularly helpful in organizing my research: Juliana Aju, Alberto Alonso Fradejas, Guicho Coy, Silvel Elías, Byron Garoz, Klemen Gamboa, Mario López Barrientos, Peter Marchetti, and Helmer Velásquez. In 2007, I enjoyed research assistance in conducting household surveys from Gloria Sucely Pop Cucul, Aura Violeta Caal Jucub, and Olga Yoland Maquín. In 2009, despite flooding, famine, and *robaniño* scares, Oscar René Obando Samos led a team of intrepid surveyors throughout Petén: Nadia Marianela Canek Márquez, Leticia Iracema Carabeo Paz, Amanda Carías González, Melyn Emérita Argentina García Castellanos, Francisco Mariano Obando Requena, Manuel de Jesús Ochaeta Calderón, Ronal Francisco Roque Esquivel, and Anita del Carmen Sánchez Castellanos.

I had the opportunity to complement my fieldwork with a diverse collection of archival and library sources. At UC Berkeley, the Earth Sciences and Map Library offered a cornucopia of maps (including the map in Chapter 4), and the Bancroft Library held a wealth of regional historical documents. In Guatemala, I gratefully acknowledge the following institutions for their access and assistance: Ak' Kutan's library; Archivo General de Centro América; Biblioteca Nacional; Cobán's public library; Centro de Investigaciones Regionales de Mesoamérica's archives and library; the CONAP headquarters library; Committee for Peasant Unity (Comité de Unidad Campesina) files; the Cooperación Española library; FONTIERRAS in Guatemala, Chisec, Ixcán, Cobán, and Petén; the National Statistics Institute (Instituto Nacional de Estadística); Inforpress Centroamericana "Colección 30 Años"; the Ministry of Agriculture of Guatemala (Ministerio de Agricultura de Guatemala); ProPetén's information center; the General Property Register (Registro General de Propiedad); the Presidential Commission for the Resolution of Land Conflicts (Comisión Presidencial para la Resolución de Conflictos de Tierra); the Secretary of Planning and Programming of the Presidency (Secretaría de Planificación y Programación de la Presidencia) archives; and the University of Rafael Landívar Cobán library. All translations from the Spanish are mine, as is responsibility for any resulting errors.

Research for this book was funded by a National Science Foundation Graduate Research Fellowship and Doctoral Dissertation Research Improvement Grant, a University of California–Berkeley Summer Human Rights Fellowship, an American Association of University Women American Summer/Short-Term Writing Fellowship, and a University of Washington Simpson Center for the Humanities Society of Scholars Fellowship.

I owe some of the ideas, insights, and interventions that reshaped this project to those who hosted presentations over the years: UC Berkeley's Environmental Science, Policy & Management Department; the University of Washington Simpson Society of Scholars; the "Dangerous Subjects" Latin American and Caribbean Studies reading group at the University of Washington; the Center for Research on Latin America and the Caribbean/York University and Libby Lunstrum's grad seminar; the Centro Universitario Departamento de Petén (Universidad de San Carlos) and Amílcar Corzo's students; and Pablo Prado's gracious invitation to present my settler colonial critique to students at the University of San Carlos in Guatemala City. Those who were the toughest crowds gave me the greatest opportunity to improve the manuscript, and I thank them.

Whether over *cafecitos* or through e-mails, I have benefited from the insights and critiques of many fellow thinkers on Guatemala throughout the years, among them Alberto Alonso Fradejas, Amílcar Corzo, Julie Gibbings, Liza Grandia, David García, Kevin Gould, Ryan Isakson, Laura Hurtado Paz y Paz, Mario López Barrientos, Diane Nelson, Catherine Nolin, Oscar Obando Samos, Norman Schwartz, Luis Solano Ponciano, and Paula Worby. Many of my favorite conversations were those that I got to listen in on at Jennifer Casolo and Peter Marchetti's place, where all are welcome and thinking for social justice is the only requirement. In particular, Jenny's unfailing generosity, incredible academic rigor, and dedication to those she works with are a way of being that I aspire to.

I owe my greatest thanks to the people I worked with in lowlands field sites. For reasons of confidentiality and safety, I cannot acknowledge many of them. Rigoberto Baq Caal and Liliana Batz were excellent, patient Q'eqchi' teachers. Rigoberto schooled me on Q'eqchi' culture and politics, and Liliana carefully assisted me in transcribing and translating muddled fieldwork recordings. Many folks accepted me, explained things to me that I should have already known, and truly took care of me, especially Maria, Rosa, Sanché, Coca, Lupe, Bernardo, Mariano, Angelina, Carlos, Rudy, Xrut, and Rodrigo. Domingo Chub' and his family made me feel like I belonged even when I didn't. Coc Choc is one of my favorite "tribal elders." We may never agree, but Romeo Euler Pacay had a profound impact on my thoughts. There were a few people who made me laugh and cry, dream and despair, but most of all left me profoundly humbled: Bernardo Coc Chub', Héctor Asig, Ernesto Tz'i' Chub', and Marcos Toc Paau. *B'antyox eere, xineetenq'a xaq.*

This book was written on the territories of the Q'eqchi' Maya people, the Muwekma Ohlone Tribe, the Grande Ronde Confederated Tribe along their trail of tears, and the Duwamish Tribe of the Coast Salish people. I hope this book goes beyond acknowledging their histories and toward supporting their futures.

Introduction

Conservation and Settler Logics
of Elimination

THIS LAND IS MY LAND, THIS LAND IS YOUR PARK?

In 2008 against the advice of development professionals to choose a less "conflic-tive" community, I decided to live in and research a community located near Lake Lachuá National Park, which today spans almost 15,000 hectares. I partnered with a sustainable development consortium, which I call the "Project," that enjoyed sig-nificant international conservation funding for reforestation easements and pro-ductive cooperatives. Both the park and the multiuse buffer zone enjoy interna-tional recognition as a Ramsar wetlands site, conservation easement funding, and inclusion in climate mitigation through reforestation REDD[1] projects. My impres-sion of these projects was fundamentally shaken by a hostage standoff I witnessed my first day on site (an incident I return to in Chapter 2). Instead of learning about the benefits of community-based reforestation, my original research question, I sought to understand how and why these seemingly benevolent projects could lead to violence. I came to see that differential processes of ownership exclusion and inclusion played a major role.

While Project employees and documentation told me that nobody was excluded from forestry benefits, the land-titling archives told another story. In the archives I found the name of one community, Quixpur (pronounced "keesh-puur"), that had legal land titles in a core park area but no longer existed on the map. When I asked the project director if he would help me contact Quixpur leaders, he first quizzed me at length about how I discovered this community's existence and what I hoped to accomplish by meeting them. The director agreed to arrange the inter-view with Quixpur leaders but warned me that they might take me hostage. He first suggested that I summon them to the Project offices, but I demurred because there was no place where they could speak without being overheard. We compromised. A Project driver delivered a letter suggesting a neutral meeting place: not the Project's office but a building that Project employees have keys to so that I could not be held hostage (as happened to a park administrator in 2005). The building was a community cooperative; Quixpur families lived in this community but were not considered part of it. Instead, they were landless, did not participate in the cooperative or local governance structures, and were excluded from reforestation projects. I was not particularly concerned about my safety, as I had never heard of dispossessed communities physically harming administrators.

I arrived at the community center in a truck with a Project driver about an hour late, and the association building was empty. The Project employee asked if we should leave, and I told him to park in the shade and wait a few more minutes. I walked away from the truck on the dusty road in the suddenly empty town, trying to look as gringa—foreign, harmless, maybe a little naive—as possible. A man walked in my direction, nice and slow, so I said (in Q'eqchi'), "Hey, you wouldn't happen to be a Quixpur leader, would you?" He stopped, glanced sideways, and said, "I got your letter." After a long pause, I stumbled through an explanation of who I am and why I wanted to hear his community's history. He said that he would see if he could find some people to talk to me. I went back to casually hanging out, a gringa by herself in the scorching sun in front of a locked association building, for more than thirty minutes, assuring the driver at regular intervals that we would probably leave soon. Just as I thought I might actually give up and leave, I saw four, five, six, seven, and then eight men materialize, carrying time-worn envelopes full of documents that had been painstakingly protected from tropical weather over decades. Although our conversation started slowly in Q'eqchi', they mercifully switched to Spanish and told gentle jokes to put me at ease. I quickly understood that they would not take me hostage as long as I didn't join any park guard/police/military patrols of their land.

I was not afraid of them, but they were afraid of what I represented. Gringos seek to work in solidarity with Indigenous peoples, wielding their political power to change a settler system that demands their death, and simultaneously support land-extensive conservation that makes their life impossible. I argue below that the indigenous right to life has no role in this kind of conservation, and I use the analytic of green wars to describe how conservation practice maps criminality onto rural Q'eqchi's and legitimates state violence. In this, I call attention to the ways that state violence works through both structural impoverishment and spectacle violence to sever Indigenous peoples from their land.

At the same time, Q'eqchi's seek the promise of gringo solidarity for survival as a people: the repatriation of land and life (Tuck and Yang, 2012). In an international conservation project that does not speak their language or respect their lived experience, these men present receipts, legal documents, and maps to anyone who might legitimate them. Their experience rests on a struggle that stretches over decades of violence, both threatened and realized, in which the military repeatedly dispossesses them of their land. Whereas many communities have only their lived experiences to rely on, Quixpur leaders showed me many documents that the National Institute of Agrarian Transformation (Instituto para la Transformación Agraria, INTA), the state land agency, had made to map out their community boundaries, which predated Lake Lachuá National Park. Even more unusual, community members paid taxes on their land and had receipts dating back to the early 1970s to prove it. When the land-titling agency first contemplated a park in the 1970s, Quixpur—a dispersed community consisting of Q'eqchi' homesteaders who practiced swidden agriculture[2] but also had cardamom plants and cattle pastures—was one of several communities that had legally recognized property rights. These are particularly important because they demonstrate investment in private property in the eyes of the liberal capitalist state. In the late 1970s, military officials and foresters arrived in Quixpur and told residents that they had to move outside the park's boundaries. When I asked how the park was explained to them, Quixpur leaders said they were told that "this is a place for animals, not people."[3] While they vociferously challenge this framework today, they did not during the 1970s. This is because Guatemala was at the height of a violent civil war (1960–1996), and challenging military officials easily led to violent death.

So, the community of Quixpur moved and built new homes, planted new crops and pastures, and completed the required down payment to receive state recognition in a "colonization zone." In return, the INTA issued them a provisional land title; they still have the original, and the copy in INTA archives was how I discovered them.[4] During the early 1980s, military officials told Quixpur residents that they had to leave their rural community for a more central village in order to prove that they were not "subversives"[5] hiding out in the jungle. Quixpur residents moved to this central village, where they still live today, but many continued to harvest crops on their land within the park, especially cardamom. They all considered themselves owners of Quixpur, and they have an uneasy relationship with the community they live in; likewise, community leaders would rather not host Quixpur "troublemakers." In the 1980s, a military cartographer came through. Quixpur leaders remember his promise that their lands would be outside the park; instead, he mapped their land inside the newly expanded park boundaries (see Figure 3 in Chapter 2). It is from this point on, they say, that they had no home they could legally return to. This is how state and nonstate conservation agencies could reframe war survivors as migrants on their own land (see Chapter 2).

By the mid-1980s, the army encouraged many people to return to their homes in the civil war demobilization. When Quixpur residents attempted to return home, however, they discovered that their interpellated identities had morphed from civil war "subversives" to "park invaders." While the park system acknowledges the community's legally recognized land rights, it asserts the primacy of its claim to administer the land in the name of the nation. Quixpur leaders say that both park and Project administrators lied repeatedly. Among other things, Quixpur leaders showed me signed copies of agreements with a National Council of Protected Areas (Consejo Nacional de Areas Protegidas, CONAP) representative that indicated they would receive titles to their land and that it would be excluded from the first 2000–2001 park measurements.[6] In a 2008 interview, a CONAP representative denied that the agency owes people compensation for the land, even as he acknowledged that they had legal title.

In the late 1990s, park and military officials began arresting people who were supposedly harming the land—a political forest that existed by decree if not in terms of trees—by, for example, harvesting cardamom crops in farm plots. Although international and national designations labeled these as core protected areas, they were working lands. In response, Quixpur residents have taken park officials hostage, burned down a building for ecotourism activities, and repeatedly stated that they will only abandon their land when the park officials kill them. These statements are poignant in both their emotion and their stark evocation of unequal power relations: land activists do not threaten others with death but assert that they are willing to be killed for their land. If land activists go to jail, bail is often higher than what a local nongovernmental organization (NGO) worker makes in one month—significantly more than a landless farmer can pay. In tracing historical continuities in standoffs between land activists and state officials, however, it becomes clear that activists' fears have deeper roots than contemporary law and order.

Park officials, in tandem with the military, utilize scorched-earth tactics from counterinsurgency campaigns. Scorched earth generally refers to harsh, take-no-prisoners counterinsurgency that characterized collaborations between the U.S. and Latin American militaries during the Cold War (Danner, 1994; LaFeber, 1993). As during the war, state officials repeatedly burn down cardamom plants, swiddens (both fallows and active plots used for maize, beans, and other food crops), cattle pastures, and any homes that Quixpur residents attempt to rebuild. During the civil war, there were over 400 documented village massacres in a country the size of Tennessee: mass killing, displacement of survivors, and burning of all crops, legal documentation, and homes. Since the 1996 Guatemalan Peace Accords, Quixpur has been in multiple hostage standoffs with park officials and police. While Project and park officials suffered significant distress from being held hostage for an hour to two days (see Chapter 2), community members have been fined, jailed, and even shot.

When I asked conservation professionals about these repeated rights standoffs, they said that it was a problem of social marginality rooted in poverty. When I asked Quixpur leaders, they told me it was racism. They asserted that the army only could evict them from their land in the first place because they are Q'eqchi' and specifically because they could not read or write Spanish. They did not speak the state's language, and so they could not claim their rights (provisional titles and paid taxes notwithstanding). Nonetheless, Quixpur leaders insisted that their dispossession was temporary and only became permanent when the military and conservation big international nongovernmental organizations (BINGOs) expanded the park and hired guards at the end of the civil war. When I asked about the possibility of reparations, Quixpur leaders flatly rejected financial compensation. They said that as long as they survive, the land is theirs.

This book does not attempt to resolve the case of Quixpur and instead makes a broader claim about the relationship between postwar law enforcement and Indigenous land activism. In the context of conservation and the wartime laws that created the protected-areas system for the Maya Forest, the fact that communities such as Quixpur have state records of their settlements, maps, provisional titles, blueprints, and even signed agreements with CONAP simply does not matter. Under protected-areas management, park officials have decided that no communities can live in core protected areas, and no communities are eligible for reparations. They have no right to their homeland or to any payments for environmental services from that land.

There was a key disjuncture between the meaning of land for the Q'eqchi' Maya community and for urban conservation and development professionals. Whereas for conservation professionals land was a source of possible conservation, housing, and ecotourism revenues, for Quixpur leaders land is more than a resource. In effect, they rejected the premise that they would cede land control for a social wage, such as financial compensation or a basic income grant (Ferguson, 2015; Hart, 2002). They take hostages not to enact harm or to ask for a seat at the negotiating table but instead to demonstrate that a project premised on taking land is not negotiable.

Q'eqchi' leaders do not accept that their ties to the land have been severed and that land is commodified. They seek survival as a people, and indigenous survival requires land. I use the term *land* here as is common in both the Q'eqchi' language and indigenous studies (Deloria and Wildcat, 2001), referring to land, water, air, subsoil, and caves. While this is related to the ways the political geography literature describes territorialization, it does not share the roots of *terroir* (Elden, 2009) and the notion that people are the only being with agency who can make rules about property relations (Agnew, 2003). Indigenous calls for decolonization demand a rethinking of people to the land, one of mutual human/land recognition. When I write about Q'eqchi' territoriality, I am also invoking a collective identity that Tuck and McKenzie (2016, 56) explain as "land is, therefore we are" (see also Bang et al., 2010). In Q'eqchi' ontologies, then, there is no amount of incentive, compensation, or social wage that can substitute for the land. Rather, the land constitutes their life chances as a people.

This book critiques the ways Guatemalan and international conservation organizations have rationalized their indifference toward Indigenous war survivors' land claims by criminalizing them as kidnappers, park invaders, and drug traffickers. This is in stark contrast to influential ethnographies that posit the limits of Maya self-determination in the neoliberal state's choice to recognize them—or not—as multicultural subjects (Hale, 2002; Wainwright and Bryan, 2009). Instead, I argue that conservation is a global project that authorizes violence in protected areas, which I call "green wars." In so doing, I evoke the longer arc of social wars—particularly the Cold War and the drug war—that map criminality onto entire peoples and authorize violence against them. Green wars limit the life chances of Indigenous peoples[7] in protected areas through their legal dispossession, denial of basic state services (such as running water, electricity, and schools), explicit military dispossession, and tacit sanctioning of private violence against "conflictive" communities.

Beginning in the 1980s, the tropical lowlands have come to be known as the Maya Forest, which must be conserved. At the same time, civil war survivors who were known as land-poor peasants are coming to call themselves Maya peoples. Today, the fight to save the Maya Forest is often waged against Maya peoples. This is only possible because state and nonstate conservation professionals interpellate Q'eqchi's as immigrants without historical ties to any land. I begin by briefly sketching Guatemala's civil war and the struggles over memory, names, and material stakes that emerged at the end of the war. Was the war about land, labor, or democracy? In the wake of United Nations (UN) determination that the military state committed genocide, are land reparations needed? If the state participated in genocide, when did genocide begin, and when did it end? Rather than restricting genocide to two distinct moments—500 years ago and the height of the civil war in the early 1980s—Indigenous land activists claim that the settler state has long been in the making, no less powerful in each iteration. In claiming the civil war as part of a longer racial project to erase Maya peoples from the Guatemalan nation, Indigenous activists called the legitimacy of the state and its *ladino* leaders into question.

I then turn to the role of territory in reworking the postcolonial, postwar state. I trace how the military state justified its intervention in the lowlands, first by taming the dangerous jungle for intrepid settlers and then by claiming that it was the protector needed to save the endangered Maya Forest. While it was primarily foreign scientists and archaeologists who envisioned the value of the Maya Forest (including naming it), the state collaborated to create protected areas as a source of income and to legitimate its claims to territory. I then explain the analytic of racialized dispossession and how this racial project works to undermine Maya territoriality by framing Q'eqchi' Mayas as little more than a needy, conflictive ethnic minority rather than an Indigenous people with territorial rights. Finally, I trace how narco-narratives articulate with racialized dispossession to authorize violence in the name of conservation: green wars. Even as the settler state subjects

Q'eqchi's to individualization and criminalization, they seek material decolonization and relationships of repair with both other peoples and the land.

IS GENOCIDE LIMITED TO GUATEMALA'S CIVIL WAR?

The creation of a protected-areas system was only possible in the midst of a civil
war with the fate of the countryside at its core, a war so violent and one-sided that
survivors were afraid to speak up for decades. A political movement for land
throughout the country emerged in the ten years of "spring" (1944–1954) when
democratically elected presidents addressed massive inequality. In the 1950s, President Jacobo Arbenz announced a sweeping agrarian reform in which the state
expropriated land from unused plantations.[8] Arbenz said that the state would pay
landowners according to the value claimed when they filed their taxes. Transnational corporations (including the United Fruit Company) and plantation owners
protested that their land was worth much more than they claimed on their tax
returns, tacitly acknowledging their tax evasion. As land reform gave to the poor
and slowly reimbursed the rich, U.S. State Department fears of spreading communism coalesced with U.S. capitalist interests in banana plantations and potential oil
production (Gleijeses, 1991; Solano Ponciano, 2005). In 1954, the U.S. Central
Intelligence Agency supported a coup d'état with a Guatemalan military dictator
who immediately rescinded the agrarian reform. The civil war officially began
when Marxist guerrillas challenged the military dictatorship.[9] Both inside and
outside Guatemala, civil war in the 1960s and 1970s was understood as a battle
between military dictators who supported capitalism and Marxist guerrillas who
tried to foment peasant revolution in the countryside. During this phase of the war
censorship and political murder were common, but massacres were not.

By the late 1970s, however, counterinsurgency shifted from targeted killings to
mass genocide. A key turning point was the 1978 military massacre of rural
Q'eqchi's who were marching for their land rights. While Greg Grandin (2004)
called this the country's "last colonial massacre," Guatemala's present-day colonial
project requires repeated violence to prevent Mayas from reclaiming the land that
was taken from them.[10] The military and paramilitaries committed large-scale
massacres that targeted the rural poor, Catholics who might have been influenced
by liberation theology (privileging the poor and empowering laity to interpret the
Bible were seen as potentially subversive), and people with Maya signifiers (phe-
notype, language, and dress). In a country with at most a few thousand guerrillas
by the military's own estimation, over 200,000 people were killed or disappeared,
and over 1 million were internally displaced from their homes for months or years.
Those killed and displaced were disproportionately Maya. One Q'eqchi' massacre
survivor (who heard his mother and sisters die violent deaths at the military's hand
when he was just six years old) told me that of his belief that targeted political

violence of *ladinos* demonstrates that *ladino* lives have value, whereas mass murder demonstrates that Q'eqchi' lives did not have value. Civil war violence peaked in the late 1980s, at which point the military declared success and demarcated the conditions for peace (Schirmer, 1998).

It was not until the 1990s that the UN successfully brokered peace processes between military and guerrilla leaders. The military and guerrilla representatives were beginning to negotiate for an end to ideological war, so it was a shock for them when Maya peoples took to the streets. Pan-Maya activists claimed that their loved ones were killed not due to Marxist ideologies but instead because of state racism. This is important, because "Maya" is *not* a "minority" category in terms of population. Demetrio Cojtí Cuxil (1992, 2007) is prominent among Maya scholars who demonstrate that the official census systematically undercounts Maya peoples.[11] He and others argue that this is because Maya peoples are probably 60 percent of the population. The application of the term *minority* naturalizes the massive underrepresentation that Indigenous peoples suffer in access to education, health care, and the country's wealth. Likewise, the term naturalizes the ways that one group, *ladinos,* dominate state institutions and purport to represent the national body politic.

The UN-sponsored Commission for Historical Clarification (Comisión para el Esclarecimiento Histórico) condemned as genocide the systematic killing of Maya peoples and policies to destroy their culture and way of life (CEH, 1999). Nonindigenous guerrillas felt betrayed by comrades in struggle (*compas* in Spanish) who alienated them by referring to them as colonial invaders (*kaxlan* in Q'eqchi'). These fissures were mirrored in the formation of a separate representative for Indigenous peoples in the peace negotiations and the splinter of peasant organizations. While many Pan-Maya activists and intellectuals have worked with and/or consider themselves Marxian thinkers, others critique the ways that class-based guerrilla recruitment hailed them as revolutionary subjects and then abandoned them to murder (Bastos and Camus, 2003; Cojtí Cuxil, 1997; Konefal, 2010; Warren, 1998a; Ybarra, 2013). Pan-Maya activists used the peace accords process as a forum to claim that the war was just the latest iteration of colonialism, beyond a three-decade struggle against capitalism. In this interpretation, military massacres of Maya villages were acts of genocide that followed a pattern of five centuries.

Across the Americas, the 1992 celebration of Christopher Columbus's supposed discovery of the Americas was an opportunity to call into question the erasure of genocide. Against a tide of politically correct claims of an "encounter," Indigenous activists condemned Columbus Day as a celebration of violent invasion. Indigenous peoples in Latin America likewise condemned Spanish speakers' celebration of Columbus Day as *día de la raza* (day of the race) because it privileges the mixing of Indigenous and Spanish peoples, claiming that all citizens have a common mixed heritage (mestizo). Indigenous peoples took to the streets to proclaim their place in the future, rejecting their relegation to the past as keepers of colorful folklore and "ancient" languages.[12] In recognition of Indigenous peoples' calls to rethink colonialism as central to the histories of the Americas, the 1992 Nobel committee awarded Rigoberta Menchú Tum the Peace Prize. Rigoberta Menchú is a K'iche' Maya who became an international celebrity after she fled military violence, calling for U.S. solidarity and activism against military repression. Her work became emblematic of the Pan-Maya movement, which calls for accountability for racial violence committed in the civil war and seeks to recuperate indigenous identity after centuries of genocide. Maya land activists argue that they cannot recuperate their identity without their land.

SETTLER COLONIALISM: GENOCIDE AS A TERRITORIAL PROJECT

While many people think that genocide is limited to physical massacres of a racialized group, the legal definition includes forcibly taking children, preventing births, causing mental harms, and inflicting conditions that bring about a social group's destruction (Article II, Rome Statute of the International Criminal Court). I argue that settler-state subjections that sever Q'eqchi's from the land constitute such a harm. According to Wolfe (2008, 108), "settler colonialism is an inclusive, land-centered project that coordinates a comprehensive range of agencies, from the metropolitan center to the frontier encampment, with a view to eliminating Indigenous societies." Just as colonialism is not a singular event that occurred when Germans appropriated Q'eqchi' territory in the nineteenth century, settler colonialism is invented and reworked every time the settler state weaves indigenous extinction into the workings of contemporary property structures, the rule of law, and everyday life. When Guatemalan conservation practitioners express sympathy for the plight of Indigenous land activists but tell me that considering changes to protected-area laws is "impractical," they are signaling that the Maya right to life is not possible in the contemporary settler state.

Scholars critique settler colonialism in the context of how British settlers created societies that were predicated on logics of native elimination in the United States, Canada, New Zealand, and Australia. Rather than a historical moment of indigenous elimination for settler life, settler logics of elimination are at the foundation of political-economic structures and can help scholars and activists alike understand why these countries voted against the UN Declaration on the Rights of Indigenous and Tribal Peoples or recognize indigenous territorial rights that are not contingent on settler benevolence.

The first prominent volume examining settler colonialism, *Unsettling Settler Societies* (Stasiulis and Yuval-Davis, 1995), was not limited to British colonialism and instead included case studies ranging from Palestine to Mexico. Latin Americanist scholars need not privilege Anglo colonial powers with the exceptional ability to impose a settler colonial project. In recent years, scholars have been delving into the nuances of settler colonialism in the Americas, including Saldaña-Portillo's (2015) pathbreaking book on formations in Mexico and the United States and a forthcoming special issue on settler colonialism in latin america in *American Quarterly* (Bianet Castellanos, in press; Loperena, in press; Speed, in press). This book does not argue that Spanish colonialism is settler colonialism. Rather, post-Hispanic independence and debates over the national body politic clearly reject Spanish colonialism while using debates over racial purity and disappearing natives to forge a new settler state (see also Gott, 2007). More than traces of Spanish colonial discourses, the materiality of Q'eqchi' moves to decolonization can only be understood in the context of the present-day settler state. I draw on settler logics of elimination to explain the military state's efforts to colonize the lowlands in the mid-twentieth century as well as subsequent claims that Maya peoples are invaders in the Maya Forest. My use of a settler colonial analysis is informed by Q'eqchi' land activists' speeches that date their dispossession back 200 years, to the liberal nineteenth century, when Spanish-descended elites wrote settler logics of elimination into land allocations to entice West European settlement (Casaús Arzú, 2010; McCreery, 1994; Wagner, 2001). Many Q'eqchi's suffered their first land dispossession in the nineteenth century when the new Guatemalan state took their territory and gave it to Germans for coffee plantations. Q'eqchi's were then forced to labor on their own land.

During World War II, the Guatemalan military expropriated lands from supposed German Nazis. Rather than return these lands to their rightful owners, the military state declared these and the rest of the lowlands *terra nullius,* an empty frontier to be populated with loyal citizens. Even though Q'eqchi's were often living on the land and investing their labor to improve it, state agencies wanted them to continue working for low wages on someone else's plantation. Nonetheless, with the exception of a few politically important cooperatives (e.g., Falla, 1993; Manz, 1988), Q'eqchi's were major participants in militarized colonization of the lowlands. When Q'eqchi's did not settle the land in centralized villages or farm according to central planners' dictates, the military increasingly imagined them as unruly and unknown subjects on the frontier. In military logics of elimination, the body politic *includes* loyal capitalist citizens who learn Spanish and improve the nation, while it *excludes* disloyal citizens who do not speak Spanish, make claims that the state should change its rule of law (to reflect indigenous conceptions of justice or property), and value reciprocal relationships over capitalist markets. This is part of a broader Latin American move toward liberal dominance and a politics of racial whitening after independence from the Spanish (Gordillo, 2004; Mollett, 2016).

By the mid-1970s, military planners marked large swaths of land encompassing many villages as "red" for elimination, killing off all people, livestock, and crops (Black, 1984; Huet, 2008; Schirmer, 1998).[13] Military and paramilitary scorched-earth massacres sent families into hiding, where they lived in the jungle for days, months, or even years. The military forcibly recruited boys and men into paramilitary patrols tasked with hunting their neighbors down in the jungle. Paramilitary leaders ruled over villages with iron fists (and the only guns in town), and people were forced to live in close quarters in densely designed model villages, where they were encouraged to spy and report on each other to authorities. In the same way that Rifkin (2009, 94) argues that a brutal "sovereign violence" was necessary for the "(re)production and naturalization of national space" in the U.S. Western frontier, military violence at once sited the jungle as a frontier and incorporated it into the Guatemalan nation. While civil war violence in Chile, Argentina, and Brazil relied on the violent spectacle of thousands but many survived their torture as a warning to others, Guatemala's military and paramilitary forces committed mass killings that numbered into the hundreds of thousands, taking on a distinctly genocidal character (Grandin, 2005; Menjívar and Rodriguez, 2005; Taylor, 1997).

Whereas the military framed the lowlands as a dangerous jungle filled with subversives in the 1970s and 1980s, state planners and international conservation BINGOs saw a tropical forest beginning in the 1980s. Even though these imaginaries seem disparate and are rarely acknowledged in the same forum, they articulate in today's green wars to legitimate violent dispossession. At first, the military state drew on settler logics of elimination to rationalize successive military campaigns. While the original intent of those campaigns was to incorporate the lowlands into a national civilizing project, conservation interests beginning in the 1970s led to a reimagination of the lowlands as the "wilderness," leaving the highlands as a site of "civilization." The community described at the beginning of this chapter was effectively written out of military narratives and erased from conservation maps before its members could move back home. While conservation BINGOs did not call for violence, their forest imaginaries were predicated on state violence that makes Q'eqchi' territoriality unthinkable.

FROM UNTAMED JUNGLE TO MAYA FOREST

This book brings together settler colonialism's emphasis on the relationship between logics of extinction and land expropriation and on political ecology's concern for the creation of protected areas as primitive accumulation, whereas British colonies in America and Africa share a history of creating parks to preserve wilderness and create elite hunting reserves. It is for this reason that the U.S. model of imagining the relationship between an urbanized civilization in contrast with the preserved wilderness, known as the Yellowstone model, is paradigmatic for how it enacts violent land expropriation while denying the capability of Indigenous peoples to understand property relations (Brockington, Duffy, and Igoe, 2008; Cronon, 1983; Dowie, 2011; Jacoby, 2001; Rifkin, 2009). The importance of fortress conservation in protecting keystone species, fostering national pride, and fund-raising has been absorbed by conservation organizations, with key personnel trained and based in the United States. These assumptions do not hold for former Spanish colonies, which mostly created national parks in a context of overlapping property rights in the twentieth century (Brockington et al., 2008; Wakild, 2011).

Beginning in the 1970s, BINGOs focusing on conservation, notably the World Wild Fund for Nature and the Nature Conservancy, began replicating the U.S. model in poor postcolonial countries. Subsequent decades witnessed the creation of a new environmental paradigm that rapidly progressed from documenting deforestation crises to creating the subdiscipline of conservation biology based on the urgent need to protect nature, today called biodiversity (Farnham, 2007). By the late 1980s, a Conservation International (CI) scientist proposed that conservation efforts concentrate on areas of high biodiversity that were endangered by logging and "shifting cultivation," referring to swidden agriculture (e.g., Myers, 1988). Conservation BINGOs participated in planning the Maya Forest, which was the centerpiece of a new national protected-areas system in Guatemala in 1990. By the late 1990s, CI focused its fund-raising and advocacy efforts around "biodiversity hotspots" (Mittermeier et al., 1998), of which the Maya Forest was the third largest in landmass.

The Maya Forest is comprised of Belize, Mexico's southeastern coast, and Guatemala's northern lowlands (Figure 1). Conservation biologists, archaeologists, and ecotourism operators focus on the similarities of the region in terms of contiguous habitat for fauna and flora, pre-Columbian archaeological sites, and adventure opportunities (Nations, 2006), but these countries have distinct historical and political trajectories. In 1981, Belize both became an independent nation and created its national park system, which today encompasses one-fifth of the nation's territory and is the foundation of a strong tourism industry.[14] The Mexican Maya Forest includes areas with high concentrations of poverty and Indigenous peoples. In 1978, the central Mexican government created the Montes Azules reserve, which U.S.- and UK-based conservationists argued only the Lacandón Mayas could lay claim to (Nations and Nigh, 1978), thus delegitimizing Tzeltal and Chol Indigenous land claims. By 1994, the Zapatista Army of National Liberation criticized the Mexican government's cooperation with international interests (corporate and conservation) to dispossess non-Lacandón Indigenous peoples (Harvey, 2001). While these three nations are distinct in terms of politics, history, and ethnicities, each nation-state manages protected areas in the face of Mayan demands for self-determination.

For its part, the Guatemalan government actively promoted homesteading in the northern lowlands beginning in the late 1950s, where landless settlers could become farmers and plantation owners through the state land-titling program.[15] In 1990, state priorities made an abrupt about-face when the legislature created a national protected-areas system that encompasses more than one-third of the

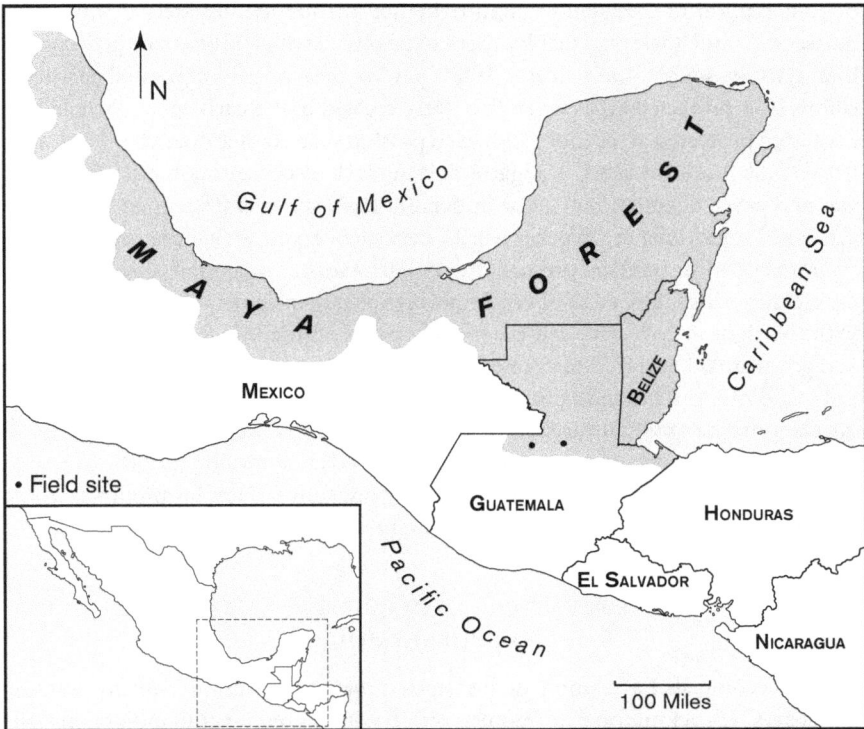

FIGURE 1. Extent of the Maya Forest, based on the Nature Conservancy and Conservation International promotional materials. (Blackmer Maps)

nation's territory. As it had been during the war, land was a central issue during the 1994–1996 Guatemalan Peace Accords negotiations. This final set of negotiations took as a given that fully one-third of national territory had conservation as its primary purpose, trumping claims to indigenous and agrarian land justice. Thus, the peace accords were restricted to debates over how to manage property in and reparations for the remaining two-thirds of the nation's territory.

In Guatemala's Maya Forest, more than two-thirds of the Alta Verapaz and Petén Departments have some protected-area status that requires land-use restrictions. The problems facing the displaced community I described earlier are all too common, as Q'eqchi's are the majority population living in the Maya Forest. Wilson (1995) estimates that more than 80 percent of Q'eqchi's in Alta Verapaz were displaced during the late 1970s and early 1980s; there are no comparative figures for Petén, as these are typically assumed to be "immigrants" irrespective of military violence. Many people were uprooted and hid in the jungle for years, many lost documentation of their land tenure (whether abandoned, molded, or burned in massacres), and it was unusual for them to negotiate with a militarized government that actively sought their death. While few people openly contested territorial claims over protected areas when they were created in the early 1990s, people have contested protected areas more with each passing year. Rather than view land activists as new "park invaders," I suggest that the lack of contestation during the civil war and peace negotiations can be understood as a survival strategy in the wake of racialized state violence. In other words, past silence was not acquiescence.

In the postwar political project, the civilian state has imagined Maya peoples as ethnic minorities in need of liberal benevolence rather than as Indigenous peoples with the right to collective self-determination as ethnic minorities. What the liberal government and military state stole collectively—land—they now reserve the right to allot on an individualized basis using conditions they declare. This bestows on the postwar multicultural state a claim to benevolence for the global good, whereby Q'eqchi's are at best supplicants with needs that may be subordinate to the need to save the Maya Forest. At worst, they are subversives, immigrants, wood-eating termites who deforest the land thoughtlessly, invaders, and even narcos.

CONSERVATION'S ROLE IN RACIALIZED DISPOSSESSION

Political ecologists have amply demonstrated that conservation leads to "winners and losers" (Brockington et al., 2008), with the losers often rural, indigenous, and poor. Lowland Q'eqchi's' territorial relationships have been punctuated with struggles against dispossession—against the Spanish, then the Germans, then military officers, and now transnational capitalist speculators (Solano Ponciano, 2013). Marxian analysis often frames dispossession as primitive accumulation, or a process that separates farmers from their land, often in repeated historical processes (De Angelis, 2001; Kelly, 2011; Perelman, 2000). While some political ecologists use the term "land grabbing" to explain large-scale land transactions that dispossess rural farmers (Alonso-Fradejas, 2012; Borras et al., 2012; Borras et al., 2011; Fairhead, Leach, and Scoones, 2012), others emphasize sedimented histories in land dispossession (Grandia, 2012; Mollett, 2016; Sundberg, 1999; Wainwright, 2008). Beyond capital accumulation, the conservation of protected areas begins with the settler's wilderness imaginary. Protected areas rest on sedimented histories of settler colonialism that prefigure the death of the indigene from whom we inherit the land (Saldaña-Portillo, 2015; Tuck and Yang, 2012).

While Marxian analysis of repeated capitalist dispossession as primitive accumulation is an important critique of capitalism as imperialism, it does not fully capture the noncapitalist ontology of territory as identity (Coulthard, 2010). Many Q'eqchi' communities understand their spiritual relationship with the land as more important than (or encompassing) their productive farming relationships. Q'eqchi's see the land as part of the *tzuultaq'a*, the spirit that grants them permission to work the land and live from its bounty. In so doing, the *tzuultaq'a* affirms their indigenous identity. Thus, processes of repeated dispossession work to alienate communities from their affirmative Q'eqchi' identity and produce a negative identity: native in opposition to the dominant settler society.

A central claim of my work is that Guatemala's protected-areas system employs a settler logic of elimination (Wolfe, 2008). This indigenous studies analytic is a way to think about settler colonialism as a geographic imaginary (Gregory, 2004; Said, 1978), a territorial project that changes even as it reproduces a vision of the native's elimination. Transnational indigenous studies scholars have critiqued the ways that Western rule of law effaces and elides accountability to its own commitments in international treaties and national peace accords. At the heart of liberal (mis)recognition of Indigenous peoples are two foundational notions: individual citizenship rights and group ethnicity needs.

First, liberal nation-states are founded on a notional relationship between individual citizens and the nation as imagined community (Anderson, 1991). Rather than individual rights, however, Indigenous peoples often focus on the needs of the entire body politic for political survival. For Q'eqchi' Mayas, justice is not about individuals being treated the same under a universal rule of law but instead is about honoring relationships with territory (*tzuultaq'a*), family, and community (Grünberg, 2003). Whereas some liberal and critical race frameworks argue that a history of oppression and marginality demands action in order to ensure equal protection, this critique still imagines the unit of analysis as the individual, a vision too narrow to encompass indigenous rights to collective self-determination.

Second, the multicultural liberal state seeks to racialize Indigenous peoples as one of many competing minority groups in need. Saldaña-Portillo (2015, 124–125) notes that Mexican elites "privileged abstract principles of citizenship, in the process reducing indigenous difference to an ethnic variation within Mexican character. But indigenous identity was produced and reproduced through specific modes of indigenous territoriality, through punctual uses of space sanctioned, in whatever abridged form, under Spanish dominion." Her intervention is salutary in that it does not privilege Anglo countries as the site of liberalism and shows how liberal models of nominally universal citizenship work to make this impossible for all but a propertied "white" man (see also Appelbaum, Macpherson, and Rosemblatt, 2003; Silva, 2007). Rather than disputing liberal frameworks of deserving/undeserving poor, Saldaña-Portillo reminds us that indigenous difference is manifest in spatial practice, including conceptions of property relations.

Racial liberalism not only articulates race, class, and religion in state subjections (Pulido, 2016; Ranganathan, 2016; Silva, 2007) but also subsumes indigenous collectives in logics of individual rights and needs. In the linked projects of militarization and conservation, the divide between individual and collective property marks *ladino* and Maya identities in a manner similar to that of racialized identities under allotment and reservations in U.S. settler colonialism.[16] In racializing Indigenous peoples, the liberal state refuses to acknowledge how identity is articulated through a relationship to land. Rather than imagine a carceral native who must be sedentary to be authentic, I mean that Indigenous peoples have ontologies that are distinct from Western ontologies and thus the rule of law; they have a different relationship to national time and space (Povinelli, 2002, 48). This relationship means that the Guatemalan state's inscription of territory into a national registry, as though it were newly created, is an act of epistemic violence. Rather than understanding how peoples' identities are defined in dialogue with place, the liberal state's racialization of Maya peoples as a minority group works to dispossess them.

The contemporary Maya Forest allows for multiple property regimes: state-owned protected areas, community-owned forestry cooperatives, and privatized landownership. This precludes the possibility of collective self-determination through territorial management. While many Indigenous people make claims on war reparations as individuals (for the loss of loved ones and land) and seek development assistance (*tenq'*, or "help"), they know that this framework recognizes them on the basis of their need and marginality and that development's trusteeship reproduces unequal power relations. Indigenous peoples may decide to participate in discursive frameworks that frame them as people to be pitied, but they may simultaneously invoke sovereignty as a positive assertion of rights claims and entitlements (Kauanui, 2008). This is not an either/or relationship to liberal states but rather a both/and relationship: Q'eqchi's accept liberal recognition as individuals and know themselves as a people. Some Q'eqchi' organizations work through current legal structures for their own ends in search of collective self-determination (see Chapter 4).

I draw on three key strands of thought to understand how conservation conflicts have normalized this level of crisis: postcoloniality, feminist political ecology, and indigenous studies. While many Latin Americanists have an ambivalent relationship with the postcolonial literature due to its spatial-temporal orientation toward post–World War II Africa (Coronil, 2008), a postcolonial critique of Occidentalism (defining the West in opposition to its Other) is helpful in letting go of the obsession with bureaucratic rationalities of capitalism or looking for the "success"/"failure" of states that haunts much of the development literature. My use of postcolonial theory draws more on works that emphasize the material implications of racial geographies than those that have a philosophical approach to decoloniality that dates to the Frankfurt School (e.g., Dussell, 1995; Mignolo, 2007; Moraña, Dussel, and Jáuregui, 2008). Postcolonial thought offers significant insights into how the national body politic is read as a racial body, one that is weak in the face of threats to the fragile racial supremacy project (Coronil, 1997; Coronil and Skurski, 2006b; Saldaña-Portillo, 2015; Silva, 2007). At the same time I read the Guatemalan national project as weak, because it is premised on the notion of a supposedly universal *ladino* settler state. From the perspective of lowland Q'eqchi's who suffer its violence, the settler state seems strong indeed. One of the goals of this ethnographic project is to explain why the same state practices seem weak from the point of view of settlers vulnerable to decolonization and strong from the point of view of Indigenous peoples subject to state violence.

Feminist political ecology offers a way to think through power relations in ethnographies of nature and conservation, particularly those that continue to grapple with the interpellation of those considered less than human. In this, I draw on the ideas of Caroline Faria and Sharlene Mollett as well as Andrea Nightingale and Juanita Sundberg in looking at power relations in nature imaginaries. White wilderness fantasies at once instantiate whiteness and masculinity (Cronon, 1995a; Kosek, 2006). Feminist political ecologists have called attention to the ways that our identities shape access and the ways that we are recognized as gendered and racialized subjects in ethnographic exchanges (Mollett and Faria, 2013; Sundberg, 2003b, 2005). In making claims about my relationship to indigeneity, land, and conservation practice, research participants were explaining their understanding of these themes and how they relate to them through difference. Even as I honor these differences, I focus on what the settler state is stealing from Q'eqchi's, both spiritually and materially. To do so, situated knowledges require us to question both what nature is (ontology) and how we can come to know it (epistemology). Following Andrea Nightingale (2003, 2016), I employ epistemological pluralism. Rather than triangulate data for complementarity, I look for divergence. It is when our results diverge that we are challenged to think of new explanations. This framework is best applied when thinking through axes of human difference in nature-society relations, even as it highlights the material urgency of the ontological underpinnings of more than human relations among peoples who have been denigrated as less than human (Pellow, 2016; Sundberg, 2014; Tallbear, 2011). In settler colonial states, it may be useful to think about multiple epistemological frameworks that operate simultaneously on the same terrain.

I complement postcolonial theory and feminist political ecology with insights from indigenous studies, which is crucial to understanding the present political structures of settler colonialism. In thinking about the importance of land beyond capital, I look to Glen Coulthard, Beth Rose Middleton, Audra Simpson, and Eve Tuck. This requires understanding land and spirituality as the conditions of material possibility for indigeneity (Coulthard, 2010; Tuck and McKenzie, 2016; Tuck and Yang, 2012). Rather than demanding state recognition and thus being defined by it, Indigenous peoples are engaging in what I call a both/and politics that engages within and beyond settler-state subjections (Middleton, 2011; Simpson, 2014). Each of these helps me suspend the urge to confine Indigenous land activism to what is practical in the eyes of the settler state and look to the horizons of new possibilities for repatriation. While Q'eqchi' interlocutors willingly discussed the damages of the past, they continually look beyond survival to an indigenous futurity (Coulthard, 2014; Middleton, 2010, 2015; Tuck, 2009).

NARCO-NARRATIVES, REMILITARIZATION, AND CRIMINALIZATION OF DAILY LIFE

Guatemala legally recognizes Q'eqchi's as an Indigenous people in its constitution, and the government legally recognizes Indigenous peoples' right to territorial autonomy (such as through ILO 169). So, why can't Q'eqchi's exercise these rights in the Maya Forest? The reason is that the nation-state's settler identity effaces indigenous sovereignty, and its logics of elimination privilege global conservation imaginaries over indigenous survival. The project of green security articulates globalized fears of the loss of the Maya Forest with national fears over the ways drug trafficking organizations use the Maya Forest as part of their trafficking networks. In Guatemala, people who might otherwise support Maya land activism are swayed by their fear of drug war violence, leading them to accept remilitarization and criminalization of daily life.

Some people in rural Guatemala say that today's drug war is worse than the recent civil war.[17] In the civil war, violence seemed to have a clear Cold War purpose with set (if covert) warriors, but in the drug war, shifting alliances mean that people understand killings as random. The idea of a "drug war" is not restricted to drug trafficking and sale. Rather, this has come to signal the vast connected networks between drug trafficking organizations and gangs that fight each other and the police over the ability to control trafficking routes for drugs, guns, people, and other contraband. The use of the war metaphor at once fails to identify who is fighting whom while signaling that those who did fight in the drug war were "combatants" who knowingly made such a choice. The problem is that sweeping narco-narratives engage in mass criminalization, which goes beyond assuming someone committed a crime to preventing them from being law-abiding (Cacho, 2012, 4).

At the same time, most people know that there is little they can do to shield themselves from violence. The global average homicide rate stands at 6.2 per 100,000 people, but Guatemala's is currently hovering around 40 homicides per 100,000 people (UNODC, 2013), on par with mid-1980s civil war levels. Many families are affected at higher rates because these statistics do not account for people who have become *desaparecidos* (disappeared) on their way north, usually losing contact with their families in Mexico. Whereas during the civil war the army took away *desaparecidos,* today migrants headed north are disappeared when they are kidnapped and family members cannot pay high extortion rates. All of this is to say that drug war violence is real, and it is scary. Fear of drug war violence shapes how people think, where and when they travel, what they say, and how they present themselves to friends and strangers alike.

On November 6, 2011, Guatemalans elected retired military general Otto Pérez Molina as president on a *mano dura* (iron fist) platform: deploy more military troops to bring security. Pérez Molina's election can be understood as public approval for the recent resurgence in militarized violence. As Guatemalans immediately recognize from the clenched fist that is the Patriotic Party's logo, Pérez Molina explicitly told Guatemalans that he would use his military experience to bring back an "iron fist" that is tough on crime. To the extent that Guatemalans now live in a culture of terror (Taussig, 1987), they may be trading what they hope is someone else's freedom for their own security. Recent years have witnessed a massive return to remilitarization. Under the previous presidency of Alvaro Colom, the administration declared states of emergency in Alta Verapaz (December 2010–February 2011) and Petén (May–July 2011); during those periods habeas corpus rights were suspended, and the military waged massive territorial campaigns against the narcos. Subsequent presidents made temporary practices and military formations permanent.[18]

But who is a narco? People who farm inside parks were accused of drug trafficking, apparently because parks were framed as ungovernable spaces. Whereas military and paramilitary forces criminalized people as "subversives" during the Cold War and then as park "invaders" when they reclaimed their lands after the peace accords, today the military is criminalizing populations as "narcos" in the drug war. While the stakes in the drug war are high enough in terms of money, lives, and territorial control, in the lowlands they articulate with what I call "green security." Lunstrum (2014, 817) identifies the resurgence in conservation violence as "green militarization," in terms of the use of paramilitary and military actors and techniques and technologies in conservation practice (see also Büscher and Ramutsindela, 2016; Duffy, 2016; Dunlap and Fairhead, 2014).[19] I emphasize the ways that green security limits life chances for people who are framed as dangerous to protected areas (Kelly and Ybarra, 2016; Ybarra, 2016). In Guatemala, this is not specific to the military but is a series of violent practices sanctioned among the military, police forces, and private security firms. When I write of limiting life chances, I draw on critical race frameworks that emphasize that racism is "state sanctioned and/or extralegal production and exploitation of group-differentiated vulnerabilities to premature death" (Gilmore, 2004, 261). My attention to Indigenous peoples' life chances moves away from state violence in general and toward the specific ways that racialization makes some people expendable in the name of conservation (see also Bocarejo and Ojeda, 2016; Lunstrum and Ybarra, in press; Mollett, 2011, 2016). When I bring in the insights of critical race theory (Cacho, 2012; Gilmore, 2007; Hall et al., 2013) to think through the ways the settler state demands indigenous death, I make a distinction from the liberal conception of life as housed in the individual. And when I write of indigenous life chances, I signal the (im)possibility of a collective Indigenous people's survival (Coulthard, 2014; Middleton, 2015; Simpson, 2014).

The logics of green security rationalize increasing militarization and also connect it with structural violence that limits life chances for people who are seen as dangerous to protected areas. In other words, green security refers to the social logics that underpin coordinated state and NGO actions to limit life chances through a series of actions, including militarized evictions from protected areas, burning subsistence crops, and arresting farmers. Courts of Narco-Activity and Crimes against the Environment find men guilty and force families to pay high fines for their release from jail. The state refuses these same families access to roads, electricity, running water, and schools for their children. I use the term "green security" to signal the ways that military troops evicting families with guns are connected to the day-to-day practices of denying basic social services to those same families, limiting the life chances of Maya children in order to save the Maya Forest.

Thus, "green wars" refers to the articulation of the drug war and green security, where narco-narratives render people as dangerous and conservation practice renders them as environmental threats. Green wars serve to strip Maya land activism of its political claims, where state and conservation BINGOs claim that drug traffickers and park invaders are simply greedy. In other words, the Guatemalan Army claims that it is not at war with rural peoples in the Maya Forest, but its claim that those same peoples are narcos means that the state does not have to engage with their territorial claims. The disavowal of politics in postgenocide Guatemala is particularly potent, because many Guatemalans are comfortable with the idea that the military does not respect the human rights of drug traffickers, but they would be concerned about the military displacing Indigenous genocide survivors for conservation.

Building on commonsense ideas from the civil war and the drug war, contemporary green wars operate in a truth regime where anyone in the lowlands jungle must be involved with drug trafficking, however tangentially. Foucault (2008) uses the analytic of a truth regime to explain how criminal justice systems can operate independently of empirical evidence. In truth regimes of social wars, policing is no longer about tracking and proving criminal *acts* but instead is about discerning the truth of who is a criminal *person*. If a person is pathologically criminal, there is no need to look further to understand his actions. In the process of arresting a Q'eqchi' farmer in a protected area and hearing his case in the Court of Narco-Activity and Crimes against the Environment, his machete is transformed from a tool that brings life from the earth into an instrument of death.

Green wars is the territorial project that makes it not only easy for the Guatemalan state to ignore Indigenous land claims but also further facilitates the criminalization of Maya peoples and the act of farming. Rather than engage with complicated histories and incomplete archival evidence, international conservationists and state agencies have posited the global good of conservation against the global evil of the so-called narco. I write to call attention to the role of the U.S.-based funding (through the U.S. Agency for International Development [USAID], the State Department, and many NGOs) in promoting what we call "citizen security" and "conservation," because they are all too often experienced as rural repression. Even though the narrative frameworks that justify global interests in mitigating climate change through forest conservation and increasing policing in the name of security seem disconnected, they work together to limit the indigenous futures that Maya activists imagine for themselves.

OUTLINE OF THE BOOK

In Chapter 1, I trace histories of how state violence criminalizes lowland Q'eqchi's. The chapter draws on Said's imaginative geographies, beginning from the proposition that there is no innocent or objective representation, and then traces how a group's representation of an Other place reveals power relations between peoples and places (Gregory, 2004; Said, 1978). I bring these together with political ecology's insights on political forests, in which the military state imagined a dangerous, subversive jungle to be tamed and eventually remade into an endangered forest to be saved (Peluso and Vandergeest, 2001, 2011; Ybarra, 2012). During the civil war, the military posited the jungle as unknown, harboring subversive guerrillas, and dangerous to the urban capitalist core. In this imaginary, the jungle and the people in it were an existential threat to the Guatemalan way of life, one that justified massive scorched-earth campaigns. While the international community disavowed this reasoning at the end of the Cold War, it is finding new purchase in contemporary drug war fears.

Chapters 2 and 3 unpack what Sundberg (1998a) refers to as the "migrant-as-culprit" narrative in Maya Forest enforcement, asking how Q'eqchi's came to be immigrants in their own land. I argue that the answer lies in the conjunctural moment when conservation organizations descended on Petén with a mandate to save the Maya Forest, while over 1 million people were still displaced by war. The liminal moment between war and peace afforded key opportunities for the military and international conservation organizations to engage in supposedly apolitical projects for the global good. Though international conservationists argue that they are not responsible for Guatemalan politics, I trace their role in advocating for the protected-areas system and framing affected communities as threats that endanger the forest.

In tracing the racialized identities of land "owners" and park "invaders," I argue that U.S.-based scientists and conservationists cannot save the Maya Forest without engaging in postgenocide politics of race and accountability. To explain why this is so, Chapter 2 shows a conservation project that cannot compete for reforestation projects because it cannot guarantee that communities will respect, much less protect, reforestation zones. The reason for this is one of radically different visions of the same park: where conservationists see an opportunity for climate change mitigation through carbon forestry, massacre survivors see their family graves and the land their fathers died for enclosed in a park. The case raises difficult questions of racism and reparations, asking how paramilitary and military authorities made decisions in drawing—and redrawing—the park's boundary lines. I argue that we must consider genocide survivors' claims that racialized repression made them into "park invaders," while those who benefited from war violence now stand to benefit from community-based reforestation payments as "landowners." While Spanish-speaking former paramilitaries dominate the community's Land Committee, Q'eqchi'-speaking massacre survivors dominate the community's Victims Committee. In this context, I argue that racialized dispossession made paramilitary landowners into *ladino* settlers and that international sustainable development partnerships with them serve to exacerbate economic inequalities and criminalize postwar land activism.

After truth and reconciliation commissions, how do killers and survivors come together as a community in conservation and development projects? Chapter 3 lays out a provisional answer, arguing that *ladinos* engage in postplantation paternalisms by claiming their role as intermediaries between international funders and poor Indigenous peoples. Whether with benign or malicious intentions, these new relationships are established on sedimented histories of unequal power relations. These families wield their historical privilege, and their children, who have grown up without land, go into politics, conservation, and development. In the postplantation era, *ladinos* step seamlessly into the role of trustee, where they know how the rural poor should live, what they need, and what is best for them. They both defuse incendiary Indigenous claims of what they are owed and offer an inventory of how gringos can help. At the same time, I reflect on what is at stake in the meaning of the *ladino* identity as a settler identity. Rather than a politics of pigmentation, the meaning of *ladino* identities is centered on their role in a property regime that posits them as owners of property and trustees of natives, who need their help to modernize and get ahead. While many *ladinos* likewise lost their land in recent decades, they have found new prosperity in their role as cultural brokers in the development of Indigenous peoples. I recognize the complicated constellations of identity politics where *ladino*, mestizo, and white have different meanings and reveal the tensions between celebrating racial mixing (*mestizaje*) and whitening the nation (*blanqueamiento*). Even as this chapter elucidates those tensions, it explores the limits of these debates by comparing with the Q'eqchi' constant that holds all of these as *kaxlan*, or settlers.

Chapter 4 traces a case of settler colonialism underneath a thin veneer of conservation, in which a European used a park-declaration process to legitimate his illegal expropriation of caves and land for an ecotourism venture. The case of Candelaria Caves National Park shows the role of protected areas in reproducing territoriality as a racialized identity practice. While the figure of "private property" was powerful in the hands of a gringo, it was revealed as worthless in the collective hands of an Indigenous community. The lesson this community learned was that the "rule of law" and private property would not be enforced on their behalf, evidence be damned, and that conforming to conservation respectability politics awarded no meaningful alliances.

In the wake of these events some people have fallen into despair, while others rearticulate a radical politics of hope in reimagining collective self-determination. Rather than choosing between the twin poles of liberal recognition and indigenous refusal, I posit a cartography of refusal[20] that rejects the authority of the settler gaze while engaging in settler legal systems. Instead of seeking legibility within the state, this entails a strategic engagement with settler legal systems that is not defined by that engagement. As with identity politics more generally, the communities I worked with do not see the need to engage in either/or strategies; rather, their lives necessitate both/and engagements with settler states to survive the present while envisioning decolonized futures. Their engagement with indigenous futures ranges from communal property titles to taxing foreign African palm oil corporations. While few attempts are entirely successful, they point to the resilience of Q'eqchi' territoriality.

In the conclusion, I apply the lessons of the civil war legacy to the present. In our present political conjuncture, what is the fate of Maya activists seeking land in a forest that the military says is full of dangerous drug traffickers? In recent years, the military has conducted many evictions under states of emergency that have suspended habeas corpus rights as part of drug war campaigns. When they clear out the forest, military and park officials claim that families are living in drug trafficking routes, so they must be collaborating with cartels. The association between park invading and drug trafficking is so strong in state imaginaries that the same court that hears drug cases also hears cases on crimes against the environment. Thus, a farmer caught planting beans inside a park is processed through the same court as a cartel assassin. Have yesterday's guerrillas become today's narcos?

In postwar Guatemala, narco-narratives work to shape the urban poor and the rural Indigenous alike as peoples who are worth more in death than in life. Civil war counterinsurgency sought communists, drug war policing seeks narcos, and green war conservation seeks park invaders—all three social wars operate on a racialized terrain that disproportionately limits indigenous life chances. I argue that racialized rightlessness limits Q'eqchi' life chances in three distinct but articulated ways: first, life chances are limited in the public health sense, where Indigenous peoples are more likely to suffer malnutrition, low literacy rates, and shorter life spans. Second, life chances are limited in the ways that Indigenous peoples are read as the affectable subject, one who cannot be rational. Third, building out from these insights, I argue that racialized rightlessness limits indigenous life chances by individualization. In treating lowland Q'eqchi's as narco-peasants, state and nonstate agents refuse to recognize them as part of a broader indigenous body politic.

In revealing the racial and geographical politics of who we let die in order to make others live and whose land we appropriate in the name of the global good, I conclude with thoughts on the responsibility of those of us whose security is ensured at the expense of others. While I enjoin English-speaking readers to rethink their relationship to conservation and indigenous rights, I conclude with a call to the uneasy and unfinished work of solidarity.

METHODS AND APPROACH

I set out to research Q'eqchi' struggles for lowland territory in the hopes that explaining how Maya war survivors are remaking their lives on scorched earth could inspire Latinx[21] solidarity and mobilize land recognition. I found myself understood as a rich European-descended woman from Guatemala City (*capitalina*) with whom conservation and development professionals assumed a shared perspective on rural Maya communities.[22] In contrast, Q'eqchi' Mayas did not accept me as a Latina because they did not share my presumption that theirs was a Latinx culture. While I sought to establish myself as a scholar of agrarian political ecology, the Q'eqchi' communities I lived in felt a distant solidarity with peasant politics akin to how they felt about me. Even as they eagerly traded gossip about which peasant group had what kind of funding and who was marching on the capital, they were not particularly interested in learning more about international peasant alliances such as Via Campesina, much less Marxian theories about them. While I asked about labor politics or invoked transnational Latinidades, my friends would gently redirect me. They asked if there were any Indigenous peoples where I lived, what land rights they had, and what their relationship was like with the U.S. government. I had read about the history of American Indian dispossession for national park establishment, but it was not until my friends expressed delight, concern, and solidarity with my thumbnail sketches of indigenous presents and futures that I sought to learn more.

My listening abilities in Q'eqchi' were good during the year I spent in the field, but my spoken skills were poor. It is telling that Guatemalans I meet in the region are often proud to spot me as a gringa—signifiers include my clothes, my height, and my accent—but Q'eqchi's often tell me that they were not sure until I greeted them in Q'eqchi', something only a gringa would do. While I still write this as a Latina who feels solidarity across the Americas,[23] my positioning is primarily that of a gringa who is concerned about the ways that global conservation practices limit the possibilities of Indigenous land activism.

Q'eqchi' leaders hailed me as a foreigner, calling on me to learn the Q'eqchi' language and Q'eqchi' history as a first step in recognizing my identity as a settler who could help them decolonize conservation. In so doing they call me *kaxlan,* a word that dates back to the description of the Spanish invasion 500 years ago, the German plantation owners who enclosed Q'eqchi' land 200 years ago, and present-day conflicts with nonindigenous Guatemalans, whom they also call *kaxlan.* For this reason, I translate *kaxlan* into "settler," as it carries the same connotations of taking what is not yours and imposing laws as an owner rather than asking permission as a guest. When I explained my proposed use of "settler" and "settler colonialism" to Q'eqchi' and other Maya activists, they approved of it. Nonindigenous Guatemalans who are offended when Q'eqchi's refer to them as *kaxlan* are likewise offended by the idea that Guatemala is a settler state.[24]

My interest in Q'eqchi' territoriality has led me to frame my work in terms of the Maya Forest, but the heart of my research—like Q'eqchi' territoriality—is in Alta Verapaz. Those who focus on Maya Forest conservation center their research in the department of Petén, with attention paid to key sites of cultural reproduction and ecotourism politics; many others, including Juanita Sundberg (1998a, 1998b, 1999, 2004) and Liza Grandia (2009c, 2012), have done this work. With a focus on land tenure, Norman Schwartz (1990, 2000) has traced the making of Petén as a land frontier, Laura Hurtado Paz y Paz (2008) has traced peasant movements in the Sierra de Chinajá, and Kevin Gould (2006, 2014; Gould, Carter, and Shrestha, 2006) and Alberto Alonso-Fradejas (2012, 2015) look at contemporary land grabbing in the context of land titling. As I explain below, this is because conservation organizations mapped and named Guatemala's portion of the "Maya Forest" in territories that overlapped considerably with that of Q'eqchi's, whom they framed as land-hungry immigrants. Given that prominent gringo scholars of the region often bring in grant funding (including CI, USAID, World Bank, etc.), conservation practitioners and scholars alike expect social scientists to focus on NGO interventions. My research included case studies of communities that had minimal interaction with international conservation and development organizations, which helped me understand how negotiations with these organizations reshape how people identify their understandings of nature, place, and themselves.

After two years as a development practitioner (2003–2005), I subsequently conducted three years of ethnographic fieldwork over the last decade, with the longest continuous period of eleven months in 2008. I spent three months each in two development poles: one where community leaders allied with the army and the other where community leaders allied with guerrillas—with the goal of land-tenure recognition. Both communities suffered massacres and are shaped by the contradictory politics of racialization and conservation. I also conducted two ethnographic cases focused on the development practice of land-tenure recognition: one with an international NGO that promotes land privatization and another with

TIMELINE: GUATEMALA'S LOWLANDS

1500s   Spanish invaders arrive in present-day Guatemala. While the high-
         lands fall to the Spaniards relatively quickly, the Tayasal stronghold
         in the lowlands is the last to fall, in 1697.

1821   Central American independence from Spain. While the federal republic
         initially included Guatemala (with a separate state of Los Altos, con-
         temporary Quetzaltenango, and parts of Chiapas), El Salvador, Hon-
         duras, and Costa Rica, these split into individual countries.

Late   The liberal Guatemalan government encourages German, Swiss, and
1800s   other West European immigration to Q'eqchi' lands. Some Q'eqchi'
         elders remember their arrival as marking the physical loss of their
         lands and forced labor on coffee and other plantations.

1944–   Guatemala's "democratic spring," in which elected presidents passed
1954   sweeping reforms. Most notably, Decree 900 (1952) would have
         expropriated and redistributed 17 percent of all privately held land
         to farmers.

1954   The U.S. Central Intelligence Agency sponsors a coup d'état in collab-
         oration with conservative Guatemalan military leaders. The author-
         itarian government rescinds all agrarian reforms and plunges the
         country into a thirty-six-year civil war.

1959   The Company for the Promotion and Development of Petén (La
         Empresa para el Fomento y Desarrollo de El Petén, FYDEP) is cre-
         ated to promote agro-industrial development and land settlement
         in Petén Department. Within ten years, people submit claims for
         over half the "available" land, which the FYDEP would process
         sometimes within months and other times left unfinished for
         decades.

1962   The Law of Agrarian Transformation (Decreto 1551) establishes the
         Franja Transversal del Norte (Northern Transversal Strip) as an
         agricultural frontier for government-sponsored colonization, with
         assistance from the newly created U.S. Agency for International
         Development.

1989   The Law of Protected Areas (Decreto 4-89) establishes the National
         Council of Protected Areas (Consejo Nacional de Areas Protegidas,
         CONAP) and the National Parks System (Sistema Guatemalteco de
         Areas Protegidas, SIGAP), including the Maya Biosphere Reserve
         (Decreto 5-90), with little knowledge or participation of affected
         communities.

1990–   The United Nations sponsors a peace accords process that officially
1996   ends the civil war. Key accords for the lowlands are the 1995 Agree-
         ment on the Identity and Rights of Indigenous Peoples, which estab-
         lished recognition and rights for Q'eqchi's as Indigenous peoples,

	and the 1996 Agreement on the Socio-Economic Aspects and the Agrarian Situation, which was meant to address land-tenure issues.
1996	Government Decree 110-96 makes Lake Lachuá a protected area with the management category "national park," without specifying its measurements.
1999	A Ministry of Culture and Sports (Ministerio de Cultura y Deportes) decree makes Candelaria Caves a national park. CONAP does not incorporate the park into SIGAP due to concerns about land conflicts.
2004	The General Property Register (Registro General de la Propiedad) inscribes Lake Lachuá National Park to CONAP.
2010	Guatemalan president Álvaro Colom declares a state of siege (*estado de sitio*) to combat drug trafficking organizations in Alta Verapaz Department and subsequently renews it (Decreto Gubernativo No. 23-2010 and Decreto Gubernativo No. 1-2011).
2011	President Colom declares a state of siege to combat drug trafficking organizations in Petén (Decreto Gubernativo No. 4-2011).
2015	Faced with national protests and significant evidence, retired general President Otto Pérez Molina resigns from office and is jailed pending his trial.
2017	Rodrigo Tot becomes the first Q'eqchi' Maya to win the Goldman Environmental Prize for defending territory against foreign corporations seeking to extract resources. Abelino Chub Caal and other Q'eqchi' land activists are still held pending trial through the Court of Narco-Activity and Crimes against the Environment on charges including land encroachment, arson, coercion, illicit association, and illegal armed groupings.

a Q'eqchi' association that promotes collective land titles. For the latter work I lived in a Q'eqchi' community for three months, traveling with community leaders on a regular basis to regional and national capitals to seek recognition of a sacred place. I present here only those cases where Q'eqchi' territoriality and conservation claims to the Maya Forest articulate.

I use pseudonyms to describe NGOs, communities, and individuals where possible. I do this for organizations because one director thought that my findings might inhibit their funding and asked me not to name them. Moreover, informal conversations with conservation and development practitioners shaped some of my ethical concerns, and I would hate to see a willingness to engage in self-reflection become detrimental to their careers. The extent to which I present a unified narrative of conservation practices reflects how national-level directors promote these projects in

Spanish.[25] That said, I would not have known to raise difficult questions had practitioners themselves not generously given me helpful nudges.

Beyond confidentiality, safety concerns mark key silences in my work. Over the last decade, I have conducted interviews and participant observation in varying contexts of violence and political uncertainty to the point that some people on my interview list have been killed—in some cases before I got to interview them—and in other cases my interview notes are haunted by the knowledge of their subsequent death. At a minimum, I have honored the wishes of any persons who asked me not to write about them. In particular, a group of Q'eqchi' women organizing for land rights withdrew permission due to fear of reprisals after I had included their work in a case study, and the book accordingly fails to address gender dynamics in territorial struggles.

I have attempted to honor the wishes of families and communities who shared their perspectives with me as a conduit to a broader audience. To the extent that the ethnography is not "thick," this is because my interlocutors expressed skepticism about the usefulness of catering to Western wishes to know our Other. Though most Q'eqchi' leaders have not read colonial ethnographies written by anthropologists and geographers, who were sometimes also plantation owners (as in the cases of the Dieseldorff and Sapper families), they nonetheless critique "a direct relationship between the expansion of [Western] knowledge, the expansion of trade and the expansion of empire" (Tuhiwai Smith, 2012, 92). As such, I am less concerned with explaining who lives in the Maya Forest than why living Mayas are unable to exercise indigenous territorial autonomy.

Following the lead of indigenous and native studies scholars, I seek to write a geography of collective self-determination that "basically, involves a calculus ethnography of what you need to know and what I refuse to write" (Simpson, 2011, 72). Since a gringa outsider cannot truly know Q'eqchi' life by walking a mile in Q'eqchi' shoes, I strive to respect the ethnographic refusal of peoples who reject the ways that gringo imaginative geographies work to limit their rights to collective self-determination. This means insisting on an emphasis on the context of racism and colonization over ethnographic storytelling, lest the reader finish with a story of damage that is vulnerable to a pathologizing analysis (Tuck, 2009, 415). Against a scholarly history of contributing knowledge to empire (Tuhiwai Smith, 2012), I call on English-speaking audiences to rethink our imaginative geographies of the Maya and seek a relationship of repair.

1

Making the Maya Forest

"CONSERVATION, UNDER THE GUN"

In 1999, the truth commission sponsored by the United Nations (UN) published its findings that the Guatemalan military perpetrated genocide against Maya peoples (CEH, 1999). Today, Guatemala has become one of few countries to put its former leaders on trial for genocide, murder, and fraud. While former military dictator Augusto Pinochet was arrested for crimes against humanity committed in Chile, his indictments, arrest, and detention occurred in Europe. When he returned to Chile, his own country made no moves to hold him accountable. In contrast, the national courts of Guatemala put their own former military dictator, Efraín Ríos Montt, on trial for multiple charges of genocide and crimes against humanity. While he spent little time in jail due to procedural issues and concerns about his ailing health, this marked an important precedent in a nation holding its own leaders accountable. As was the case with popular ideas about Pinochet after his death, the 2016 trial of former president Otto Pérez Molina seems to signal mass frustration at his participation in corruption and stealing government funds—not his leadership role in killing civilians during the civil war. Long and winding court cases reveal that many Latin Americans see state violence against a nation-state's own citizens as paradoxically justifiable for "security."

Less acknowledged is how recent genocidal violence shapes contemporary conservation practices. It was not until after the protected-areas system was created that the peace accords process, which the UN insisted was the only way to ensure that rural and indigenous sectors could have a political voice, addressed fundamental questions of land rights. The park system was created in a process that was undemocratic and so lacking in transparency that baseline surveys conducted in 1990 and 1991 revealed that most residents did not know the Maya Biosphere Reserve existed, even though it encompassed half the Petén Department (USAID, 1995). This set protected areas as the stage for postwar agrarian conflicts in the lowlands.

While the protected-areas system was declared without community participation or physical boundary markers, enforcement began and increased through the 1990s. In 1997, around sixty community members took over Conservation International's (CI) field station in Laguna del Tigre National Park (part of the Maya Biosphere Reserve), taking thirteen CI employees hostage. They also burned down CI's seven-building field station complex.[1] The global CI annual report recounts the story in a section titled "Conservation, Under the Gun":

> The raid on Laguna del Tigre has its origins, ironically, in the 1996 peace accords that ended Guatemala's 36-year civil war. That welcome end to bloodshed had an unintended effect—it sparked an illegal land grab in some of the country's most sensitive protected forests. Guarding park borders was once the job of the military. But now the Guatemalan Army's role has been drastically reduced, and land-hungry refugees are streaming into the preserves, hoping to turn pristine forest into farmland. (Conservation International, 1997, 14)

CI's anger at the burning down of field stations is the first claim I have seen of land grabbing, something that was taken up with gusto by peasant scholars in the 2000s (Borras et al., 2012; Vidal, 2008). While contemporary peasant studies scholars use the term "land grabbing" to refer to big private companies taking lands from peasants by force and corruption, CI uses it to refer to poor farmers trying to "grab" land from state-protected areas. In this narrative the civil war was not a problem, and the role of the military in building roads, burning down forest, and taking over land for cattle ranches is not mentioned. Likewise, the park's declaration and subsequent building of field stations by and for international scientists on supposedly pristine forest goes unremarked. Rather, *peace* was the cause of the "illegal land grab" threatening the Maya Forest. CI claims that 700 families moved into the park since the peace accords, but what the annual report does not acknowledge is that (1) the park itself was created only seven years prior, as part of a broader conservation project that claimed more than half the land in Petén Department (Ybarra et al., 2012), and (2) there were already families living in the park prior to its declaration. This is important, because there were 42,000 legally recognized refugees who were negotiating a return to Guatemala in the late 1980s and more than 1 million people who were displaced from their homes within the country.

Conservationists decried what they called "an aggressive and rapid program of human settlements" in the biosphere reserve, including purchasing privately titled cooperative land for refugee resettlement (Ponciano, 1998, 107). In pitting the National Council of Protected Areas (Consejo Nacional de Areas Protegidas,

CONAP) against the UN high commissioner for human rights, the conservation studies director for the national university, Universidad de San Carlos, claimed that "this resettlement process also brings investments by international organizations in infrastructure [including schools and homes], creating the possibility for further destruction of natural resources" (Ponciano, 1998, 109). Some of the people living in Laguna del Tigre National Park were displaced by the military's scorched-earth campaigns during the civil war. Still others were moving in alongside roads that were built to facilitate oil exploration. (Many of those families have been subject to subsequent eviction, but oil exploitation, transportation infrastructure and cattle ranching remain unaffected.) Most of these families did not have official land titles, but neither did parks: as of 2016, not all protected areas in the Maya Biosphere Reserve had been mapped and entered in the General Property Register.[2] While CI's annual report is correct that these are sensitive forests, most participants saw themselves as protesting for land rights, not "raiding" them.[3]

More important, CI framed the reduction of the army in the parks as a negative outcome, as there were not enough military "boots on the ground" to protect the forests from returning refugees. Why was the Guatemalan Army's role so drastically reduced? According to the findings of the UN-sponsored truth commission, the army played a key role in creating the refugee crisis as part of a genocidal counterinsurgency campaign. Without acknowledging the need for accountability for wartime atrocities, less than one year after the peace accords ended the civil war CI already advocated increasing the military's budget and its presence in parks. While the slippages in acknowledging context may go unnoticed by U.S.-based funders, conservation organizations' advocacy on behalf of the military is a key reason why rural war survivors associate international conservation with violence.

Finally, the report demonstrates that conservation big international nongovernmental organizations (BINGOs) knowingly criminalized civil war survivors. The 1997 report acknowledged that many people are war refugees, but even so CI qualifies this—calling them "land-hungry refugees." This articulates with local elite claims that Q'eqchi' refugees are wood-hungry termites, a racialized stereotype. Rather than Indigenous peoples reclaiming land in the wake of genocide, CI positioned these as poor people in need of humanitarian aid, preferably outside the 1.6 million–hectare reserve. In explaining who is in the park and why, CI claimed that "squatters" are "reportedly organized by a band of smugglers who trafficked in drugs, tropical birds and timber," without offering evidence to back its claim (Conservation International, 1997, 14–15). While drug trafficking was not the prominent problem in 1997 that it has since become, conservation BINGOs were already making inflammatory and unsupported accusations that park squatters work for drug traffickers. As Bocarejo and Ojeda (2016) suggest, these kinds of accusations go beyond unfortunate coincidences and unintended consequences in the global struggle for conservation—rather, they are an explicit call for remilitarization using criminalizing narratives with racialized consequences. These narco-narratives fore-close the possibilities of political change and eat away at solidarities, as all individuals fend for themselves in twenty-first-century green wars.

Even at the time, not all conservation professionals agreed with CI's official narrative of why affected communities burned down the station and held CI employees hostage. While Liza Grandia largely agrees with CI's account, she shifts the focus toward the ways that "Guatemalan staff risked their lives defending the property after loggers tricked local communities" into burning down the biological station (2009b, 12). Grandia's account centers on the power that Washington-based CI wielded to the detriment of Guatemalan conservation practitioners,[4] but even her more sympathetic portrayal does not treat local communities' political claims as legitimate. The language that local communities were "tricked" is part of a longer trend of discounting Maya political activists who were "tricked" (engañados) by outsiders (Marxists, loggers, drug traffickers), which is a rationalization to ignore their political claims (Nelson, 2009). As she was living in Petén at the time, Grandia probably has good reason to suggest that illicit actors were involved. Still, a simple trick (whether truco or engaño) does not explain why more than ten years later the relationship between conservation organizations and affected communities is still "difficult, conflictive, and sometimes physically dangerous" (Grandia, 2009b, 11). Claiming that Indigenous land activists were "tricked" by greedy capitalist outsiders is a just-so story, one where if Maya peoples only knew how important the Maya Forest is to global conservation, they would concede their homelands.

Whether they argue that these connections are nefarious or manipulative, both portrayals use the role of illicit actors to avoid territorial politics. CI's former vice president, Jim Nations, acknowledges that conservation organizations frame "conflicts" in terms of criminality in his recounting of how CI's country director (of Guatemalan nationality) defused the hostage situation. He claims that the director "played his cards brilliantly," reporting a case of kidnapping for cash ransom to the police and the press. When the hostage takers saw that the newspaper depicted them as "kidnappers rather than political leaders" (Nations, 2006, 193), they gave up. According to Nations, CI lost the biological field station (later rebuilt) but won the war of representational politics. Conservation BINGOs' strategy to win the war is one that systematically undermines the political demands of affected communities. Rather than territorial claims and shared rights to negotiate, CI and other organizations have represented returned refugees and displaced peoples as criminals who take advantage (aprovecharse) of international aid. In presenting them as common criminals, conservation practitioners elide the political implications of their collaboration with settler states in creating and enforcing protected-areas rules.

In this chapter, I draw on political ecology, postcolonial, and indigenous studies literatures to demonstrate how conservation can become a racial territorial project.

Racial projects interpret racial dynamics in ways that facilitate resource distribution (Omi and Winant, 1994; Pulido, 2015, 2017). I apply the concept of a racial
project to postwar Guatemala to show how racializing Maya peoples also individ-
ualizes them, stripping them of collective territoriality. Racial projects bring
together Orientalist imaginaries, everyday practices, and political structures to
institutionalize racism: this is how the scary figure of the narco gets mapped onto
a Q'eqchi' farmer. In preempting other territorial claims, Guatemala's protected-
areas system has become a racial territorial project that distributes resources away
from Indigenous peoples. The creation of the national protected-areas system and
repeated militarization to save the Maya Forest is the articulation of two imaginaries: first, the U.S. depiction of the Maya Forest that employs colonial and imaginaries of Maya places and peoples to write a new spatial relation using tropical logics
of conservation (to paraphrase Mbembe, 2003, 25–26), and second, Guatemalan
depictions of the subversive jungle that represents a security emergency. In this
articulation, conservation acts as a racial territorial project where conservation
BINGOs, Guatemalan military, and even the U.S. Drug Enforcement Administration employ imaginaries of tropical forest and dangerous jungle to create an
isomorphism between Maya peoples with the two-faced Indian (Nelson, 2009),
guerrilla, and/or narco subject. In other words, the imaginary of the Maya Forest
simultaneously represents Maya peoples as a threat and authorizes violent, racialized actions to protect the forest in the name of global conservation.

"COME TO THE CONQUEST OF YOUR OWN TERRITORY!":
INVITING IMMIGRANTS TO THE LOWLAND FRONTIER

Land for Those Who "Work" It

While many Latin Americanists point to the Spanish invasion as the key colonial
moment, for Q'eqchi' lowlanders there were three pivotal moments in Guatemala's
settler colonialism. While the Spanish did arrive and conquer territory, Q'eqchi'
leaders brokered a deal with the Catholic Church, agreeing to mass conversion and
maintaining relative territorial autonomy. It was not until independence and nineteenth-century nation building that Q'eqchi's were confronted with massive territorial dispossession. In this, creole and *ladino* elites in Guatemala's new capital gave
away their land and their autonomy (billing them as *colonos,* or serfs) to European
immigrants. While some new plantation owners embraced *mestizaje* (racial mixing) to create a better nation, most embraced *blanqueamiento,* a politics of whitening that prefigured the demise of Indigenous peoples (Euraque, Gould, and Hale,
2004). Scholars regularly refer to landowners and would-be landowners as *ladinos,*
but many of them reject or contest this term, as I discuss below and in Chapter 3.
Even though Q'eqchi's spoke only an indigenous language and wore traditional
indigenous clothing (*guipil* and *corte*), highland Mayas often considered them less

indigenous because they lived on European-owned plantations (e.g., Rigoberta Menchú in Burgos-Debray, 1984). Over time, this means that ethnographers of living Maya peoples study the highlands (especially K'iche's and Kaqchikels), while archaeologists look for the demise of ancient Maya peoples in the lowlands. It is possible that the relative dearth of scholarship on indigeneity in the lowlands led conservation and development nongovernmental organizations (NGOs) to uncritically embrace the narrative of Q'eqchi'-as-migrant (Sundberg 1998a).

It was not until the mid-twentieth century that the *ladino* state opened up the possibility of landownership to Q'eqchi's. In this, both the progressive reformers (1940s–1950s) and conservative dictators (1950s–1970s) embraced a liberal program that can be summed up as "land for those who work it." Today, peasant organizations such as Via Campesina have taken up the call of land for those who work it and have sought to reframe its liberal and Lockean history as a rejection of land markets that facilitate the dispossession of the poorest farmers (Rosset, Patel, and Courville, 2006; Wolford, 2010). As with the nation-building phase of Latin America, however, this allows the World Bank and states to only see—and value— some forms of labor (Appelbaum, Macpherson, and Rosemblatt, 2003; Sundberg, 2008). Settlers do not see Q'eqchi' work as labor, nor do they see Q'eqchi' land management as a material property claim. These misrepresentations facilitate racialized dispossession among both land-hungry capitalist speculators and land-poor farmers seeking new land.

At the end of World War II, an alliance of landed and military elites, together with urban workers, forced authoritarian dictator Jorge Ubico to resign, opening up a space for a ten-year "democratic spring." Democratically elected presidents enacted a series of sweeping reforms. The most dramatic of these was Decree 900, passed in 1952, a large-scale plan to ameliorate land inequality by expropriating more than 500,000 hectares of unused or fallow land (approximately 17 percent of privately owned land in the nation) and allocating it to 100,000 farming families in just eighteen months (Brockett, 1998). U.S. corporations had significant land interests, notably the United Fruit Company, which had large fallow landholdings and a growing interest in oil exploration in the country (Schlesinger and Kinzer, 2005; Solano Ponciano, 2005). These material interests, together with rising Cold War fears of communism (Gleijeses, 1991), led the Central Intelligence Agency (CIA) to cooperate with the Guatemalan military to overthrow President Jacobo Arbenz. In 1954, U.S. president Dwight D. Eisenhower authorized the first-known solo CIA coup d'état of a foreign government. The immediate success emboldened U.S. forces to intervene in other Latin American countries, even as the long-simmering conflicts boiled over into a civil war.

The installed military government immediately overturned reforms that would have purchased lands from foreigners, Guatemalan elites, and transnational corporations. Beyond that, the military government rewrote the constitution to facilitate foreign national resource extraction, with the portion relating to oil extraction published in English apparently so U.S. oil company representatives were assured of the terms (Solano Ponciano, 2005). At this time, lists of communities making land claims as part of the state-sponsored agrarian reforms became lists of potential "subversives" (Weld, 2014), which had political consequences for organizing and land titling in decades to come.

For those who would work it, the military government framed the lowlands as a new frontier for settler colonialism.[5] The first major colonization project proposed for the lowlands had the goal of "decongesting the agricultural land of the highlands [and] promoting migration" (Gobierno de Guatemala, 1964, 8–9). In 1962 the military passed the Law of Agrarian Transformation (Decreto 1551), designating the lowlands as an "agricultural frontier" and offering land, credit, and technical assistance to rural settlers. This law split the frontier into two regions: the northern department of Petén and the dryly named Northern Transversal Strip (Franja Transversal del Norte). Guatemala institutionalized colonization through two new agencies, the Company for the Promotion and Development of Petén (La Empresa para el Fomento y Desarrollo de El Petén, FYDEP), which focused on the entire northern department, and the National Institute of Agrarian Transformation (Instituto para la Transformación Agraria, INTA), whose first major colonization zone was the Franja, stretching out east to west along a new highway. The nascent U.S. Agency for International Development (USAID) collaborated with the Guatemalan state with the primary goal of natural resource extraction, seeking timber, oil, and minerals such as gold (Grandia, 2012).

An army major and colonization official in Petén waxed poetic, imploring "Come to the conquest of your own territory!" to "men who are willing to burn in the sun, or leave their life for an ideal of conquest and liberty, but always to be a *conquistador*" (Samayoa Rivera, n.d., 5–6). Military planners explicitly hearkened back to the Spanish conquest, calling on "men" to burn in the sun and take over the conquest of territory that was already Guatemala but not (yet) settled. Much as the U.S. state told poor white men in the nineteenth century to "go West, young man" and stake a claim in American Indian territories, USAID worked with Guatemalan planners to imagine the lowlands as "underutilized" lands that could be an "escape valve" for land-poor peasants (Hecht and Cockburn, 1989; Jones, 1990).

From its inception, the military planned to entice landless communities in the highlands and the southern region to settle the lowlands frontier. Military planners believed that highland Mayas were the most politically volatile and open to Marxist rebellions, so they sought to co-opt them through colonization projects.[6] This exclusion points to colonization as a political project, one that partnered with familiar, legible, and politically active groups while reproducing the historical exclusion of others. In terms of relationships with the *ladino* state, K'iche's in particular acted as a kind of synecdoche for all Maya peoples, where their understanding of property relations and political representation stood in for all Indigenous peoples (Grandin, 2000). More generally, highland Mayas were more likely to speak Spanish and have higher formal education levels than lowland Mayas. K'iche's in the highlands were indeed a land-poor population, but military planners favored them over equally landless Q'eqchi' plantation workers. Even as "[l]adino reformers believed that Indian ethnicity needed to disappear for the nation to progress" (Grandin, 2000, 142), they created a process of differential inclusion into the *ladino* body politic.

This territorial vision meant reproducing the fiction that nobody laid claim to these lands as individual property, governed territory, spiritual home, or region of refuge against forced-labor campaigns (Aguirre Beltrán, 1979; McCreery, 1994). The rationale was that the lowlands had a relatively high amount of parcels that were still *baldíos*, a legal term for unowned land parcels that also describes them as wastelands, idle and unimproved. It is here that the liberal conception of improvement is so important: Q'eqchi' lowlanders with mixed swiddens using long fallow periods were seen not as knowledgeable stewards of the subtropical forest but instead as nomads squatting on wastelands. Given that their land uses were not understood as "improvement," they were not understood as owners. This follows the pattern that political ecologists have long identified that criminalizes extensive land uses and erases associated property relations (Craib, 2004; Kosek, 2006; Peluso, 1992; Ybarra, 2011b).

In claiming that the lowlands were "unknown to Guatemalans" (IDS, 1961), the military state stripped lowlands residents of Guatemalan citizenship.[7] While planning documents regularly note that there were sparsely populated regions, there is no indication in either the Petén project documents or the Franja Transversal documents that any attempt was made to speak with those populations, much less ask them about their land use. This is probably because military planners only spoke Spanish. A careful read of project documents, however, reveals that there were existing communities that were only reluctantly incorporated into cooperatives and former plantation serfs who sought to become landowners.

In the case of the Petén Department, Schwartz (1990) has traced the ways that traditional Peteneros who had land rights as rubber tappers, loggers, and farmers lost their land in the colonization project. Likewise, Sundberg traces the claims for recognition and land rights among the Itza' Mayas in Petén. Q'eqchi's, however, are regularly represented as "gringos" of the lowlands, naturalizing their dispossession as a thirst for travel while framing them as immigrants (e.g., Grandia, 2012, chap. 2). This is common on both the political Left and Right, as exemplified by the case of leftist cooperatives that suffered war violence as supposed subversives in Petén, Alta Verapaz, and Ixcán.

In a famous example of agrarian cooperatives that effaced Q'eqchi' lives, Beatriz Manz tells the story of K'iche's who worked with *ladino* and gringo Catholic priests to establish a cooperative and gain land in the Franja Transversal. When they arrived in Ixcán, "they encountered seven [Q'eqchi'] families in the practically uninhabitable area who were hospitable" (Manz, 1988, 130) and received, fed, and taught new arrivals how to manage subtropical forest lands. Manz does not mention whether these families considered themselves owners of the land or if they gave the cooperative permission to settle it. Indeed, Q'eqchi' opinions of new settlements were irrelevant in peasant imaginaries. When I learned about these cooperatives, I likewise admired the courage of new settlers, lamented the state violence they suffered, and celebrated the hope of their right to refugee return (Falla, 1993; Manz, 2004). It was not until I met Q'eqchi' elders from the Zona Reyna who described having their land taken over by *kaxlan* settlers who fought among themselves and brought conflict (*cha'ajkilal,* also a reference to counterinsurgency) that caused them to abandon their homes that I thought to look back and wonder what happened to those families who lived in the supposedly uninhabitable area. Why did cooperative leaders ask for food but not for permission to settle the land?

When families tell me the stories of their struggles for land and state recognition, I am reminded of the indigenous studies rule of thumb: immigrants ask for permission, but settlers claim that they discovered the land and invented property relations where none existed before (Wolfe, 2008). This same phenomenon was at work when *ladinos* settled land near Lake Lachuá (see the introduction and Chapter 2), acknowledging that Q'eqchi' families were already living and farming the land but refusing to acknowledge that they had property claims to it. Another community in Chisec attempted to form its cooperative according to Q'eqchi' property relations, in which one must ask permission to join a community. When they refused to give up the land to a would-be plantation owner, they were massacred (Ybarra, 2011a). Where policy makers and other scholars see immigrants, I ask if we might see natives. In seeing natives, I read these as histories of racialized dispossession and indigenous struggles for territorial recuperation, not gringo-like expansion.

I suggest that scholars and policy makers should understand moments of supposed settlement as attempts to recuperate land lost through centuries of racialized dispossession. Guayo's story is typical of Q'eqchi' community elders in the lowlands. His father traveled extensively during Ubico's forced-labor campaigns in the 1930s and spent time fishing and hunting throughout the lowlands (Chisec, Raxruhá, and northern Cobán) as a child. When he was older, Guayo regularly traveled from the highlands to the lowlands to work in Petén as a rubber tapper. When he heard the news that the state would help people gain legal title to these lands, he and a small group of men from his village staked out some land in what is today Raxruhá, with their wives and children joining them after the first few months. From Guayo's point of view, this was sacrifice and risk. Families tried to research what land was available for titling, but they could not speak or read Spanish, much less afford a trip to the capital to comb through the General Property Register. They staked their home and a claim by building humble houses with wooden walls and *manaque* leaf roofs. When they first built their homes, they sought to be walking distance from each other but "not too close." Guayo told me that he regularly visited both the army base and the INTA office seeking to legalize his land title and gain recognition as a community that could apply for benefits such as a school where their children could learn to read and write Spanish.[8] One could interpret Guayo's story as that of a Maya gringo who fearlessly explores and settles new land—indeed, this is how he told me the story of founding Setzuul (see Chapter 4). When I asked him why he chose to leave his home, however, he framed this same history a different way: first, as a child, his family escaped forced-labor campaigns and a vicious plantation system; then, his family was expelled from their homes for the development of Semuc Champey as a tourist site; and finally, he settled in Setzuul in the hopes of state recognition that would prevent his dispossession. While he likes the idea of being "like a gringo" in terms of travel, Guayo also asserts that it is the *kaxlan* who take land, not him.[9]

Settlers into Citizens, Jungles into Farms

In conceptualizing raciality and citizenship in Brazil, Denise Ferreira da Silva (2007) traces two key logics: the logic of exclusion and the logic of obliteration. Her analysis is particularly salutary in its recognition that most national projects employ both logics, which are not mutually exclusive. Drawing on this, one way to explain the differences in the lowlands experience is not to say that Q'eqchi's did not suffer racism but that during Spanish colonialism rulers employed a logic of exclusion, one that left open territorial imaginaries for what they classified as "wastelands." It was not until independence that the Guatemalan state began to employ a logic of obliteration, one that engulfs the Other in the name of civilization in a process where consent is impossible (because the Other is not a rational subject) and the only goal could be a whiter society (McCreery, 1994; Silva, 2007). I consider these ideas to be in keeping with indigenous studies' critique of the ways that the native supposedly will inevitably miscegenate and assimilate into whiteness (Wolfe, 2006).

When the military dictatorship took up the banner of improvement in the name of forging what it called a "National Guatemalan Culture,"[10] its goal was to promote assimilation and citizenship in the lowlands. While the National Guatemalan Culture was not initially predicated on genocidal massacres, it did employ a vision of *mestizaje,* or racial mixing, that drew on older logics of improvement. In the foundational moment of the Guatemalan nation, creole elites who were of European heritage debated between social Darwinism's claims that civilization could only be inherited and Lamarckian ideas that people could acquire civilized traits and pass them on. Lamarckian ideology draws on the idea that a giraffe acquired its long neck through repeated stretching for leaves at the top of a tree and then bore children with longer necks. Similarly, social Lamarckianism posited transmutation and the ideas that tropical jungles could be improved as farmland

and that people could learn to be good citizens who would pass on their knowledge to their children (Rabinow, 1989; Stepan, 1991). These would be the "always already slightly tanned" citizens who are "essentially" European, notwithstanding their black and Indigenous grandmothers, as Silva (2007, 241) acerbically remarks. At the founding of the nation, the term *ladino* subsumed all previous caste identities (*mulato, pardo, zambo*) to refer to people of mixed African, Indigenous, and/ or Spanish heritage who spoke Spanish (Martínez Peláez, 2009; Taracena Arriola, 2004). While the reference to African heritage has been dropped over time, the notion of *ladino* as a nonindigenous person who speaks Spanish remains. In this book, I call them "settler" in English and *kaxlan* in Q'eqchi'.

The lowlands were considered the frontier of the Guatemalan national project, and the military proposed to incorporate them into the nation through a goal of creating concentrated villages laid out on a grid, which project documents called "population nuclei." These nuclei, visible in rural communities with urban centers (*cascos urbanos*) today, were built on a longer history of Spanish colonial practices in the highlands (*reducciones*). As I discuss in the next chapter, these projects were largely unsuccessful until imposed by violence during counterinsurgency practices (*polos de desarrollo*).

In a key military document for the Franja Transversal, known as the Sebol Project, the military proposed "awakening" rural people to the possibilities of capitalist development in agriculture. To do so, Project planners proposed a "morphological method . . . to achieve a change in social habits by *altering traditional social and physical structures that created the lag [condicionaban el atraso]*."[11] The end of the phrase highlights the confluence of modernization theory and Lamarckian narratives of improving the population. U.S. modernization theory represented all of rural Guatemala as lagging behind the developed world, or as a kind of Latino nation that was racially inferior. *Ladino* planners, for their part, saw Indigenous people living in rural areas as the problem that needed to be fixed and that could best be fixed by creating an environment where they would cease to be Indians and become Guatemalans. While their visions were different, U.S. and Guatemalan planners called for similar actions.

The Sebol Project envisions colonizers in this way:

> With respect to the social, cultural, and economic qualities of the colonizers, broad criteria were established, limited only in terms of: a) the adults should speak Spanish [*castellanizados*]; b) favor the most needy; with a firm belief that good assistance, in all aspects of development, will produce in just one human generation, the necessary assimilation for the progress of the settlers [*conglameración social*]. . . . In plantations and the respective Population Nuclei, we will strive so that the Ladinos and Indians live together [*convivir*], without any discrimination. The positive values of both cultures will be exalted in schools, in sports, and in social relations, undoubtedly this will produce the fusion of both cultures to integrate a National Guatemalan Culture.

Although the language of the document at first glance offers an optimistic hybridity, the planners assume that there are only *two* groups—*ladinos* and Indians—such that the differences among each of the twenty-one Maya peoples are collapsed into a single, racialized Other. As the plan states, the fusion of cultures would occur in Spanish. The nuclei were to be centralized, hierarchical villages that allocated land to entrepreneurs as private property (Decree 559, 1956), with centralized market hubs for export agricultural products. In other words, there would be no discrimination because settlers would discard any language, cultural, or spiritual beliefs in favor of assimilation to the National Guatemalan Culture—as envisioned by the *ladino* settler state.

Much to military planners' chagrin, Q'eqchi's transformed the jungle not into Green Revolution farms but instead into extensive tropical swiddens. By the 1970s, the lowlands were populated with settlers who were not performing the state's vision of the improved National Guatemalan Culture. The military-USAID project to colonize the frontier with new citizens and transform jungle into farmland began with this optimism and then slid into something darker. There is a key tension in the Lamarckian understanding of racial hygiene. In the same ways that Latin American leaders debated whether their population could become productive citizens, they worried about whether the tropics could weaken the body politic. If the jungle was dangerous and full of exotic diseases that make men weak (Slater, 2002; Stepan, 2001; Stoler, 2002), could it really become the nation's breadbasket? In the darker vision, life is pathos and resists the challenges of its environment, deforming itself to survive (Rabinow, 1989, 129); from this stemmed the fear that tropical degradation might lead to politically suspect settlers living on the lowlands frontier.

SCORCHED EARTH: DEATH-DEALING DISPLACEMENT IN LOWLANDS GENOCIDE

There was no genocide in Guatemala.

—RETIRED MILITARY OFFICER AND
FORMER PRESIDENT OF GUATEMALA
OTTO PÉREZ MOLINA (SANFORD, 2013)

Who Must Live and Who May Die

In 1978, the military massacred over thirty Q'eqchi' Maya land activists gathered in a public demonstration in the center of Panzós, sparking domestic and international outrage (Grandin, 2004). USAID planners who had been collaborating with the military on colonization projects began to wonder about their relationship to state violence, particularly given that the executive coordinator for the Franja development scheme, Fernando Romeo Lucas García, became president in unfree and unfair elections in 1978. USAID consultants reported that when he was still executive coordinator, "[Lucas García] visited the project group on occasion and showed interest in the work going on and the prospects of settling people in 'his' area" (Fledderjohn and Thompson, 1982). Within the military state, moving from a commitment to colonization and entrepreneurial farming on the lowlands frontier toward becoming the military dictator that presided over the most openly bloody phase of scorched-earth massacres was a logical career trajectory.[12] Likewise, at the same time as he was expanding his plantation holdings in the lowlands and speculating on oil, Lucas García was giving land to "his" people. Despite USAID consultants' grave concerns, the U.S. president, military, and Congress continued funding for the dictatorship.

According to the military state's narrative, marauding guerrillas began dropping south from Mexico and spreading throughout the lowlands colonization sites by the late 1960s. Even at the height of the violence, however, the military estimated that only 1,200 people were actually guerrillas (Schirmer, 1998). There is a great degree of consensus among scholars that military violence was totally out of proportion to the threat; around 200,000 people were murdered, and 1 million people were displaced due to the perceived threat of a few thousand guerrillas at most. So why did the military recruit people to settle the frontier and then kill them?

There was no separation between state-sponsored development and state-sponsored genocide in Guatemalan government. Rather, the death of unfit and disloyal subjects was part and parcel of a project to make the national culture live. Violence is still implicated in development and politics today, as evidenced by the president's declaration—in defiance of both UN-sponsored truth commissions and a recent Guatemalan Supreme Court finding that there was no genocide in Guatemala (Sanford, 2013). President Pérez Molina was not a disinterested actor in these judgments, as he oversaw a military campaign in the Ixil Triangle during the civil war, and witnesses in the 2013 genocide trial in question implicated him in genocide.[13] For the military, then and now, promoting the colonization of the frontier and killing off anyone who did not promote its vision of the National Guatemalan Culture is a singular development project. This is best understood as a Foucauldian biopolitics where the state's right to "make live" is intrinsically tied to the right to "let die" (Foucault, 1978, 2003; Stoler, 1995). In order to produce a new National Guatemalan Culture and incorporate the frontier into national territory, the military settled loyal communities and eliminated anyone who threatened those communities.

The presence of monolingual Q'eqchi's on the frontier, however, presented the military with a body politic that was historically excluded from the *ladino* nation and therefore might not act in its interest. Once the representation of space as a National Guatemalan Culture failed, the military elite's primary stated goal became to save the nation from the communist threat. In the succinct words of Ríos Montt (military dictator, 1982–1983), "When the Indian is ended, Latin America will be free."[14] In signaling the importance of death in biopolitics, Foucault (2003, 81–82) explains that "state sovereignty thus becomes the imperative to protect the race. It becomes both an alternative to and a way of blocking the call for revolution that derived from the old discourse of struggles, interpretations, demands and promises." The military identified suspected subversives who had become dangerous because of their lack of allegiance to the *ladino* state project. In this way, the military reworked its failure to incorporate the Franja into the geobody of the nation by deeming the territory and the population, the entire milieu, as degenerate and therefore vulnerable to the disease of communism.

Discourses of security threats facilitate a slippage that moves from an external threat to the nation—whether Cuban revolutionaries or Mexican drug traffickers—to an internal threat, one that ultimately interpellates an individual subject. Stuart Hall (1978) describes how these subjects become an "enemy within," and Foucault (2003) describes a national imaginary of a singular race that is threatened by a "subrace" that supposedly will infect and weaken the national body politic. Perhaps the reason why postwar politicians reject the label of genocide is the ways in which state racism is "not so much racial *elimination,* but the *purification and protection* of the worthy stock from the unworthy" (Crampton, 2007, 233). The perception of an internalized threat can become exacerbated on national frontiers, which have a powerful ideological valence (Coronil and Skurski, 2006a; Watts, 1992), as they can be seen either as key to the national identity itself or at the margins of state power. At this time, state leaders seem to have viewed the entire lowlands as a dangerous, subversive place, as were all the people who inhabited it. The frontier is not only a place of possibilities, a field of intervention on which the state can write its representation of space and shape its people into citizens; it is also a dangerous unknown.

When counterrevolution becomes counterinsurgency, state discourses on modernization reshape colonial discourses, associating the state with civilization and insurrection with barbarism and resting these ideas on categories of people (Coronil and Skurski, 2006b; Mbembe, 2003; Saldaña-Portillo, 2015; Schirmer, 1998). By the mid-1970s when the military's counterrevolutionary project to colonize the lowlands did not seem to go according to plan, the military enacted counterinsurgency violence as part of a larger development project. This new territorial project took away the land from supposedly undeserving subjects and placed it back in the hands of the racial state, which later rewrote it as wilderness. While it may seem to an outsider that scorched-earth massacres are a disturbing example of overkill writ large, biopolitics and necropolitics operate through deep-seated fears whereby institutions act in violence in what they may believe is a matter of their own security against an unknown Other that is too close for comfort. The driving force that brings racism into genocide is a "fatal coupling of difference and power," one in which the powerful misrecognize their repression because they act on "fear—the terrifying, internal fear—of living with *difference*" (Hall, 1992, 17). When those who wield power are afraid of vulnerable people, this fatal coupling can result in a death-dealing displacement (Gilmore, 2002).

Even when they operate according to logics of obliteration, the Guatemalan lowlands demonstrate the ways in which biological and demographic conceptions of racial formations are socially constructed and highly contingent. U.S. settler colonialism often imagined that all Indigenous peoples could be absorbed (albeit violently) into the dominant white population using ideas of ever-disappearing peoples in dwindling blood quanta, while supposedly hewing to a one-drop rule to ward off the threat of blackness (Kauanui, 2008; Morgensen, 2011; Smith, 2012). In contrast, many Central American countries allowed peoples of African descent (called *pardo, zambo,* or mulatto) to become part of the dominant settler population (Gudmundson, 2010). This is why Guatemala is among relatively few Latin American countries to employ the term *ladino* (which is inclusive of people of African descent on condition of Spanish-language proficiency and other "civilizing" signifiers) instead of the term *mestizo* (which denotes a mix of Spanish and Indigenous heritage but not African). In a way that is perhaps similar to how Mexico classified borderlands Indigenous peoples into "civilized" and "barbarous" (Jacoby, 2008; Mora, 2011; Saldaña-Portillo, 2015), Guatemala came to understand western highland Mayas as relatively "civilized" in terms of their legible hierarchies, clearly demarcated altars, and sedentary agriculture. Perhaps unsurprising, lowland Maya peoples who were not as easily conquered did not practice sedentary agriculture (employing a mixed swidden system more apt to tropical soils), practiced spirituality that revered territorial relations writ large and was centered in natural formations, and resisted plantation labor were understood as less civilized. By the twentieth century the existence of African peoples had practically melted into the *ladino* nonindigenous identity, but the highland/lowland binary that differentiated highland Mayas from lowland Maya, Garífuna, and Xinka peoples remained. Whereas the black population was successfully "absorbed" into the Guatemalan body politic and effectively evicted from the national imaginary, Q'eqchi's were the largest of the lowland Maya peoples who were still an Other, one that seized twentieth-century colonization as an opportunity to take back their territorial holdings, parcel by parcel.

The end result of what the state called "spontaneous migration" was that the Franja became predominantly indigenous (82 percent), and that proportion was even greater around the wider Sebol sector in northern Alta Verapaz; of Indigenous peoples, almost half were monolingual in a Mayan language (Comisión Interministerial, 1980). INTA promoted few modernizing colonization projects in these communities. Even in Ixcán, the county with large-scale projects led by both the Catholic Church and USAID, consultants found that "the flow of spontaneous settlers continued with little or no order in placement, formality in land-tenure arrangements or supporting services. Also, two groups placed by INTA earlier in the proposed project were bitter about their plight and hostile towards visitors."[15] By the time of their 1978 field visit, consultants noted ominously that "the army maintained a presence in the area and kept in close touch with events" through interrogations, relationships with community leaders, and informants (Fledder-john and Thompson, 1982, 9).

From the central state's perspective, these "spontaneous" communities were a threat. Rather than fill out paperwork and go to the place INTA assigned them, these were people who already settled the land, and INTA often didn't know exactly where villages were or how many people lived there. This was partly because homesteaders organized themselves into dispersed communities, not a centralized nucleus with each house mapped out on a rectangle plot and identified by owner. Many community leaders did not speak Spanish, much less the majority of the community. Finally, community members practiced swidden agriculture, using rotating plots of land over four to twelve years. This land-extensive practice is relatively well suited to thin subtropical soils but only as long as plots have sufficient fallow periods. While Q'eqchi' communities adopted some Green Revolution techniques, particularly in regard to pesticides and fertilizers, and experimented with export crops such as coffee and cardamom, they did not conform to the state's vision of entrepreneurs creating a Guatemalan national culture.

While the planners' vision of centralized villages was realized in resettlement following scorched-earth massacres (as in development poles, discussed below), one key element was not incorporated until the creation of the protected-areas system. In Petén, government planners designated a forest reserve that was sporadically enforced until the creation of the Maya Biosphere Reserve in 1990, which both expanded and enforced this national territorial claim (Schwartz, 1990). In the Franja, Sebol Project documents suggested that one-quarter of all land should be held in forest reserves. Only one reserve was created, that of Laguna Lachuá, which comprised approximately 4 percent of the total forest reserves that the Sebol Project claimed were needed (see Chapter 2). Titled communities were supposed to hold 10 percent of their land in a community forest reserve, but this was unevenly practiced in the titling process. When I interviewed NGO fieldworkers on land formalization in 2008, they were unsure about how many communities are actually required to map out a forest reserve to obtain title to their land, often suggesting that this was less than half of communities. Meanwhile, extensive landholdings such as cattle ranches and plantations are effectively exempted from a conservation requirement (Grandia, 2012). For land agencies (INTA and FYDEP) and USAID alike, conserving forests simply was not a priority until the late 1980s, when it became an emergency.

Taming the Subversive Jungle

Peluso and Vandergeest (2001, 2011; Vandergeest and Peluso, 1995) describe the ways that jungle-based insurgencies sparked militarized counterinsurgencies that involved massive spatial reorganizations of populations and the territorial rezoning of property rights. In particular, counterinsurgency territoriality fostered the creation of a political forest whereby the state declares land as national forest, regardless of actual foliage or competing land claims. Peluso and Vandergeest's intervention is crucial for understanding that the political forest was often a central state claim for power that did not emanate from environmental or conservation concerns (see also Neumann, 1998; Slater, 2002).

Guatemala's Maya Forest stands in stark contrast to Southeast Asia in one crucial regard: there was less active insurgency in the jungle. Given the low number of actual guerrilla fighters, this was a one-sided war. In Petén, guerrillas would successfully stop oil pipelines, and then the military would retaliate against noncombatant communities. There were also a series of noncombatant leftist groups known as Communities of Population in Resistance (CPR) who were displaced from their homes by counterinsurgency and claimed allegiance with the Left. The CPRs were also located in lowlands jungle bordering Mexico, including settlements in Uspantán, Ixcán, Chisec, and the Sierra de Lacandón (Falla, 1993). The military considered all of these to be subversives and occasionally led campaigns in the jungle against them.

In order to defend Guatemalan society as a whole, the military saw it as urgent to wipe out the deviant, "spontaneous," unmapped Q'eqchi' communities supposedly populated with Mayas whose loyalty was unknown. Decades later, even rural paramilitaries who collaborated closely with the military recounted their gripping fear of attending meetings at the Cobán military base and of answering to military leaders who challenged their loyalty as well as their families and their entire communities. The military elite ceased to discriminate among the Mayas, speaking instead of the urgent need to "drain the sea" of Maya people as a way to kill the "fish," or Marxist guerrillas. The difficult work of counterinsurgency intelligence became unnecessary once the military legitimated itself through biopower, killing suspect Mayas indiscriminately in order to make a loyal population live.

In 1980 the Guatemalan military released its National Plan of Security and Development, which was based on the "beans and bullets" premise: 70 percent of the rural population could be rehabilitated and would receive food aid and development (beans), and 30 percent of the population was irrevocably damaged and had to be exterminated (bullets). The long-term plan was part of the military's greater attempt to imbricate itself further in developmental processes and state agencies in order to ensure a modicum of control, even as it ceded executive office to a civilian.[16] The main objective of the plan was to provide "development within a context of rational and effective security," because "the war must be fought on all fronts: military, political, but above all socio-economic" (National Plan, cited and translated in Schirmer, 1998, 24).

Rather than specific campaigns against well-organized armed guerrilla groups, however, the military was much more likely to lead counterinsurgency campaigns against noncombatant villages. These were targeted campaigns, as terms such as *jungle* (*selva*) have strong negative political valences, which quickly become associated with racialized subjects. In the lowlands, this was so direct that the Q'eqchi' word for "guerrilla" is *aj rub'el pim*, or "people from the jungle." When I asked, nobody seemed to know where the Q'eqchi' term came from, although one group of elders speculated that this was because guerrillas seemed to appear from the jungle, ask to buy food, and then return.

For the 70 percent of the population that military planners decided to "make live," the military intended to reshape this population, to mold them into citizens proud of the National Guatemalan Culture. Schirmer describes the military's efforts to reincorporate what she calls "sanctioned" Mayas, those whom the military state decided to make live as loyal subjects, into a newly reborn nation. She argues that on the ashes of scorched earth, military leaders eagerly returned to a "view of the Indigenous community as a child needing to be disciplined, 'ladinoized,' entrepreneurized—that is, 'forged' to fit the 'new' modern Guatemalan state" (Schirmer, 1998, 114). In training sessions that lasted for hours, the civilian affairs unit (S-5) taught rural communities to sing the national anthem, march with guns (using sticks for those populations who had yet to prove their loyalty), and hate communists and also taught that the scorched-earth campaign was regrettably necessary to discipline wayward communities (Nelson, 1988; Padilla, 1990; Wilson, 1995). Military institutions themselves participated in broader Cold War indoctrinations throughout Latin America, which they then brought home (Gill, 2004).

For approximately ten years, from the mid-1970s to the mid-1980s, the military employed a scorched-earth strategy: at least 400 villages were burned to the ground, including people, livestock, crops, and homes. Many survivors report that the military burned their land titles and legal paperwork; indeed, one postwar development project was devoted entirely to helping survivors get new identification cards to replace those that the military had stolen or destroyed. The military's goal was to wipe the slate clean by killing subversives as well as the jungle and civilians they used for cover. Once the guerrilla threat was eradicated, the military planned to repopulate the jungle with loyal citizens in strategic hamlets.

By the mid-1980s, the military proceeded to operate in a kind of "peace of the graveyard" (McAllister and Nelson, 2013, 17), repopulating selected areas through a "development pole" program to resettle people in centralized villages. This was related to the rise of General Ríos Montt, who led a coup in 1982 and then continued his predecessor's counterinsurgency campaign, infusing it with his evangelical Christian beliefs (Garrard-Burnett, 2010). In June 1982 he announced a thirty-day "amnesty" for people to turn themselves in to the military, promising a "state of war" immediately afterward.[17] For a brief period, planes flying over the lowlands stopped dropping bombs and started dropping propaganda. Survivors hiding in the jungle explained that they joined the concentration camps in central Chisec (the *cabecera*) awaiting resettlement because the military recorded community and church leaders promising the "amnesty" in both Q'eqchi' and Spanish. The planes flying over used their voices on the loudspeaker, saying "Come back, y'all [*muchá*], the army isn't killing people anymore." In accepting the "amnesty," villagers effectively conceded to the army's judgment that they conspired with guerrillas and needed the state's forgiveness. In return the army placed them in camps, where it oversaw "reeducation" and resettlement into dense villages (Nelson, 1988; Padilla, 1990).

There were no more than fifteen to twenty development poles in the counties of present-day Chisec and Raxruhá (most of which were included in the Sebol Project), but they are significant for signaling the villages that the state permitted to be resettled. All settlements had to register with the planning agency, participate in a census, and centralize their homes in an "urban center" (using the same plans as earlier population nuclei), away from agricultural plots. In interviews, some people recounted that they were not allowed to resettle areas that were too "isolated," too "dangerous," or "evil" because they had too many caves. Counterinsurgency here brought together evangelical condemnations of animist practices that involved drinking and dancing in caves at night with Cold War fears of guerrillas planning state overthrows in cave meetings at night. The military's villagization program directly imposed grid-like patterns that separated nature, human settlements, and agriculture in ways that few Q'eqchi's chose for themselves.

The army's goal of clearing out guerrilla havens created a political forest as a secondary effect. The military massacred over 400 villages, but even more affected communities in "red" areas disappeared en masse; some returned to their highland communities of origin, some became refugees in Mexico, and others fled to the jungle. According to Alfonso Huet (2008, 77), who worked in the Verapaces during the counterinsurgency campaign, "The objective was clearly to create a no-man's-land, a territory where neither the presence of human housing nor anyone's entrance was permitted, with the military purpose of declaring as enemies all people who moved there, persecuting them and systematically destroying their sources of food, in order to force them to turn themselves in or be eliminated." Military planners relied on simplifying assumptions to police the no-man's-land, even if they could not quite control it. All told, as many as 1 million people were internally displaced by war violence; they did not have homes to return to, nor did they have anywhere else to go. In my study area, as many as 80 percent of rural communities were displaced (Wilson, 1995). In other words, many Mayas hoped to return to the same farmlands and homes that international conservationists simultaneously envisioned as endangered tropical forest.

The military did not plan for a massive protected-area system, but the spatial practice of counterinsurgency tamed the jungle and collected survivors in concentration camps. The violence that emptied out the jungle facilitated its imaginary as a political forest. While the actual forest experienced deforestation due to counterinsurgency campaigns (including burning), antinarcotics maneuvers (including spraying), and logging, these helped create the Maya Forest emergency. Below, I describe how conservation BINGOs imagined poor people's land claims as national protected areas.

LOOKING AT SCORCHED EARTH, IMAGINING THE MAYA FOREST

In 2004 Mac Chapin, an anthropologist who works with Indigenous peoples to map and conserve their lands, issued a public challenge to conservation organizations. He argued that the major conservation organizations (the Nature Conservancy, the World Wildlife Federation for Nature, and CI) "begin with the need to establish protected areas that are off-limits to people," and "if they include Indigenous peoples in their plans, they tend to see those people more as a possible means to an end rather than as ends in themselves" (Chapin, 2004, 21). In other words, conservationists care about indigenous plants and animals more than about Indigenous peoples. Chapin criticized conservation BINGOs for their unwillingness to support Indigenous land-tenure battles as "'too political' and outside their conservationist mandate" (2004, 21). Since then, social scientists, policy makers, and practitioners have struggled with the question of how to think about Indigenous peoples' rights in relation to global conservation.

Below, I shift analysis from military territoriality to that of conservation BINGOs to show how they articulate in the imaginary of the Maya Forest. Conservation here is a territorial practice, one in which U.S.-based environmentalists pay for Guatemalan park enforcement to reinforce counterinsurgency's territorial projects. While many international conservationists see themselves as apolitical and while some Guatemalan conservationists consider themselves on the political Left, there is no such thing as an apolitical ecology (Carroll, 2015; Robbins, 2012). Taking Chapin's critique a step further, I argue that it is not simply that conservation practices fail to protect Indigenous peoples but rather that current protected-areas practice rely on alienation of people from their territory through settler colonialism.

Rain Forest Emergencies

While biodiversity today is a key term that shapes scientific subdisciplines and conservation practices in poor countries, it emerged as a meaningful idea only in the early 1980s, since which its use has grown dramatically (Farnham, 2007). As a biodiversity hot spot, the Maya Forest reflects these broader trends. Biodiversity emerged as an advocacy tool in the popular environmental movement through the works of Paul Ehrlich, who wrote *The Population Bomb* (1968) and *Extinction* (1981) to argue that poor people were overpopulating the planet. Likewise, Norman Myers published *The Sinking Ark: A New Look at the Problem of Disappearing Species* in 1979, focusing on the degradation of tropical forests and sounding the alarm that they were quickly disappearing. Myers began his career as a British colonial administrator who became a freelance writer on African wildlife after Kenyan independence.

When he coined the term biodiversity hot spot, Myers (1988) identified a way for conservationists to concentrate their efforts in combating the "mass-extinction episode" he identified, highlighting the environmental emergency by juxtaposing pictures of major logging and "shifting cultivation." Myers recommended focusing on tropical forests as key intervention sites, and his seminal paper first characterized these key sites as biodiversity hot spots to describe their proportionately high endemic species and vegetation loss. CI, which had just been founded the year before, quickly partnered with him in publishing a new agenda around biodiversity hot spots including the Maya Forest (Mittermeier et al., 1998),[18] raising awareness and directing donor attention to tropical forests through partnerships such as the collaboration with MacDonald's to create the first "Rain Forest Happy Meal" in the early 1990s. As in their agenda, the Happy Meals featured endangered, charismatic megafauna in tropical forests without human populations. In just six years, CI's "hot spots" strategy saw overall annual expenditures more than triple (Rodríguez et al., 2007).

In Guatemala, the rain forest emergency narrative described an important empirical problem. Satellite mapping shows that the department of Petén had 50 percent less forest cover in the 1990s than it did thirty years before (Ponciano, 1998). Jim Nations (2006) reports that conservation BINGOs used these satellite images to convince Guatemalan president Vinicio Cerezo to create a national protected-areas system in the late 1980s. Before 1990 there was only one NGO working in Petén,[19] but work began quickly because "the conservationists who designed the [Maya Biosphere Reserve] believed they had a narrow window of opportunity in which to act" (Schwartz et al., 1996, 2).

President Cerezo was not only willing to act because he was afraid that Mexican loggers were destroying his national patrimony. While he was one of the first civilian leaders seeking to usher in an era of peace in Central America, the military refused to agree to minimal human rights guarantees, and the peace talks stalled. Peace could not be Cerezo's legacy, but parks could (Arias and Nations, 1992). Guatemala passed its Law of Protected Areas (Decreto 4-89) and the law establishing the national protected areas-system and the Maya Biosphere Reserve (Decreto 5-90). In this conjunctural moment, the Guatemalan government was newly a legitimate political actor in the international community, but the continued war meant that activism was dangerous, and citizens were still afraid to speak up for their land rights.

As shown in Figure 2, the region that conservationists came to call the Maya Forest in Guatemala overlapped significantly with the colonization zones of the Petén Department and the Franja Transversal del Norte. These, in turn, had significant Q'eqchi' Maya populations who sought land in the face of military and paramilitary violence. For decades, peasants defended their land from military elites and cattle ranchers, only to find that the spoils of war went to gringo conservationists who did not even fight for it. As of 2017, the UN-sponsored reparations process is *still* evaluating claims of war losses more than two decades after the establishment of protected areas. The park system was created in a process that was undemocratic and so lacking in transparency that baseline surveys conducted in 1990 and 1991 concluded that most people living in Petén did not know that the Maya Biosphere Reserve existed, even though it encompassed half the department (Sundberg, 1998a, 1999). While some people did not know that the state had made their land into a protected area, others simply could not find a way to stop their racialized dispossession.

I insist on recounting so many different hostage standoffs because they illustrate the crisis that is daily life for affected communities struggling for sustainable livelihoods in the Maya Forest. According to CONAP, there are more than 30 "population invasion fronts."[20] When the park system was created, CONAP's "approach was to impose and enforce the law" as it saw fit (Sundberg, 2003a, 725), which did not include educating the affected population about what kind of rights they had under new conservation and protected-areas laws. Instead, CONAP officials viewed the military as an ideal support agency because it is "respected" (Sundberg, 2003a, 726). While this statement seems inflammatory given the Guatemalan military's poor international reputation with regard to human rights, park guards and conservation professionals refer to "respect" as a way of signaling that the military is the only agency that can police effectively. In the context of the civil war, I suggest that displaced communities did not regard protected areas as legally sanctioned but instead regarded the areas as part of a longer history of injustices in which powerful people used an armed military to perpetrate whatever actions they wanted without regard to justice. Whether for counterinsurgency or conservation, their experience of dispossession is strikingly similar. The repeated violent imposition of wilderness is anything but natural.

In the same annual report that posited conservation professionals as heroes "under the gun" against the "illegal land grab" of civil war survivors, CI explained why it focuses its investment in countries such as Guatemala: "Poor countries, desperate to acquire foreign currency in order to pay off debts or raise the living standards of their people, are throwing open their wild lands at bargain basement

FIGURE 2. Fieldwork sites and the Franja Transversal del Norte. (Blackmer Maps)

prices" (Conservation International, 1997, 3). In other words, conservation BIN-GOs can save biodiversity hot spots from poachers, loggers, and land-hungry refugees on a shoestring budget. At the same time, CI relied on U.S. government money and Guatemalan laws to buy land at "bargain basement prices." In this chapter, I suggest that the bargain basement prices were not because people did

not know the value of their land but because the sellers were not the rightful owners. Today at least half of the lowlands and more than two-thirds of the Petén
Department are under some protected status.

Unsettling Racialized Dispossession

While agrarian political economy fundamentally asks "who owns what?" (Fairhead, Leach, and Scoones, 2012, 241), this is already a narrow reading of territoriality that excludes indigenous ontologies by assuming human property relations of
access and control. While Indigenous peoples sometimes see land as a resource,
their relationship to the land is also one that constitutes their indigenous identities
(Coulthard, 2010; see also ILO 169). The ownership question itself assumes that
the alienation of natives from their territory was successful. As Marxist revolutionary calls proved time and time again in Latin America, the focus on labor
serves to reproduce the notion that settler dispossessions are "settled," something
that Q'eqchi' Mayas refute. While it may be that the settler never leaves, the settler
colonial project is unfinished where the settler fails to exterminate the indigene
(Simpson, 2014; Wolfe, 2008). Rather than a teleology that moves from indigenous
social relations to capitalist social relations, some Maya peoples live both realities.
As in the case of Quixpur (see the introduction), Q'eqchi's understand the material
act of their dispossession as one that racializes them, excluding them from the
ladino state and a capitalist ownership society as an underdeveloped people. At the
same time, they reject the kind of fee-simple ownership that makes it possible for
either states or individuals to sell land without community approval.

Analyses of conservation and capitalism tend to see a profit motive in their
assessments of winners and losers, but what about cases where the investments will
never pay off? In this case, the backbone of racialized dispossession is in settlers'
anxious maintenance of racial hierarchies. A key constitutive element of racialized
dispossession is white wilderness imaginaries, which erase natives and their labor
from landscapes (Cronon, 1995b; Denevan, 1992; Kosek, 2006). Likewise, the two
imaginaries of the Maya Jungle/Forest sketched in this chapter are about both more
and less than financial imperatives. As a jungle that must be tamed, the Maya Forest
represented the danger of the unknown native, tropical disease, and dangerous animals that threatened the health of the national body politic. The military state's
greater goal was to physically eliminate natives and their labor from landscapes,
ostensibly to produce a more productive landscape and people.

When conservationists imagined the Maya Forest that must be saved, theirs
was a project of recuperation. More than an economy of repair, conservation biologists, development practitioners, archaeologists, and tourists sought an authentic
experience of the Maya Forest that could only exist in this place. Even though a
completely authentic experience is lost in the wake of deforestation, fears of continued danger can increase the value and importance of the ever-disappearing for-

est. This experience is grounded in its affective potential, which entices settler fantasies that we have inherited the Americas from our ancestors, the Mayas. It is this assumption that legitimates the idea that a biodiversity hot spot is a global good, one that all members of the international community share a right to. It is only through the assumption of "vanishing Indians"—framing *all* inhabitants in the Maya Forest as settlers—that international conservationists were able to make moral judgments about which ethnic people is more environmentally sustainable than another, erasing Q'eqchi' Maya territorial claims by framing them as settlers with unsustainable farming habits (e.g., USAID, 1990). In this cruel twist of fate, conservationists use the repeated history of settler colonialism that ripped the Mayas from their territory as a rationale to strip them of their indigenous territorial rights today. Guatemalan state officials and conservation professionals refer to communities such as Quixpur as "invaders" in misrecognition of their territorial rights. Likewise, a critique of conservation as primitive accumulation tacitly accepts that the settler colonial project of alienation was successful. This critique might call for reparations, but it does not call for decolonization.

Indigenous land activists understand all too well that they suffer from repeated racialized dispossession, but they strive to renew their relationship with lowlands territory. When the Quixpur leader told me that he would not leave the land until a park official killed him, he rejected the premise that the settler state has the right to dispossess him of his home. Repeated hostage standoffs are an act of desperation, but they are also an act of hope.

2

We Didn't Invade the Park,
the Park Invaded Us

INTRODUCTION: "THEY'LL CALL IT A MASSACRE"

In 2008, I traveled to the village I call Sepac to work with a European conservation nongovernmental organization (NGO), the Project, to trace the roots of social conflict in a land-formalization project.[1] From the Project's perspective, Lake Lachuá National Park[2] is an internationally recognized wetlands site that is threatened by oil exploration and "disputes over the allocation of natural resources."[3] To alleviate these threats and promote sustainable development, the Project incorporated the park and fifty nearby communities into an ecoregion. The Project's goal was to map and formalize landownership to promote "land-tenure security" and mitigate "invasions" into disputed park territory. Conservation big international nongovernmental organizations (BINGOs) provided funding for this multiyear project because they hoped that protecting Lake Lachuá would offer ecosystem services to mitigate climate change and that both local landowners and park management could achieve economic sustainability through REDD+ climate mitigation. This program gives consumers in countries such as the United States and Japan the opportunity to offset the carbon they emit when they fly by paying ecoregion landowners to reforest their land.

While the Project has inclusive intentions, some communities flatly rejected notions of inclusion that did not allow for land-tenure transformation. This fierce resistance was evident not only through lackluster participation in projects that offered financial incentives but also in repeated park "invasions" and harassment of Project and park employees alike—as Project "beneficiaries" believed that the two entities had the same goal of formalizing wartime dispossessions. At the

54

Project's invitation, I lived in one of the most "conflictive" villages for three months, interviewing community leaders and writing a report to the Project director. As with most Project employees at the management level, the director was born in the nearest highlands town (Cobán) and attended university in the national capital (Guatemala City). Employees without decision-making power, such as drivers and cleaning and security staff, were from local villages. In addition to being sited as a potential host for ecotourism ventures and organic fair-trade cooperatives, Sepac was also a major administrative hub during the civil war, and its history shaped that of the entire ecoregion.

On my first morning in Sepac, I had just found the women's bunk in the Project offices and staked out a bed and mosquito net when word passed through the office that we were being evacuated. Project gossip spread that an angry mob of locals had taken park employees hostage. I reluctantly tossed my backpack and myself in the back of the pickup truck for a bumpy four-hour ride back to the place I had just left at five o'clock that same morning. The technician in charge explained that everyone affiliated with either the Project or the park had to leave. Earlier that morning, a patrol team of park guards, armed police, and soldiers confronted a group of "invaders" at their maize and bean crops inside park boundaries. When officers attempted to arrest two farmers, a group of forty men, women, and children reportedly brandished machetes and took twelve law enforcement officers hostage.

No Project employees were held hostage, but the Project director was called in to mediations with the park director, the police, a representative from the Secretariat of Agrarian Affairs (Secretaría de Asuntos Agrarios, SAA), and invader representatives. On our ride back to town, some Project employees riding in the truck bed complained vociferously that their boss would not stand up to the invaders. When I asked why it mattered so much—the Project is, after all, a separate organization from the park—one insisted that they should "stand with them" because they were "our brothers."[4] In other words, Project employees wanted to stand with park employees as brothers, against the park "invaders." It surprised me that sustainable development NGO employees were so adamantly opposed to the communities they were supposed to be supporting.

Another project technician was angry that the army would not kill the hostage takers, because "if you kill them, then they'll say it's a massacre." In other words, he implied that the army should kill hostage takers and that the label "massacre" was inappropriate to describe state forces killing dozens of men, women, and children. This technician was also present while I asked questions and learned that community members carry machetes but that only state employees (park, police, and military) would have guns. Given that this happens a few times a year, it also stands to reason that he would know that there were women and children who did not even have machetes, as most were there to weed crops. (Weeding crops is what the farmer on the book cover photo was doing just before he posed for the picture.) I was shocked that he resented human rights condemnations of massacres; Sepac is a confirmed civil war massacre site. To call into question the validity of political designations of massacres in a community of massacre survivors—even indirectly—seemed to efface survivors' identities. I did not ask the technician further questions because it was my first day, but I later confirmed that project technicians know about Sepac's civil war history, even those who are not from the region. Indeed, it was this massacre's history that was spilling over into the present in the hostage situation.

There is almost no traffic on this one-lane road (*brecha*), and mud often makes it impassable during the rainy season. We slowed down when we saw a truck headed toward us that was bringing the director from Cobán to participate in hostage negotiations. As I watched the employees nod and seem to agree sagely with the director's stern warning that the most important thing is not to escalate the situation, I began to revise my understanding of Sepac. I also realized that my relationship with the Project was far more politically fraught than I had thought. Whereas the Project was less than a decade old and offered significant financial and administrative benefits, those benefits were distributed in a way that rubbed salt in civil war wounds.

The standoff lasted over forty hours and ended in a stalemate. The police did not arrest anyone, but they subsequently filed warrants for kidnapping charges (for four men out of perhaps forty people). Since community members did not know who was named in the warrants, all the men involved went into hiding.[5] Park guards asserted that the "invaders" had beaten and threatened to kill them. The "invaders" vehemently denied this, although they did admit to mocking them. The prosecutor did not file assault charges.

When I was allowed to return to Sepac a few days later, nobody from the Project would tell me who the "invaders" were; some people claimed it was for my protection, while others implied it was for their own. In the meantime, Project technicians set up my first interview with the president of the Community Development Council (Consejo Comunitario de Desarrollo, COCODE) in the Project office, where I had a cubicle. When I asked the president about the COCODE's relationship with the Project, he startled me by saying simply that many people wanted to burn the Project offices down. Seeing the look of surprise on my face, he hastened to assure me that most people did not want to burn anyone alive inside the buildings. It hadn't occurred to me in the moment that they would burn Project employees—or me—alive, but this was how some families from this village had been massacred in the early 1980s. This distinction was to note that dispossessed community members would not harm people, in strong contrast with others who committed violence. There was a long, awkward pause as we both looked around the Project office to see who might have heard his statement. While the COCODE president did not explicitly tell me that the building housed difficult memories, the way he described the Project offices made me wonder if his negative associations with the building predated the Project's short tenure.

After our interview, I found my answer on a crude map (*croquis*) that I found in land-tenure archives. In the 1970s, the military built a modern office for its primary paramilitary civil defense patrol, the Civil Self-Defense Patrol (*Patrulla de Autodefensa Civil,* PAC), at the same time as it mandated that paramilitaries surveil all families and force them to live in a centralized village on a grid. Today, the paramilitary headquarters building is the Project office. While these were nominally "civil" patrols that men could participate in, in practice all boys age twelve and up were forced to patrol for "communists" during the early 1980s or risk being killed themselves. The coercive nature of paramilitary participation, together with regional war dynamics, meant that many PACs were largely peaceful, while others committed some of the most violent acts in the war. Sepac's PAC was renowned as one of the most violent in the region, and its members were rumored to have been prime actors in vicious massacres in both Cobán and Ixcán. Although I could not confirm this in state archives, locals told me rumors that the PAC held community members prisoner, possibly torturing them before transfer to a military base; after that, they were disappeared and never returned. When people were disappeared they joined more than 200,000 people killed in state violence, many of whom have never been identified and returned home for proper burial. When approaching lived memories of violence, I rarely discussed this articulation of paramilitary patrols and sustainable development territoriality with community members. When I asked, some people shrugged this off as the past. Others, with a sideways glance and a lowered voice, would ask if I knew about the history of that place. When the Project took over the PAC offices, it seems to have also inherited the political alliances to formalize the military's boundaries for parks, communities, and landownership.

I continued to meet with Project and park technicians for interviews in the Project offices, but I never interviewed another community member there, nor did I stay in the Project bunks. Instead, I rented a room from a wealthy family and conducted interviews in their garden (which land activists preferred over the Project office, even though the owner was related to paramilitary leaders), at a soccer field, or in other people's homes. While I maintained my formal affiliation with the Project, including writing a field report at the end of three months and meeting with the director to review it, I did my best to present myself as someone who knew Project officials but was not one of them.

I had a few names of people I had found in archival records of unsuccessful land petitioners at the end of the civil war (in the late 1980s and 1990s), and I wondered if some of them were the same families that were planting crops inside the park. One morning I decided to walk around and ask some questions on the street, the fastest way in a small town to get the word out that I was looking to talk. I wandered the muddy road in sweltering heat, asking elderly women for directions to the houses of people I had not met. It was a kind of quid pro quo—in exchange for my story of how a Q'eqchi'-speaking gringa came to be standing on their porch, they would point me in the right direction. Eventually I had the good luck to slide down a very muddy hill and land unceremoniously on my butt in front of a group of laughing children who confirmed that their father, Rodrigo, was the man I sought. They disappeared to tell their mother, who sent them to question me. I answered that no, I was not the park director (one of few female professionals in the region), and no, I did not want to arrest their father; I was just a gringa studying land tenure and wanted to talk to him so I could write about his story. "Ohhh, a gringa," they said, "like Peace Corps." When I explained that I used to be a Peace Corps volunteer (2003–2005), the mother must have decided that I was harmless because she came out herself to tell me what time I could meet her husband.

When Rodrigo returned home from tending his crops inside the park, we had our first interview. I told him that I was interested in land titling in Sepac, not the politics of the park. While I hoped that this claim would lower the law enforcement stakes of my research, Rodrigo instead paused and looked at me for a long moment before replying that these were one and the same thing. Even as the Project director and I had framed my research as one that took park boundaries as given and sought to understand titling outside those boundaries, Rodrigo and others repeatedly pointed to the establishment of park boundaries as exacerbating land conflicts. Over the weeks, Rodrigo and other farmers who planted in the park told me how they became "invaders," while other people became "owners" because of racial, religious, and economic inequities that shaped the park's boundaries. Shaping the park boundaries not only designated "owners" but did so in a way that racialized the dispossession of those who have become "invaders."

While most Guatemalan conservation professionals told me that they did not think scorched-earth massacres are related to protected areas, to Rodrigo they are. He leads groups that attempt to reclaim land held in protected areas, but the army arrests them; burns their homes, possessions, and crops; and then camps on the ashes, as it did after massacres in the 1980s. Although I set out to study the politics of land titling and agrarian change in a separate sphere from conservation, Rodrigo and other community leaders insisted that these are two aspects of a single racial territorial project. Postwar land conflicts are contemporary resource struggles, but they are also struggles over the meaning of civil war violence. When these struggles take place over park boundaries, conservation BINGOs have become the arbiters of property, thus simultaneously spatializing and racializing marginalization in deciding whose historical land claims merit recognition and/or compensation. In naturalizing their dispossession, conservation BINGOs made indigenous territorial rights unthinkable.

In her ethnography of conservation practice in Guatemala, Juanita Sundberg (1998a) critiques the "migrant-as-culprit" narrative. In the last chapter, I argued that the transformation of the lowlands into a political forest was only possible during the liminal moment between war and peace, when over 1 million people were still displaced. Rather than a homeland to be restored, the Guatemalan government and conservation organizations passed protected-areas laws, making the Maya Forest into deforested land that needed to be reforested. This chapter looks at the complicated case of many communities that became one—Sepac—and many people who became park invaders on their own land. I trace both how Q'eqchi' war survivors came to be understood as migrants and the ways that their framing as "culprits" draws on powerful civil war interpellations. In Sepac, landless families say that they have been framed: first as subversives, then as park invaders, and today as narcos. They claim that community leaders have collaborated in making them culprits in order to avoid violence, secure land tenure, and reap development benefits.

To explain how this is possible, in this chapter I trace the history of this region, and in the following chapter I reflect on the meanings for racialized development. Rather than a single community history, I found the story of many dispersed communities whose members were forced to move into a paramilitary center to save their lives. Even as they hoped to return home again, the central military government declared a 10,000-hectare park. In the midst of civil war machinations, massacres, and mapping, the park expanded to its current awkward shape and expanded by another 4,500 hectares. Survivors vociferously contest this expansion, which is met with a collective shrug by protected-area administrators because they are not obligated to respond. I explain how this tense relationship bleeds into development projects and argue that these made it a region vulnerable for criminal activities. Rather than victims, the state already frames survivors as culprits. While protected-area administrators claim that they are migrants who should seek land somewhere else, survivors demand recognition that they are home.

TEMPORARY MEASURES: SURVIVING MASSACRES, CENTRALIZATION, AND SURVEILLANCE

Due to subversive actions to kidnap population groups and integrate them into their armies . . . a great number of people suffered the destruction of their homes and fields for cultivation by these subversive groups. . . . This situation caused the creation of the [Playa Grande military base], whose principal objective is to establish conditions of security for the population and, in this way, make viable the return of the inhabitants of this area to their place of origin.

—GOBIERNO DE GUATEMALA (1985, 27–29)

TIMELINE: LAKE LACHUÁ

1950s   Two men from opposing families (Portillo and Mendoza) say that
             they founded communities. Their descendants acknowledge that
             there were families who already lived there and/or used the land
             as hunting grounds but argue that they did not have valid legal
             land claims.

1970   First archival record of ruling families claiming that the land is an
             unowned *baldío* and seeking ownership from the departmental
             government.
             The Playa Grande military base is established.

1975   The first government declaration of "Area of Lachuá Reserve," listed
             as ten square kilometers but with no measurements specified.

1976   First physical measurements done for the reserve.

1977   *Escrituras públicas* (public documents recognizing legal rights) are
             issued for the two cooperatives but do not include land rights.

1978   Families that lost land in the cooperative titling process establish
             other communities.

1979   General Benedicto Lucas García, the military dictator's brother,
             ordered a second measurement of the Lake Lachuá Reserve,
             which Sepac community members assert expanded to enclose
             their land.

1981–1983   The most violent period of the civil war in the region.
             Q'eqchi' survivors assert that the army displaced them from pre-
             sent-day Lake Lachuá National Park as "subversives." The army
             also confiscated identity cards from men throughout the region
             and told them to go to the Playa Grande army base; many fami-
             lies of the disappeared resettled in Sepac to wait for them.
             Sepac paramilitaries participated in a brutal massacre of over
             eighty children, women and men.
             A few months later, members of the Guerilla Army of the Poor
             (Ejército Guerrillero de los Pobres, EGP) retaliated in a targeted
             massacre of Sepac men who participated in land dispossession
             and paramilitary leaders who participated in the massacre.

1984   Sepac y Tal is legally measured and inscribed in the General Prop-
             erty Register (Registro General de la Propiedad) as a community.

1989   The Guatemalan government makes the reserve an "Area of Special
             Protection" but does not specify its measurements (Decreto
             4-89).

Sometime   The third measurement of Lake Lachuá National Park includes
between   an "annex" of more than 4,000 additional hectares. It is not
1986 and   written into the General Property Register and thus is still
1998   technically a *baldío*.

1996	Government Decree 110-96 makes Lake Lachuá a protected area with the management category "National Park," without specifying its measurements.
2000–2001	Fourth measurement of Lake Lachuá National Park.
2002	Provisional land title is granted to Sepac and Tal as a collective agrarian patrimony, which requires titleholders to have equal land rights.
2004	Lake Lachuá National Park is inscribed in the General Property Register to the National Council of Protected Areas (Consejo Nacional de Areas Protegidas), the national parks agency.

Something happened in Sepac to make this town—with access to a road, cash crops, and other development opportunities—a dangerous place to live. When I asked, development professionals explained that these communities had long been "conflictive," almost ascribing paramilitary violence as inherent to the region. For their part, anthropologists have tended to focus their energies on recuperating the historical memories of communities that survived massacres and now live apart from those who committed them (Huet, 2008; Viaene, 2010; Wilson, 1995). When I prepared to live in Sepac, one anthropologist professed ignorance, telling me that he preferred not to work in a community run by known killers. This is because elites actively sought a deal with the military to transform the town into a major development pole and themselves into paramilitary leaders. Former paramilitaries described this as a kind of deal with the devil, where they agreed to carry out violence against other villages to save themselves. They did so proactively in order to gain land-tenure security, as I describe below.

When Project technicians took me on a tour of Sepac, they showed me productive projects and emphasized the ways that the cooperative would serve to the long-term benefit of the entire community of Sepac, thus addressing my concerns about inequality. When I asked about the successes of projects thus far, they admitted frustration that attempts up to that point were failing, suggesting that this was because the men in charge of the cooperative were not committed to its success. When I asked the COCODE president about the history of the cooperative, he asked which one I meant. Whereas cooperatives are sometimes celebrated as grassroots moves to promote development and community solidarity, in Sepac they were legal mechanisms that would-be plantation owners used to make claims on land that was already in use. During decades of counterinsurgency, people from more than four communities and two legally separate cooperatives found themselves living in a centralized surveillance site, known as a development pole. While Sepac was not created as a development pole, the military's designation, infrastructure investment, and land-tenure legalization made it into one. Sepac was a hub not only for military resources, including access to farmland, but also for military and para-military cooperation in surveilling the resettled residents as potential subversives. By the mid-1980s, some families took the chance to ask leaders of the Playa Grande military base to return to the "subversive jungle" (see Chapter 1), which they must have thought was safer than staying in the development pole. The problem is that these supposedly temporary measures became permanent for those survivors who lost their land to the park and today live as neighbors with those who stole lives, livelihoods, and land. Conservation and development practitioners who today bemoan the "conflictive" nature of Sepac nonetheless reinforce the military's desig-nation of this land as a single community, upholding one cooperative's claims to land and leadership to the exclusion of others.

As a development pole, Sepac paramilitaries carried out violence against nearby communities and then forced the survivors to move into the centralized grid for ease of surveillance. More than once, I would meet leaders from nearby communi-ties who bitterly described childhood memories of living in Sepac temporarily while their mothers waited in vain to see if their husbands would return from the military base. When the men did not return they became disappeared, and survi-vors would eventually return to find their homes ransacked, their horses stolen, and their crops burned. One Q'eqchi' leader explained that Sepac paramilitaries' denial did not matter, because they kept souvenirs that were proof—jewelry, belts, and horses—that he recognized as belonging to his murdered neighbors. He blames Sepac for exacerbating the brutality of counterinsurgency for the entire region, which I recount below.

Sepac's official history began in the 1950s, when two *ladino* cousins were violently expelled from nearby plantations to prevent them from making inheritance claims.[6] In search of fortune, the cousins attempted to establish two separate plantations in what they called "pure jungle." Pancho Mendoza had two Spanish surnames, but José Portillo's second surname was Q'eqchi', and today some Portillos claim Q'eqchi' eth-nicity, which is hotly contested (see Chapter 3). Descendants admit that neither man intended to found a "community" but instead wanted to establish a plantation with Q'eqchi' workers. For their part, some Q'eqchi' families had already settled the land and considered themselves owners. Many Q'eqchi' families recall that their parents left nearby plantations during forced-labor campaigns in the 1930s (see Adams, 2001), establishing six dispersed communities. Some Q'eqchi's remember when the Portillos and Mendozas arrived and attempted to impose a plantation regime where Q'eqchi's were treated as serfs. Though these attempts ultimately failed, they set the tone for coercive relationships that persist into the present.

The state's archival records for this period no longer exist, but community lead-ers say that Sepac's claim stretched 3,600 hectares; park administrators insist that it was never more than 2,250 hectares. All parties agree that Sepac never reached as far north as Lake Lachuá, but they differ on its extent into that direction. When the military included that land in the Franja as a "Zone of Agrarian Development" to incentivize settlement of the northern lowlands, the Portillos and Mendozas sought title as a "community." When that failed, Pancho Mendoza decided to form a cooperative. A member of the Mendoza family explained to me that they understood the meaning of "community" and "cooperative" as the same in terms of property rights, but they heard rumors that the Lucas García dictatorship was more likely to approve cooperative land title applications.

A few months later, the Portillos realized that the Mendozas were seeking title to a cooperative without them and were livid. When I asked why this happened, a Portillo explained that the Mendozas held themselves "very apart"; they were better educated, more *ladino*. When I interviewed the Mendozas, they told me that the Portillos were "all military commissioners" and were responsible for bringing violence to the region. Beginning in the early 1960s, Portillo plantation owners became regional military commissioners, and they appointed family members in Sepac as well. When the regional military commissioner, a Portillo, was killed in the early 1980s, the Portillo family took this as confirmation that they were in a kill or be killed war and acted accordingly.

In the 1970s, then, there were two cooperatives, one run by the powerful Mendozas and the other run by the paramilitary Portillos. Both had government connections, spoke and wrote Spanish, and were Seventh-Day Adventists.[7] In each cooperative (which today make up the single community of Sepac), controlling families charged "entrance" fees to homesteaders.[8] Families that paid these fees told me they did so because they believed (incorrectly) that the community had legally valid land titles. Families from the four communities who were working on establishing legal land rights were told that they would either have to pay the fees or leave. Instead of continuing separate legal processes as cooperatives, the Portillos and Mendozas hired a cartographer and a lawyer to map and title their land as a single community. Land was allocated into 10- to 100-hectare parcels without regard for existing crop holdings. Most people farmed only a few hectares spread over a large area, but the ruling families assigned them contiguous plots of land that did not include their cardamom plants, a crippling income loss. According to current members of the Land Committee, Portillos and Mendozas allocated land "according to one's capacity to pay" rather than equitable plots as the law required.

The ruling families insist that only a few families lost their land during this process, but a regional leader whose family left Sepac after his father was killed and he lost his land-inheritance claim told me he believed that almost half of contemporary families were dispossessed. One way to trace how bitter people were after the illegitimate land titling and dispossession is through the deaths that followed in its wake. Of the three men who ran the titling process for Sepac, one died and two fled the country.[9] Those who received land through this process have paper titles and a sketch (*croquis*) of their parcel. Today, Portillo leaders tell me that everyone knew the titles were not legal. For their part, most Q'eqchi' families said they could not speak or read Spanish and ask why they would have paid money for useless land titles. At any rate, the men who collected the money, including one man whose name was also listed as the "previous owner" on the paperwork, were killed in a Guerilla Army of the Poor (Ejército Guerrillero de los Pobres, EGP) assassination in 1981.[10] In a rare convergence among interviews, everyone remembered that conflicts over this first land "titling" angered many people, some of whom subsequently joined the EGP guerrillas. The only people who said that it did not matter were park officials (who were themselves from the department or the national capital); they instead asserted that because the paperwork had no legal standing, its history did not matter.

Conservation officials are correct that the paperwork had no legal standing. The reason why the paperwork doesn't matter, however, is that conservation officials use protected-areas legislation to make this paperwork matter less. The government (FONTIERRAS) regularly collects and uses informal, illegal, or fraudulent paperwork in legalizing land claims (see Chapter 4). It is here that conservation's exclusions reproduce power relations that are imbued with the historical production of race, place, and violence. Representatives of state agencies—the National Council of Protected Areas (Consejo Nacional de Areas Protegidas, CONAP), the National Forestry Institute (Instituto Nacional de Bosques, INAB), and the SAA—direct conservation BINGO money and the global good of conservation when they decide what paperwork traces histories worthy of recognition and what paperwork has no legal validity and therefore represents traces of stories not worth listening to.

A FLOATING DECLARATION, AN EXPANDING PARK

In 1975, the national government declared Lake Lachuá a 10,000-hectare reserve shaped like a square. Today, the park has expanded by half to approximately 14,500 hectares, and it looks like a rectangle extending south, with an odd bite taken out of it (Figure 3). That bite is Sepac's land, or (so they say) what is left of it. What is at stake here is whether the land agency *intended* to appropriate more than 10,000 hectares and when government agencies communicated this intention to affected communities.

The "Maya Forest" did not yet exist, nor did Guatemala have a protected-areas system or agency to manage it (see Chapter 1). Rather, this was a "forest reserve" that the national government declared and placed under the auspices of the INAB, ostensibly because of the lake's recreational potential. Community leaders claim that the reserve was strategically located to fend off Mexican border encroachment or guerrilla attacks,[11] but park officials claim today that the location was designated

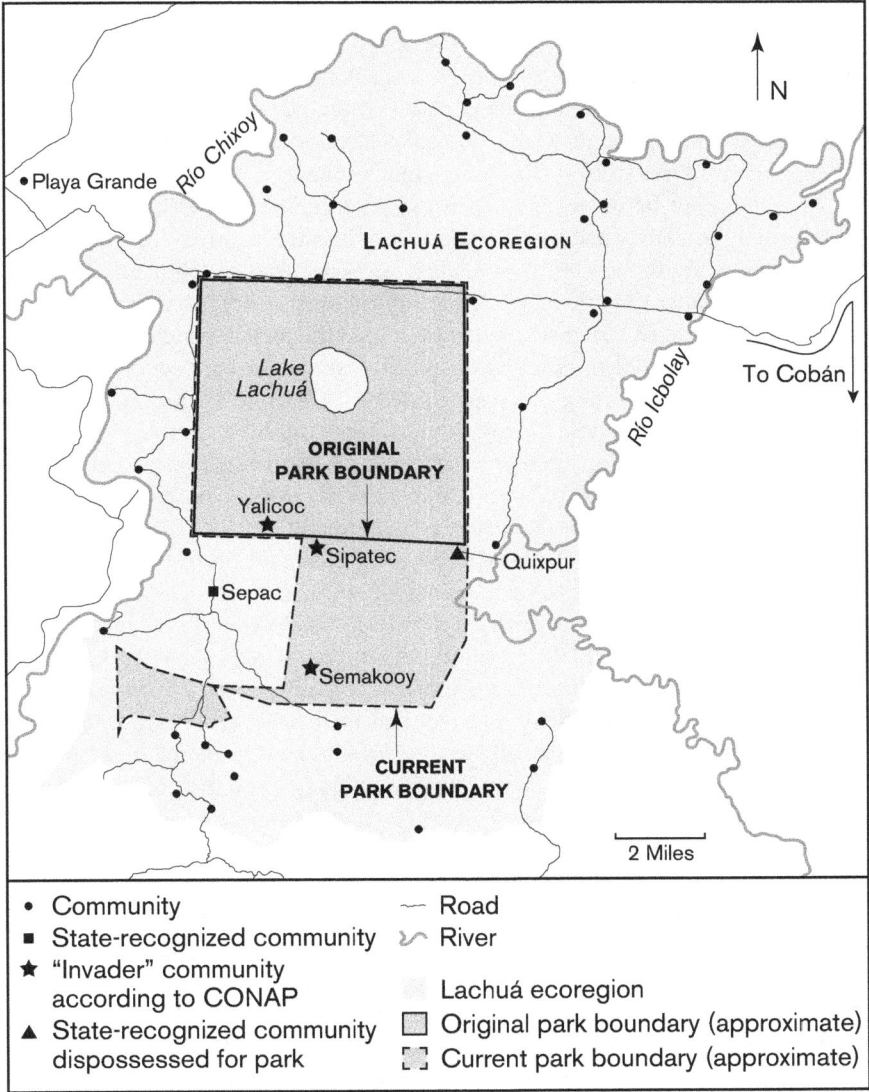

FIGURE 3. Original and current boundaries of Lake Lachuá National Park. (Blackmer Maps)

due to its value as a conservation location. Here is where the park's location becomes problematic; the maps were not based on fieldwork with corresponding coordinates, so "ten kilometers squared" was a floating declaration that hung over the region without cohering to lived places. Moreover, the park was not legally titled, nor was it listed in the General Property Register. To any agricultural home-steader, the land was still a *baldío:* empty and available.

At some point between 1975, when the state declared the original park, and 2003, when the state issued legal title, the 4,500 hectares south of the original polygon affected many families' land claims. As Sepac leaders tell it, the park was declared as 10 square kilometers, but military engineers were like greedy *finqueros,* throwing down boundary markers that expanded the park beyond its current borders. At one point, they say, the state wanted to expand the park south, closing the rectangle and dispossessing everyone in Sepac. A Portillo leader attributed this attempt directly to the Lucas García brothers, who coordinated the Franja. Romeo Lucas García was president/military dictator and had previously been coordinator of the Franja, while Benedicto Lucas García studied military counterinsurgency in France and became chief of the army high command, Jefe del Estado Mayor del Ejército, under his brother's government, in which capacity Benedicto ran the major massacres, including those recounted in this chapter.

As ruling families remember it, their historical trajectory was shaped by their success in defending their land from military interests. Since Sepac was not titled through the National Institute of Agrarian Transformation (Instituto para la Transformación Agraria, INTA) or inscribed in the General Property Register, they discovered that the community did not legally exist. A colonel suggested that they should legalize their agricultural cooperatives because the process might be faster than actual land titling, and Lucas García's own policies favored cooperatives.[12] By 1979 both the Portillo and Mendoza cooperatives were legal, although they did not have formal land titles.

While the paperwork did provide some legal recognition, without land titles the cooperatives were still vulnerable to dispossession. As poor Q'eqchi' families tell it, elite families cut a deal with the military: land for loyalty. Former paramilitary leaders emphasize their lack of power in relation to the army, but their loyalty was gruesome. Sepac *ladinos* have a reputation as one of the most violent paramilitary forces in the region; they killed, raped, and dispossessed people of their land, and then survivors often had to resettle in Sepac, living under their surveillance.

Resettled families say that the military evicted them in the 1970s as "subversives" living in the "jungle," and only when they attempted to return home in the late 1980s did the military begin calling them "park invaders." Park and Project officials classify all four groups as "invaders." The groups refer to themselves as "communities," a term that park and Project officials say gives them unearned legitimacy. Due north of Sepac, military officials also told people in another community that "we don't want people here, this will be a place for animals."[13] Some of these families moved to a community north of the park, while others moved south to Sepac. When I asked why they did not protest their removal, a former paramilitary leader and current landowner scoffed that "at that time, you could accept or not, the result was the same." Invader families agreed, with a proviso—they believed that their dispossession, like the rest of the civil war, was a temporary measure. It was only with the articulation of conservation and settler logics of elimination that they found that the indigenous right to life has no place in protected areas.

"Self-Defense"

With wide eyes, former paramilitaries recount that EGP operatives arrived in the late 1970s to recruit people for the revolution. Although incidents of guerrilla murders amounted to only 3 percent of total wartime violence (CEH, 1999), to hear Sepac *ladinos* tell the story, their homes were the epicenter of guerrilla fronts, and this is one of relatively few documented sites where guerrillas committed a massacre. Broadly speaking, there were two kinds of development poles: one was a community that suffered counterinsurgency and was allowed to rebuild under militarized supervision (Wilson, 1995), and the other acted more like a hub for multiple communities where displaced peoples from the region would gather under military supervision as they awaited permission to rebuild their communities elsewhere. Sepac fell into the latter category, becoming a place where survivors of scorched-earth counterinsurgency would turn themselves in, risking military torture and extrajudicial killing in the hopes of food and shelter. The Sepac military also turned men into the military base at Playa Grande for questioning, so the town swelled with families waiting to see if their loved ones would return from the base. Some men returned, and some did not; if not, these men were disappeared (*desaparecidos*), and their families never heard from them again.

While historical remembrance is infused with present politics, I learned two reasons why EGP guerrillas targeted Sepac. First, Huet (personal communication, 2008) pointed to the possibility of direct retaliation for a two-day massacre on Río Negro. Sepac paramilitaries raped, tortured, and killed an entire community of men, women, and children with little official military presence or overt supervision. The blatant brutality of the massacre meant that surviving family members, some of whom joined the EGP, vowed vengeance. At the same time, EGP leaders apparently threatened Sepac leaders because of their reputation for charging exploitative "entrance fees," collecting money from poor people without giving them land titles in return. Both of these were probable reasons for a relatively rare massacre on the part of Marxist guerrillas, one that was targeted against injustices. Whereas military and paramilitary massacres killed elderly people, women, children, and even livestock with a focus on inflicting long-term pain and shame, the EGP massacre killed twenty-six men, a relatively small proportion of the community. (Sources agreed that this was a number far fewer than the massacre that the Sepac PAC committed along Río Negro, which is consistent with the findings of Guatemala's Commission for Historical Clarification [Comisión para el Esclarecimiento Histórico, CEH]).

The massacre was marked with a strange familiarity: the killers knew the homes of the local mayor, military commissioners, and paramilitary leaders. In meting out retribution against these leaders, EGP killings were a racially framed practice that marked families such as the Portillos and Mendozas as *ladinos* who had oppressed poor, Indigenous peoples. This racialized targeting was consummately intimate, as people who had lived in Sepac were probably among EGP operatives. One former paramilitary shook his head, saying that "they came to attack their own people." This signals a key breaking point—while this former paramilitary was still calling his neighbors "*su propia gente,*" this violent act points out that they were not (if they ever had been) the same people. If boundary making on the land was a way to fix racial identities, murders made racial identities how one lived and how one died. Q'eqchi's suffered rape, torture, and prolonged pain in death and were often unable to bury bodies and mourn loved ones. *Ladino* men suffered quick deaths with unmutilated bodies left that they photographed, mourned, and buried in public. A Q'eqchi' leader who left Sepac as a child after paramilitaries killed his father and burned down his land alluded to this only by saying that he believed that this act of retribution was too small in relation to years of violence across the countryside. This former neighbor grew up as a child knowing that these were not his people. Today, this lack of kinship is signified in his casual assertion that someone might one day kill the *ladinos* in Sepac, even as those same men claim him as one of "their people" and deny that they are *ladinos* (see Chapter 3).

While Sepac never came together as a social unit, it is around this time that government agencies designated it as a single community (*aldea*). Although commanders at the Playa Grande military base authorized families to live in the urban center beginning in the late 1970s, the Portillo and Mendoza cooperatives split the urban center down the middle, and each family treated half of the town as their own. The army did not recognize this cross-town split. Army leaders only made one agreement with paramilitaries and built only one "self-defense" center that housed paramilitary authorities and PAC patrols.

Representatives from both the Portillo and Mendoza families claim that they had been trying to get the land-titling agency (INTA) to map their cooperatives since the 1960s. It was only after officially becoming a development pole in the mid-1980s that the military authorized mapping Sepac. When engineers arrived, they were from the civilian affairs section of the army (G-5). A Portillo leader told me that they mentioned the cooperatives but did not insist that these be designated two separate communities because they feared army reprisals. Instead, army engineers mapped one set of boundaries for a single community named Sepac that included the Portillo cooperative, the Mendoza cooperative, and a nearby smaller village (*caserío*).

INTA designated this community eligible for land titling as communal property (*patrimonio agrario colectivo*), such that each family has legal rights to an equal land parcel.[14] The Portillos and Mendozas were alarmed by this turn of events. As they believed that they owned most of Sepac's land, equitable shares amounted to a loss for them. While they successfully lobbied military engineers to wait to conduct the census (until displaced families left, relinquishing their land claims), the engineers mapped in only 2,150 hectares of their land claim, less than two-thirds of Sepac's cooperative claims. Leaders were frustrated that they might lose land and were enraged about the possibility of equal shares, but they were too afraid to directly challenge military engineers. As a result, they focused their energies on giving themselves the best land that was least vulnerable to park claims and allocating the claims of neighboring communities into the parcels that military mappers designated outside of Sepac community boundaries.

Improvement Committees: Betterment and Violence

Institutions created during wartime violence were built on the foundation of older paternalistic relationships. In this region, civilian military commissioners were more likely to come from plantation families, whose earlier relationships established them as intermediaries between centralized states and Indigenous peoples. Just as these relationships did not begin with the civil war, they did not end with it. Rather, they continue on through institutions that mediate participation in conservation and sustainable development projects. One of the first interviews I conducted in Sepac, which I recounted earlier, was with the leader of the COCODE, a community association that coordinated closely with the national park and the Project. Here I explain how militarized relationships are at the heart of this community association's history and why I argue that contemporary development and conservation practices must account for these histories.

When development poles began as "strategic hamlets," the military had significant leverage over the population. People lived in fear, as scorched-earth campaigns made clear that one did not have to be a guerrilla to be massacred; one only had to be suspect. The problem is that suspicion inhered in people who were poor, rural, Indigenous, and/or Catholic. When the military told survivors to move to development poles and warned them that if they returned home they would be killed as "subversives," military officers ensured their ability to monitor these populations and their economic control over displaced rural farmers.

In Sepac, *ladinos* with military ties became local mayors, paramilitary leaders, and members of the Pro-Improvement Committee (Comité Pro-Mejoramiento), the precursor to contemporary COCODEs. Displaced people were subject to "customary" labor requirements that the Pro-Improvement Committee mandated as well as training and patrolling with the PACs. When PACs were not searching for guerrillas in the jungle, they performed basic labor for development projects, including road construction and irrigation projects, without remuneration. Military dictator Ríos Montt had made famous the "beans and bullets" strategy of killing some of the population and feeding the rest in a coercive trusteeship, but this strategy predated and outlasted his reign. Agencies that funded food-for-work programs included the U.S. Agency for International Development[15] and the World Food Programme, but people in development poles remember only the army.[16] This is because the army accepted food aid on behalf of Guatemala and then distributed it through the paramilitary system. As the 1980s progressed the army lost some of its funding from major aid groups due to bad publicity, but it gained funding from Protestant churches. Evangelical churches send U.S. parishioners on vacation missions to fund and help build infrastructure projects to the present day, a practice that some Guatemalans associate with militarized development. This also coincides with a massive shift away from Catholicism, part of a broader Latin American phenomenon (Stoll, 1990).

Contemporary reports show that the army had a less direct presence near Sepac because the military at the nearby Playa Grande base had strong relationships with evangelicals and *ladinos* who acted as spies (*orejas*), reporting on their own neighbors. Whereas the guerrillas tended to impose their own institutions, the military was eager to work with and transform existing systems of nonreligious traditional authority (Le Bot, 1995). However, as a Portillo former paramilitary explained it to me, in Sepac the military killed Catholic and Q'eqchi' traditional authorities who threatened the counterinsurgency agenda and then replaced them with evangelical authorities who supported a counterinsurgency agenda.

In the 1990s when international conservation organizations began transforming the "paper" park into a "real" park, Sepac's attitude was notably different from that of other communities in the park's vicinity. This was true even with potential funders who came in to meet with communities and ask them about the possibility of investing in a long-term sustainable development project (IUCN and INAB, 1997). This is not because they are inherently "conflictive" but instead because Sepac's land claim included much of the additional 4,500 hectares that were included in the expanded national park. As with other communities in the new ecoregion, 100 percent of Sepac residents noted that the national park has benefits including oxygen, water, and a source of protein (from hunting and fishing).[17] According to the survey to outline the scope of work for the Project, however, "[Sepac residents] object to the expansion (*ampliación*) of the reserve of the [park], because this was taken from them, according to some of those interviewed, large extensions of land, which makes them upset (*molestos*), because not only do they have problems with the distribution and tenure of land, but these events make them worse off" (IUCN and INAB, 1997, 20). This language is awkward not because this is a bureaucratic report but because of the nature of the national park itself.

In 1975, the state declared a 10,000-hectare forest reserve. When park rangers began patrolling in the late 1980s, they say they also patrolled an expansion reserve (*reserva de ampliación*) adjacent to the 10,000-hectare forest reserve (*reserva*). This is the only case I am aware of in Guatemala where officials claim that a "reserve" had its own "reserve" (INAB, 2003)—this makes as little sense in Spanish as it does in English and seems to confuse everyone except the park and Project officials who repeatedly told me that it was not confusing and was a perfectly normal practice. When I asked if the expansion reserve (*reserve de ampliación*) was a buffer zone (*zona de amortiguamiento*), a park guard told me that the buffer zone was later, expanding the realm of conservation even farther. In their meetings and survey participation with conservation professionals in 1997, then, Sepac respondents did not protest the existence of the 10,000-hectare park but rather the assumption that the park would expand by an *additional* 4,500 hectares, cutting directly into community lands.

Agreements with newly arrived park guards beginning in the late 1980s afforded rights and privileges to some Sepac community members but not necessarily those who originally planted the cash crops. When I interviewed people about resource extraction, some people said that paramilitaries harvested cardamom inside both the original park and the expansion/reserve. They did not have rights to these products (because they did not plant the seeds), but they took advantage of the fact that rightful owners were either dead or too scared to reclaim their rights. At least some of the people harvesting cardamom in the 1990s were former paramilitaries, and I am not sure when others began to (re)claim their families' alleged crops and land. It is unlikely that former paramilitaries would have planted maize inside the park, as they were more likely to have larger parcels more conveniently located to the town center. As for current "invaders," their status as landless was in flux, and it was still relatively easy to "borrow" or rent land outside the new park boundaries.[18] Correspondingly, satellite maps suggest relatively little clearing for planting maize or beans in the park until the late 1990s.

In the same 1997 survey, some people mentioned that they were angry with park guards due to confrontations with people inside the park. The report is vague about who was inside the park, why they had confrontations with park guards, and why this made other people angry. Beginning around 1988 two park guards were stationed in Lachuá, and they quickly got into confrontations with multiple communities. Park guards acknowledged that residents had cardamom plants inside both the original and expansion/reserve lands. In one signed agreement in Sepac's COCODE *Libro de Actas,* the park administrator told residents that they could continue to harvest their cardamom but could not plant any more maize.

My understanding is that Sepac residents never respected this agreement and continued to plant, harvest, and hunt in the park. When I interviewed park guards they contextualized this event, pointing out that there was massive logging going on inside the park in the late 1990s, and they believed that people in Sepac also participated in large-scale illegal resource extraction. They never acknowledged the issue of cardamom and coffee plants, the existence of which is commonly accepted evidence of historical land rights (*mejoras*, or "land improvements") that can be approximately dated. At first, the two park guards who arrived in 1988 insisted that no farming occurred until well into the 2000s. Our conversations continued over the course of a few months, during which time community members from both Sepac and another community, Quixpur (see the introduction), gave me copies of agreements dating from the late 1980s through the 1990s that these same park guards had signed stating that they could continue to harvest cardamom and coffee plants. The next time I saw the park guards, I told them that I had reviewed the paperwork and mentioned that I thought I had seen their signatures on agreements about harvesting inside the park. One park guard said nothing, and the other acknowledged that the signatures I saw were his. They both stopped claiming that nobody had farmed in the expansion zone until the 2000s. Likewise, they were more reticent to share histories with me after that. I understand this as tacit acknowledgment that community leaders' claims about historical agreements were at least partly true.

In the absence of a competing land claim, communities with historical land rights, signed state paperwork and physical land improvements (*mejoras*) would be able to get formal land titles. The arrival of global conservation imperatives to this national park, however, reworked settler colonialism to extinguish Indigenous people's rights—if not the evidence—to the land. Below I explore the consequences of articulating settler logics of extinction with conservation practices in the workings of property relations, the rule of law, and everyday life.

KILLERS AND SURVIVORS, OWNERS AND INVADERS?

[The Indian] is only one two-faced figure haunting postwar Guatemala, waiting to be unmasked. Another is the war perpetrator, who committed dastardly deeds and then, seemingly acknowledging their badness, covered them up by "disappearances" and clandestine cemeteries, and by hiding ill-gotten gains off the books.

—NELSON (2009, 10)

Juanita Sundberg (2004) describes identities in the making, drawing on feminist and post-Marxist theory to emphasize the role of contingency in identity formation (Gibson-Graham, 2006; Laclau and Mouffe, 2014; Nelson, 1999). Rather than taking binary identities such as killer/survivor, Q'eqchi'/*ladino*, etc., as a coherent assigned identity, this chapter examines how a series of decisions and discourses became fixed first through civil war violence and then through a recapitulation of these identities in a conservation project that relied on private land titling. Conservation and sustainable development organizations took the identities of landowners outside the park and invaders using land illegally inside the park as fixed, as this helped legitimate park boundaries. In so doing, I argue that they hardened the simple wartime binaries of *ladino*/Q'eqchi' and subversive/loyal. Present-day landowners argue that these binaries are not useful because they fail to account for the ways that most people in the community are actually cousins across racialized binaries, but the landowners are able to hold themselves above ethnic identities, arguing that they are neither *ladino* nor Q'eqchi'. Meanwhile, "invaders" are always recognized as Q'eqchi', not *ladino*, even by those who know about cousins, bloodlines, and genealogies.[19] This makes sense to those with lived experiences of intimate tyranny (Mbembe, 1992; Stoler, 2002). "Invaders" argue that it is their unshakable indigeneity that limits their life chances and criminalizes them.

When I began fieldwork in 2008, the SAA official told me that there were three "invader" groups based in Sepac planting in Lake Lachuá National Park (see Figure 3). To the north of Sepac is Yalicoc, a community of Q'eqchi's who claim to have descended from families that the military forced to regroup in Sepac in 1976 when they first established the park boundaries. Most people in Sepac claim that the original ten-square-kilometer park's boundary was set farther north than it is today. Along that slice Yalicoc families care for old homes, a cemetery, and various plants, all of which they use to point to their historical relationship to the land they farm communally today. To the east of Sepac lies Sipatec, where families farm land and claim historical rights. Although some people told me that their fathers died in the war at the army's hands, truth commission reports suggest that the EGP killed them in retaliation for taking land under the auspices of the Portillos.

The third group claims a different history, farming land called Semakooy to the southeast of Sepac (farther into the present-day park). These Q'eqchi' families claim that they were dispossessed from Sepac's land-titling process in the late 1970s, then moved east to establish a new community. A few years later, the army killed their community leaders as "subversives." The army told the survivors that they were living in subversive territory (jungle), accused them of living in a guerrilla camp, and forced them into the Sepac development pole—thus making them landless. Today, they claim that their status as genocide survivors means that they deserve land as reparations, and they eschew association with the other two groups.[20] Although all three groups tend to plant maize and beans communally, only Semakooy has homes inside the park. Every time the judge orders an eviction from the park, the military burns their crops and their homes. Every time the land is burned, residents rebuild on scorched earth.

All three groups insist that their status as park "invaders" stems from Sepac's unjust and illegal land-titling process. Indeed, the Project's promise to formalize landownership and raise land values through sustainable development reforestation programs triggered expanded use of the park as farmland. When owners began holding land in reserve for reforestation rather than rent to neighbors, landless farmers had nowhere else left. In this narrative, paramilitaries committed massacres and terrorized neighbors, and the military rewarded their loyalty by making them community leaders. When the Project titled their lands, community leaders successfully excluded other people from ownership. Paramilitary violence served to legitimate land dispossession, at least in the eyes of the military. For their part, genocide survivors, people who lost family members to the war under the army's policies that disproportionately affected Catholic Q'eqchi's, claim that their dispossession is a continuation of the army's racialization. Q'eqchi's do not claim racial animus on the part of their neighbors; rather, they claim that community leaders exploited institutions of racial violence for personal gain. The intimate nature of violence in no way undercuts their critique of institutionalized racism and genocide. While state militarization has ebbed and waned since the civil war, the racial state has continually been renewed (Goldberg, 2002; HoSang, LaBennett, and Pulido, 2012).

While landowners and park invaders trace the legitimacy of their claims in different ways, neither group accepts the legitimacy of the park beyond 10,000 hectares. These families are only invaders if one accepts that the park's claim on the land supersedes theirs. Today, owners and invaders alike declare that "we didn't invade the park, the park invaded us!" While racial animus infused the racial state, it was not until international conservation that racialized dispossession was fixed. Below, I explain how this process occurred.

Did Killers Become Landowners?

When I asked Project employees how some people became owners and other people became landless, at first they told me that everyone was included on the title. Anyone who claimed to be landless was actually the child of a landowner and could expect to inherit land. When I insisted that there were families who were not included in the land title, they told me that these families must have arrived after the land-titling process began in 1985. The Project employees never acknowledged that this was during the civil war and that many communities in the region were seeking to return home through the late 1980s. For their part, Sepac paramilitaries described their landownership as a reward for loyalty, a harrowing and long-term relationship with the army that they entered into to save their land. Finally, landless people in Sepac assert that they were repeatedly excluded from their land rights under threat of violence. Eventually the Project paid to formalize their dispossession in formalizing the rights of the rich and the forest instead.

The first historical process of exclusion was when the Portillos and Mendozas formed cooperatives and paid professionals to map land. Families that could not pay their share (with prices set by ruling families) lost their land. The 1970s maps were neither legally nor cartographically valid, but former paramilitaries fight for their recognition because this is when they made claims to larger parcels of land than their poor and monolingual Q'eqchi'-speaking neighbors. Before the Project's intervention, the military and INTA both refused to formalize these claims.

Instead, the military directed INTA to map Sepac's claim in 1985 as part of the process of declaring it a development pole. On the official INTA map, it lists the land to the north as "Lachuá National Park." Although the park was not legally inscribed in the General Property Register, INTA included the 10,000-hectare park on all its maps. To the east, the 4,500-hectare reserve/expansion was still listed as empty terrain (*terreno baldío*). Sepac leaders wanted thirty *caballerías* of the empty land to be inscribed as part of their claim, but INTA cartographers (military men who reportedly carried guns) refused. Sepac leaders claim that this refusal was not because of the park but because of some other reason that INTA did not give. According to FONTIERRAS records, including reports from the cartographers, INTA refused Sepac's large land claim because it would have allocated twice as much land per family as the law allowed for. In keeping with INTA's policy for the region, INTA designated Sepac as eligible for a land title as a collective agrarian patrimony (CAP). Although other kinds of land titles allow for differential, privatized holdings, CAPs give titled owners equal parts of land (*partes alícuotas*). INTA told paramilitaries that they could not title 90 hectares for themselves and only seven for their neighbors, but they would have to split the difference such that each family would end up with perhaps 15 hectares.

Paramilitaries fought this law, demanding that INTA halt the process until there were fewer families claiming land. In 1989 because displaced people had returned home in the intervening three years, INTA returned to Sepac to conduct a census of all families, who would become equal owners. When INTA employees attempted to conduct the census, however, paramilitary leaders threatened to kill them if they included all residents. According to archival records of a subsequent meeting, an INTA representative told Sepac that they would not get land titles unless all families were included. After this, Sepac's land-titling process fell into a stalemate. When the Guatemalan Peace Accords disbanded the PAC system that afforded paramilitaries power, they reorganized into the Land Committee, which charged residents money and pursued titles for the same exclusive group unsuccessfully over the next decade.

In the late 1990s, the Project received funding to title the park and more than twenty surrounding communities. Sepac quickly emerged as a "problem" community, and the Project attempted to address its land conflicts through its Land Forum, where the Project would mediate land conflicts with all interested parties as part of the titling process. Project administrators told me that they had no records of any Land Forum meetings and that it was impossible for me to contact the Land Forum administrator.[21] Park employees said this person meant well, but they fired him because he was a troublemaker; he told local communities that the park was still a *baldío*, or land without an ownership claim. When I interjected that he was correct and the park was a *baldío*, one guard's response was "It was a *baldío*, but it wasn't." When I asked why it was not a *baldío*, he said that the state had already claimed that land for the park and the expansion zone but just had not formalized its claim. As a sustainable development consortium, park employees believed that the Project's Land Forum should have increased the legitimacy of the park, not revealed its weaknesses to landless families making counterclaims.

For their part, many Sepac community members scoffed at the Land Forum, saying that it was a waste of time because there was a lot of talking but no decision making. Project administrators were supposed to be the neutral forum facilitators, but I think this was impossible. The Project's funding was contingent on its support of Lake Lachuá National Park, including the legalization of the park's expansion. Also, some Project employees were from one of the two ruling families. Unless they had been excluded from participating in Sepac's case (which they were not), it is hard for me to see how they could not have influenced the resolution of this case in their families' favor.

Despite the fact that it remains illegal according to the laws for Collective Agrarian Patrimonies, the Project paid for the formalization of inequitable land tenure in Sepac. FONTIERRAS issued a title that asserts that all titleholders have equal rights to the land. In 2008, the Land Committee president (a Project employee who is also a Portillo family member) told me that he rode around town (using a Project motorcycle) to tell people with land titles in progress that "if you don't pay for your land, we'll give it to the invaders." The Land Committee tells people how much land they can claim and then forces them to pay their share of the land's cost on that basis or risk losing it.

Here is where I argue that we need to critically interrogate the "two-faced" war perpetrator in the same way that anthropologists have exhaustively interrogated the figure of the "two-faced Indian" (Nelson 2009, 10). Diane Nelson's work enjoins us to look for the figure of the war perpetrator who committed bad deeds but then "covered them up by 'disappearances' and clandestine cemeteries, and by hiding ill-gotten gains off the books" (10). In this framework, it is important to note that the two-faced Indian is a racialized Other, while war perpetrators are unmarked by race. This could be because of the ways that people who seemed to take on agency in committing genocide *became ladinos* (Remijnse, 2002). While race has no essence, racism does, and the fatal couplings of power and difference are at the height of spectacle in enacting a massacre in the name of the *ladino* military state

(Gilmore, 2002). In this case, contra Nelson, war perpetrators do not hide their acts, and they barely acknowledge their "badness." The people who buried entire communities in "clandestine cemeteries" were not the paramilitaries but rather surviving family members who overcame their fear to clandestinely honor their loved ones, sometimes in the dead of night. Even today, they rarely speak of these acts. Rather than hiding, Sepac leaders flaunted ill-gotten gains and demanded that the Project formalize them. While I discuss the *ladino* imaginary in Chapter 3, I will say here that open acknowledgment, and in some cases pride, in committing genocidal massacres is why surrounding communities call former paramilitaries *ladino,* regardless of language or family genealogy.

Did Survivors Become Invaders?

Paramilitary killers and their families own the most land—this is widely understood, and no respondent disputed or qualified this statement when I made it. It is much more controversial, however, to say that today's park invaders are yesterday's genocide survivors. In terms of the politics of positionality, a former paramilitary leader is secretary of the Land Committee and a landowner, while the leader of the official civil war Victims' Committee is a member of one of the invader groups, Semakooy. The purpose of the Victims' Committee is to collect documentation and advocate for proper burials, dignification, and financial compensation for state violence during the civil war, especially military massacres. As landowners seem more likely to have bloody war histories, invaders seem more likely to be in the process of receiving financial compensation because the military disappeared a family member.

Still, the Project director expressed gentle skepticism when I raised the possibility that the land-titling process was disproportionately dispossessing Q'eqchi' genocide survivors. The two park guards who had been working in Lake Lachuá National Park since 1988 were openly hostile to the idea that "invaders" might be telling the truth when they claim historical rights that the army illegally took during civil war repression. It is important to understand that the claims of marginalized people are often difficult to prove by design. Many surviving families were forced to join the development pole when the army confiscated the identification cards of the male heads of household; families were told to wait in Sepac while their men went to the Playa Grande army base for questioning, but the men never returned (CEH, 1999, Case Study 17). It was impossible to live without identification during the war, and even today the police regularly pull all men off the bus and ask them to show their identification cards, bringing people to the station who cannot produce one. Without these, people could not claim their lives or their livelihoods. Likewise, many "invaders" claim that the army took their land-tenure paperwork. Indeed, one of the benefits that the UN-funded National Reparations Program offers Victims' Committees is help getting national identity cards to replace those confiscated or lost—but not finding land records that were likewise confiscated, lost, or destroyed when people's homes were burned down.

The only way that one can prove land tenure that supersedes a park is to have a file registered with INTA that predates the park's legal creation. Nonetheless, INTA/FONTIERRAS is notorious for losing people's files. For example, Semakooy representatives have a card that INTA issued with their case number from the 1980s, which they claimed would show that they asked INTA to legally redress the military's violent dispossession of their lands. FONTIERRAS was unable to locate the corresponding file, so park guards' assertions that these families never farmed inside the reserve/expansion until after 2000 stand as accepted fact—even though the park did not have any guards until 1988. As mentioned in the introduction, Quixpur has legal ownership over land that CONAP will neither let them access nor compensate. Every time "invader" leaders would show me their scant documentation, they were careful to remind me that Sepac leaders received legal land titles with the exact same documentation—the difference is that their titles were located outside the park.

If one discounts the paperwork because of its lack of legal status, all the last two groups have is physical evidence of tenure inside park lands (Figure 4): ruins of old buildings (foundation posts on the left), cemetery plots (marked by crosses and flowers), and cardamom and coffee plants still growing. When they took me on a tour in 2008, we entered the park illegally. I only knew this because the farmers acting as my tour guides told me—there was no fence, there was no boundary marker, and there were no signs. While they first talked among themselves about whether I was afraid in Q'eqchi', they laughed when I interrupted their conversation to tell them (in Q'eqchi') I was not. They showed me the graves of their parents they carefully tended, and they showed me the plants they had left with pride. While the Spanish speakers took turns telling me their history, those who only spoke Q'eqchi' periodically wandered off to clear paths and weed crops. One man was weeding his beans when a guide saw my camera and waved at him to look up; the man posed for the camera with his machete held high. As he held the machete high, the guide told me that he would die before he gave up his land. Once the picture was taken, the farmer went back to weeding with his machete, barely looking up as we walked on.[22] This is the picture on the cover of this book.

Park administrators assert that there is no way for "invaders" to show that they are the same families as those who established tenure in the 1960s (a decade before the forest reserve was declared), and at any rate they lost their land rights to the national park. To return to Diane Nelson's (2009, 10) claim about the Indian as a figure haunting Guatemala waiting to be unmasked, these land activists seek to be unmasked as Indigenous genocide survivors. They call for solidarity subjects such as me to recognize their ties to place and to read their participation in Sepac community life and paramilitary patrols as coercion and war violence rather than

FIGURE 4. "Invaders" point out a grave and church ruins as evidence of their historical land claims inside park boundaries. (Photograph by the author)

loyalty to a *ladino* state. In other words, they claim that the couplings of power and difference have limited their life chances (Gilmore, 2002). Burning down maize and bean crops of rural Q'eqchi' families limits their life chances in terms of both their material ability to feed themselves at harvest and the spiritual harm that burning sacred maize causes. For Q'eqchi's, it is their difference manifest in language, appearance, and access to powerful media outlets that makes them vulnerable to military patrolling, burning, jail and forced resettlement.

Each side—park administrators and farmers—has progressively hardened its stance. Where there were opportunities to negotiate solutions when the Project began, those opportunities disappeared when the boundaries of Sepac and the park were formalized in the 2000s. Every year families plant in the park, as they have nowhere else to plant. Every year park guards organize to arrest them with military patrols, as it is their job to protect the park. Enmity grows on both sides as hostage situations take their toll, and the SAA cannot find a solution. This tacitly opens the door for violent evictions. This cycle repeats with evictions approximately twice a year and may escalate, as most families farming on park lands stated bluntly that they had nowhere else to go, and they would die before they stopped farming in the park. For so-called invaders, it is the state and development agencies that created the fictional community of Sepac using military maps. While their racialized dispossession occurred in the context of the civil war, they believe that it was the arrival of sustainable development agencies that allied with Sepac leaders to formalize Lake Lachuá's park boundaries. In so doing, development formalized their dispossession.

"EVERYBODY LIES": DEVELOPMENT,
DRUGS, AND OTHER RUMORS

When people in Sepac say that they want to burn the Project down, they implicate current sustainable development work in wartime experiences of violence. Although influential development ethnographies emphasize benevolence in the will to improve (Li, 2007) or claim that harm emanates from capitalism in development (Goldman, 2005; Wainwright, 2008), this is not how people in places such as Sepac see the situation. They are not mystified by the fairy tales that development professionals tell themselves; rather, they understand development as politics. Conservation politics have different meanings in different places. In this community conservation politics have become racial politics, where the formalization of landownership for some and landlessness for others creates a fatal coupling of power and difference.

Before the civil war, people's marginalities came from the articulation of class, ethnicity, and religion. During wartime violence, families with marginal lands had to seek refuge in Sepac, begging for food and shelter, thereby physically ceding their land claims. After the war, many families claim that environmentalism is just a new mechanism for injustice, making them into park "invaders." They declare that "we didn't invade the park, the park invaded us!" Land activists embrace their Q'eqchi' identity, which they strongly associate with surviving civil war violence. As I discuss in the following chapter, those who committed violence in return for land have a more ambivalent relationship with their racial identities.

People's belief that paramilitaries won the war has implications not just for the past but also the future. When I was living in Sepac in 2008, I heard rumors about a giant plantation run by "Mexicans," code for Zetas cartel drug traffickers, replete with military men, guns, and shady security. I asked a gringa Peace Corps volunteer what she thought about these rumors. She said that she had heard them but laughed and said, "You can't believe everything you hear here. Everybody lies, you know." I realized that I had heard a version of this refrain from everyone I talked to about Sepac. Conservation and development practitioners repeatedly explained to me that I should not spend much time asking questions about the past, as locals were taking advantage of my gringa naïveté. At the same time, former paramilitaries and massacre survivors alike asserted that outsiders lie—park administrators, NGOs, the military. When everybody lies, there is nobody to trust.

Even if everybody lies, kernels of truth are powerful. Quietly but insistently, people whispered about the drug trafficking den just down the way from Sepac and whether there would be violence. In March 2009, national newspapers revealed that Guatemalan police and the U.S. Drug Enforcement Administration (DEA) raided a narco-plantation. Two Mexican Zetas commanders and thirty-seven trainees fled the plantation, leaving grenades, rifles, and ammunition behind. Authorities believe that the primary purpose of the plantation was for former Guatemalan special forces Kaibiles to train Zetas recruits (Castillo and Martoccia, 2011). While everybody from Sepac knew sordid details about the narco-plantation and its parties—even me—nobody reported it to the authorities. One newspaper claimed that the way the DEA found the narco-plantation was through those same parties, based on the idea that only the Zetas would be willing to pay so much to import massive quantities of Mexican beer.

I never got a chance to ask the Peace Corps volunteer what she thought about the narco-plantation (she finished her service in 2008), and in the summer of 2009 other volunteers in the area had not heard about the raid on the Zetas narco-plantation. I talked to a few Sepac community members, all of whom doubted that anyone would be brought to trial. A Semakooy leader told me that he thought "they" (unspecified) would find it away to use it against land activists. It would seem that he was right. During the 2010–2011 "state of emergency" that suspended habeas corpus rights in the name of clearing the Alta Verapaz Department of Zetas, the military did not arrest any major kingpins or raid narco-plantations. Instead, they raided the corn and bean fields I visited in 2008, burning them to the ground, shooting and arresting landless activists as so-called narco-peasants. While none of the Q'eqchi' land activists died in the military raid, the consequences of their arrest and potential solidarity support is hampered by the claim that they are narcos. I return to how narco-narratives limit the horizons of Indigenous land activism in Chapter 5.

3

———

Rethinking *Ladinos* as Settlers

BLOODLINES AND WAYS OF BEING

During my second interview with a key community leader in Sepac (see Chapter 2), Ramón Portillo, I horribly offended him. In our first conversation, Ramón explained to me the history of two families fighting over land and how this led to his role as a leading figure in paramilitary massacres.[1] He spoke easily about how his family plantation ties facilitated his military relationship and why he took on a leadership role as a military commissioner. While he never admitted responsibility for leading massacres in the region, he did not seem offended by my questions. When we began our second conversation, I showed him a draft of his family tree that I had drawn and asked if he would answer questions to help fill in some of the blanks on the branches. He seemed impressed that I made an effort to understand the genealogical underpinnings of his community's conflict. We pored over the drawing, talking of cousins, land, and inheritance for a while, when suddenly his countenance turned cold. He may have participated in mass murders, but Ramón was too polite to end the interview when I offended him. When I tried to talk to him about *ladino* identity, he called to his wife in the other room to tell her that we were almost done talking and he would be ready to eat soon. He did not invite me to join them, a signal that I was no longer welcome in his home. As the conversation drifted on, I wondered to myself, what did I say? I think I offended Ramón because I referred to his family members as *ladinos*.

When I interviewed former paramilitaries about land politics, I was worried that they would be close-mouthed or would simply refuse to talk to me because gringos are notorious for judging Guatemalans over civil war atrocities (while failing to judge U.S. actors for similar atrocities). As both military and civilian para-military leaders have been convicted of crimes against humanity, a stunning change from the army high command's assumptions of impunity just years before (Schirmer, 1998), the power of human rights seems to grow in the countryside. While the international human rights community bemoaned the Guatemalan Supreme Court's 2013 decision to overturn the genocide conviction of former military dictator Ríos Montt,[2] the Guatemalan community was shocked to see that the court formally declared that the 1986 constitution's blanket amnesty was invalid.[3] Today, former paramilitary leaders in places such as Sepac know they might not enjoy immunity for their war crimes.[4]

In Chapter 1, I argued that the Maya Forest is a racialized territorial project that interpellates and dispossesses Q'eqchi' Mayas as environmental criminals and then redistributes resources to others on that basis. In Chapter 2, I traced the history of one community where the articulation of the civil war and park creation culminated in racialized dispossession, such that genocide survivors became park invaders. Here, I argue that scholars can fruitfully understand the *ladino* identity as that of settler. Rather than a politics of pigmentation or blood quantum, the meaning of *ladino* identities is centered on their role in a property regime that posits them as owners of property and trustees of natives, who need their help to modernize and get ahead. While many *ladinos* likewise lost their land in recent decades, they have found new prosperity in their role as cultural brokers in the development of Indigenous peoples. I recognize the complicated constellations of identity politics where *ladino,* mestizo, and white have different meanings and reveal the tensions between celebrating racial mixing (*mestizaje*) and whitening the nation (*blanqueamiento*). Even as this chapter elucidates those tensions, it explores the limits to their meanings by comparing them with the Q'eqchi' constant that holds all of these as *kaxlan*—as I explained in the introduction, there has been a seamless move from applying this term to Spanish invaders, to German colonizers, and now to gringos in the twenty-first century.

Ramón's cousin returned from a visit to Europe a few days later, and I took the opportunity to ask him the questions I was afraid to ask Ramón. I asked him to draw on international perspectives because I knew he had been traveling as an international human rights organization representative, and he had extensive experience with European development professionals. Ramón's cousin invoked Q'eqchi' identification based on identifiers of language and blood quantum. He explained that their grandmother was Q'eqchi' and that everyone in the family spoke at least some Q'eqchi', and therefore the entire family was Q'eqchi' Maya. I explained to him why I described the Portillos as *ladinos:* they spoke Spanish as their first language, they invoked a paternal history of Hispanic landownership, the family rejected Mayan spirituality, they had strong military ties, and none of the women owned indigenous clothes (*traje*). While they spoke some Q'eqchi', everyone knows that plantation owners (*finqueros*) speak Q'eqchi' as a way to control their workers.[5] To me, I joked, this made them *puro ladino*. Ramón's cousin responded with a deep belly laugh. The joke is that there is no "pure" *ladino*, as the identity is so often understood as "not indigenous" rather than signifying a positive identity. I was one of few people who knew that he represented himself as Maya internationally and that he was understood as *ladino* locally. Equally important, he is called *kaxlan* in Q'eqchi'.

In moments like these, *ladinos* expect me to act loyal to them as on the basis of a shared nonindigenous identity. My increasing reluctance to do so has led to racial resentments and frustration. In sharp contrast to this, once they realize that I understand the settler colonial implications of being called *kaxlan* and the imperial implications of being called a gringa but that I am not offended when they call me by these terms, my Q'eqchi' friends are fascinated. They have so many questions about gringos (Why aren't we all white? Why are we offended to be called "gringo"?), Indigenous peoples in the United States (Do gringos recognize Indigenous land rights? Is it true that we killed almost all of them? What is a reservation?), and the politics of whiteness in the United States. In turn, I asked them why some people are okay with being called *ladino* and *kaxlan* but others are not. My Q'eqchi' friends love using me as a prop, explaining to Guatemalans that they are *kaxlan*, like the gringa. When my non-Q'eqchi' friends protest this term, saying they are neither invaders nor imperialists, Q'eqchi's shrug nonchalantly in disagreement.

While the production of a singular Mayan identity has long been questioned (Bastos and Camus, 1993; Burrell, 2013; Velázquez Nimatuj, 2012; Warren, 1998a), the ambivalent relationship that Guatemalans have with a *ladino* ethnic identity is less studied (cf. Euraque, Gould, and Hale, 2004; Hale, 2006; Taracena Arriola, 2002). *Ladino* has been the term commonly used to mean "nonindigenous" after nineteenth-century specific caste categories that often implied blood quantum measurement (mestizo, *pardo, zambo,* etc.) fell out of use. Whereas Mexico emphasized a positive move to *mestizaje* as the development of a "cosmic race" from Spaniards and indigenes, Guatemalan liberals spent significant time and effort on promoting racial whitening (*blanqueamiento*) through West European immigration. German families were focused on their highland landholdings through the mid-twentieth century, so elites in the lowlands hold together two contradictory identities: both European plantation owner and Indigenous.

Although two of the Portillos I interviewed claimed a Q'eqchi' identity, most did not. Everyone else I asked, both inside and outside Sepac, agreed that it was appropriate for me to refer to the Portillo family as *ladinos*. At the time, I thought that those two men claimed a Q'eqchi' identity in order to mitigate claims that they were *ladino* paramilitary leaders who had killed their Q'eqchi' victims under the watchful gaze of a racist state. In this way, articulations of identity are also social and political claims, or a settler move to disavow genocide while appropriating Indigenous peoples' territory (Smith, 2014; Tuck and Yang, 2012).[6]

When I returned a year later, I discovered that these claims were about more than a revisionist past; they also stretched into the future. In the summer of 2009, I called a professional lands conflict mediator to catch up.[7] He told me that the major gossip was about Sepac—the Portillos were asking for the Committee for Peasant Unity's (Comité de Unidad Campesina, CUC) representation in a land conflict. He knew this would surprise me, because the CUC was the emblematic peasant rights organization that was directly affiliated with members of the Guerilla Army of the Poor (Ejército Guerrillero de los Pobres), the same guerrilla group that killed Portillos in a massacre in the early 1980s (see Chapter 2). So, the same family that had reported people as guerrillas to be killed, allegedly played a leading role in multiple rural massacres, and ruled a development pole for years with impunity was now working with the CUC against a cattle rancher they said was a violent *ladino* outsider. I scoffed and said, "So what, they're Indigenous peasants now?" We also exchanged barbs about peasant organizations that come in from the capital without understanding who they represent.[8] This frustration with revolutionary *ladinos* co-opting Indigenous politics is common in Central America (Euraque et al., 2004). My colleague was one of a few development professionals (*técnicos*) who speaks Q'eqchi' as his first language and is from a rural community, not the departmental capital. In 2008, he told me that he finds it frustrating when people try to take advantage (*aprovecharse*) of ethnic identity in postgenocide Guatemala for personal gain. In return, his jokes affirmed me as someone who had spent enough years working in the region to be able to discern an "authentic" Q'eqchi'.

At the time I dismissed this as a form of political opportunism, one where *ladinos* revive rumors of a Q'eqchi' great-grandmother to claim marginalized status when it benefits them. This draws on notions of bloodline, where genealogy determines belonging. Like the U.S. context, people who want to "play Indian" do so in Guatemala by referencing matrilineal heritage, upholding colonial masculinities even in claiming indigenous roots (Deloria, 1998; Sturm, 2011).

Since the 1990s Guatemalan Peace Accords, the nation-state has recognized Maya peoples on the basis of ethnolinguistic identities. Indeed, the national census tended to count people as Indigenous only if they were unable to speak Spanish (Cojtí Cuxil, 1997). While this may work as a commonsense heuristic in the western highlands, it fails miserably in the lowlands. As *ladino* friends mournfully explain over *micheladas,* in Cobán one must speak decent Q'eqchi' in order to get a job as a bank teller—many people who meet these qualifications do not self-identify as Q'eqchi'. Meanwhile, in Flores, the departmental capital of Petén, second-generation (and earlier) Peteneros claim a like-indigenous identity in terms of ties to the land and political legitimacy (Schwartz, 1990; USAID, 1990). While we all claim to have moved beyond crude measures such as phrenology, key physical identifiers of indigeneity include skin color, hair color, shorter height, and broader bodies (Cojtí Cuxil, 2004, 195). *Ladinos* mourn the ways they are defined by their lack of indigenous traits (e.g., lighter skin, taller height, Spanish only, and wearing indigenous patterns only as cultural appropriations) and how they suffer indigenous resentment without elite privilege (González Ponciano, 2004; Morales, 2004).

While Anglo and German notions of identity draw strongly on bloodlines to determine identity (King, 1974; Wagner, 2001), most Q'eqchi's are more interested in performative work. I came to understand what this means through my own work as an ethnographer. When I studied the Candelaria Caves land conflict (see Chapter 4), I stayed in a community that was strongly split along religious lines: evangelical Q'eqchi's who demanded that I renounce the devil and join them to be reborn in the river waters and Q'eqchi's with an ambivalent relationship to Christianity (either Catholic or nonreligious) and a positive relationship with animist spirituality. The evangelicals told me that unless I was willing to forsake the devil and temptation in the form of dancing to honor spirits in the caves at night, I was going to Hell and would no longer be welcome in their church. I refused rebirth through baptism and did not attend church again. When I asked my Q'eqchi'-language teacher about cave rituals (*mayejak*), however, he explained to me that what mattered was not what I believed in my heart but whether I performed my duty as a community member.[9] I asked Javier, a local community leader, what he thought, and I couldn't make him understand why I felt a moral dilemma about participating in the rituals. When I told him I wasn't sure I believed that the spirit was actually animating the cave in a particular moment, there was an awkward pause while he waited for me to explain more. Finally, he asked if that meant I didn't want to participate next time. I said I would still like to participate in the *wa'atesink* and *mayejak*. He nodded and then asked me if there was a problem. I laughed and said it didn't seem like it. My limited Q'eqchi' skills failed me, but I think my language teacher was right—the rituals are not about me as an individual and my internal beliefs but instead are about my participation. In sharing the rituals, I demonstrate respect for the land, the spirits, and the people. Because Q'eqchi's emphasize the survival of people and place over an individual, acting in favor of a community matters more than any specific belief, much less one's blood quantum. In a way, the invocation of genealogical heritage reflects a *ladino* and/or European mind-set, one that carries weight mostly with other *ladinos* and/or Europeans (Casaús Arzú, 2010; King, 1974).

Identity is not a unified essence, but you can only become who you are by taking up the identities that others interpellate you into and then acting on them (Hall, 1995, 65). While *ladinos* sometimes claim indigenous roots today, Q'eqchi's will not interpellate them as Indigenous subjects. Unmoored in a sea of identity assertions, I relied on a simple question: you know your tribe, but does your tribe know you? (Sturm, 2011, 14). Neighbors' insistence that Portillos were *ladinos*, not Q'eqchi's, carry much weight in my analysis. The angry rejections that Q'eqchi's had of the Portillo family as Q'eqchi' both unsettle simple binaries—settler/native, individual/collective, legible/illegible—and reproduce them. Debates over *ladinos*, mestizos, and creoles are all in Spanish. Conversations in Q'eqchi' begin from the premise that all of these—*ladinos*, mestizos, and creoles and those who refuse an ethnic identity, claiming that they are "Guatemalan"—are *kaxlan*. At its heart, the *ladino* identity is that of the settler, defined as one who is not indigenous. When I call people *ladinos* and they reject that meaning, this calls both their identity and the larger ethnopolitical system into question.

PROPERTY MAKING AS RACE MAKING

It wasn't necessary to reform the land, nor to eliminate a political system, because there had never been one.

—CASASOLA (1968, 56; IN GRANDIA 2006, 111)

In U.S. critical race theory, whiteness itself is understood as a property relation (Du Bois, 2007; Harris, 1993). A key distinction between race and property relations in Guatemala and the United States is the role of blackness. While Guatemala did indeed have African diaspora slaves, the role of slave emancipation and the ability to become *ladino* means that darker-skinned peoples (*pardos, morenos,* etc.) were legally able to own private property and become entrepreneurial citizens earlier and at a higher rate than in the United States (Gudmundson and Wolfe, 2010a). Today, Guatemalan elite families see themselves as better than *ladino*, naming themselves creole and invoking pure bloodlines (Casaús Arzú, 2010). Creole disdain plays a major role in facilitating the *ladino* disavowal of advantages over Indigenous peoples and perhaps toward explaining why poor *ladinos* and Indigenous people do not collaborate in class alliances. Here, I follow Cojtí Cuxil (2004, 193) in acknowledging that there are multiple forms of discrimination at work in contemporary Guatemalan society but privileging what he calls the "creole-mestizo racism" toward Indigenous peoples. Building from this, my analysis emphasizes the ways that *ladinos*, mestizos, and creoles collaborate in imagining a settler state that they built, not one that they stole.

In the repeated invocation of the lowlands as a frontier with neither land-tenure regimes nor political systems, military leaders such as Casasola (1968) declared that settlers were the first property owners and that settler law was the first law. Indigenous and nonindigenous peoples alike became *ladinos* in settling the frontier. Likewise, the erasure of Indigenous peoples from the land, the law, and historical memory was meant to eliminate them. While the promise of land and law often goes unfulfilled, *ladinos* cling to unearned advantages while rejecting racial and/or colonial analyses that explain their historical basis.

Ladino *Is Not Mestizo*

At the end of the civil war, anthropologists and activists alike recognized the importance of a national Pan-Maya movement that reclaimed space for indigeneity beyond class affinities (Cojtí Cuxil, 1996). In postwar multicultural politics, many *ladinos* felt that they were condemned as racist murderers by international outsiders who knew nothing of the conflict (even if, as in the case of the United States and Israel, they helped fund it). *Ladinos* are often understood as agents of the state and/or as playing an intermediary role in elite efforts to control the rural, Indigenous poor (Nelson, 1999; Smith, 1990). Postwar accusations of genocide have articulated with older Hispanic prejudice such that as photographer Diego Molina asserts, "Ladinos are liars, traitors, charlatans, thieves, hypocrites, cowards, co-opted, sold out, and always taken advantage of" (Nelson, 2009, 11). In other words, even as *ladinos* commit the violence of stealing native land, they do not reap the benefits of this violence, and they resent blame without benefit.

Most Latin Americanists are familiar with *mestizaje,* the idea that the political project to build the Mexican nation was also a racial project to promote the miscegenation of Spanish and Indigenous peoples to produce a single "cosmic race" (Graham, 1990). This notion has been celebrated as a way to bridge racial difference and produce unity through hybridity (Anzaldúa, 2012). Whereas Anglo settler colonialism imagines that one drop of African blood condemns a person to inferiority, Mexican coloniality imagines that native territoriality decreases simultaneously with an ever-diminishing blood quanta among Indigenous peoples (Saldaña-Portillo, 2015). While *mestizaje* celebrates instead of fears mixing, this is arguably due to the erasure of African heritage in Latin America, focusing instead on the teleology of the disappearing Indian who bequeaths the nation to her mestizo child.

The figure of *ladinidad* differs from *mestizaje* in a few key ways (Euraque et al., 2004). *Ladinos* in Guatemala were not called "mestizo" precisely because this signifies people of mixed Spanish and Indigenous descent, whereas African diaspora peoples were an important part of the middle strata of Central American postcolonial classes (Gudmundson and Wolfe, 2010b; Lovell and Lutz, 1995). Beyond miscegenation, the *ladino* identity facilitated a social whitening of *negros, mulatos,* and *zambos* (mixed African and Indigenous descent) into a singular category of the civilized non-Indian. In Guatemala, the national project of improvement incorporated blackness into the identity of the nation, positing that this problem could be resolved through decreasing blood quantum, whereas the stain (*mancha*) of the Indian might reveal itself at any embarrassing moment (Hale, 2006).

In order to communicate overwhelming evidence of genocide (CEH, 1999; REMHI, 1998), the international human rights community simplified complex articulations of race, class, history, and belonging into a *ladino*/indigenous binary. For mestizos or Germans (whom I offend by calling *ladinos*), the situation is complicated in the Verapaces. Nelson (2003, 135) describes *mestizaje* as something that differentiates mestizos from "*white* aggressors, including internal elites and external (read gringo) interventions." Even this is a kind of conceit; U.S.-based scholars have an unfortunate tendency to write as though gringos are the only foreign white aggressors—heirs apparent to Spanish colonialism. From Guatemalan independence through World War II, however, German and Swiss immigrants held a higher social rank that distinguished them from *ladinos* or gringos (Casaús Arzú, 2010; King, 1974).[10] This newer set of immigrants was so reticent to become Guatemalan that many plantation owners lost their land because their parents registered them as German citizens (not Guatemalan), even though they had never been to Germany (Wagner, 2001).

When I partnered with development organizations that specialized in land titling, I found that most of my colleagues self-identified as German Q'eqchi', not *ladino* or mestizo (as is the case of Alfredo, below). While Q'eqchi's suffer a 500-year history of colonialism dating to the Spanish invasion, the first 300 years were mostly unsuccessful attempts by Dominican Catholic missionaries to move them into dense urban towns (but see Grandia, 209). Q'eqchi's regularly fled Dominican dominance and forced labor, fleeing into lowland jungles. Guatemala became an independent nation in 1821, and *ladino* elites embarked on a project to whiten the nation (*blanqueamiento*), but 50 years later there were only 6 *ladino* families among over 10,000 Q'eqchi's in the entire county of Cobán (King, 1974, 26). As was the case in the U.S./Anglo context, Spanish colonials found extensive and overlapping territorial rights particularly troublesome to recognize. Whereas the United States attempted to reduce those rights via treaty, the Hispanic mode of colonialism simply denied their existence (Craib, 2004; Rifkin, 2009). Highland Mayas were coded as more civilized because their property rights were more legible to the Hispanic property system, whereas lowland Mayas were coded as troublesome wanderers.[11]

The settler state declared that it was the first owner of the land and then broke its territory up into pieces of private property. The language for this practice is evocative—much like Black Hawk described the privatization of American Indian land as the dismemberment of a corpse that was ripped from his soul (Rifkin, 2009, 86), the Hispanic process first summoned the existence of land into being on the General Property Register, then dismembered it into pieces (*desmembración*). As there were relatively few *ladinos* from the highlands interested in moving to the lowlands, elites offered the opportunity for German traders to become plantation owners with coffee and sugar crops. Germans were familiar with the area and had begun to experiment with crops in the early nineteenth century, and they were seen as a bulwark against English traders and planters who were steadily settling the frontier that Guatemala eventually lost to Belize. Today, people in the Verapaces refer to the Europeans collectively as "Germans," reflecting their dominance in an immigrant wave that also included English, Belgians, French, and Swiss migrants.

To facilitate racialized dispossession, Guatemalan elites invited Germans to make the land work and teach Indigenous peoples how to work it. Marxian scholars have long interpreted dispossession as enclosure and profit as primitive accumulation, claiming that capitalism inevitably means that the rich take from the commons and give to themselves. While capitalism is a factor, it falls short in explaining why Guatemalan elites worked so hard to give away land in the late nineteenth century. The open invitation to Germans both reproduced notions that Indigenous peoples were not yet citizens and established racialized land rights stamped with dissymmetry. *Ladino* elites did not take land for themselves and instead gave it away with the goal of improving the Guatemalan national race with European settlers.

As this was specifically a project of racial improvement, national elites sought plantation owners who would become part of the nation—not absentee landowners who would not improve the land and their people. By 1897, German citizens owned at least 270,000 hectares in Guatemala (Wagner, 2001). Many German merchant houses and plantations were blacklisted during World War I, but they still owned about half of all coffee-producing acreage, most of which they ran through German trading houses (King, 1974).

When Germany declared war on the United States, the Office of Strategic Services (OSS), precursor to the Central Intelligence Agency, identified Guatemala as a "Nazi center in Central America" and deemed it a threat because of the importance of Guatemalan coffee in U.S. markets (Wagner, 2001, 173). In 1942, a Guatemalan dictator sent 115 Germans and 1 Italian to U.S. detention camps to exchange as prisoners of war (King, 1974).[12] The OSS issued an official blacklist of German-owned firms operating in Guatemala, targeting German-owned coffee plantations in production. As shown in Figure 5, the OSS blacklist was inexact, and the United States enjoined the Guatemalan government to research and discern which people were disloyal and merited dispossession of their land and their selves. This prefigures the relationship between the United States and Guatemalan security forces in the subsequent Cold War and the drug war. In 1944, the state expropriated German-owned properties. The actual extent of German dispossession is unknown, because most plantation owners resisted dispossession using a variety of techniques, including simply returning after the war and retaking land (King, 1974).

Many German descendants claimed land by racialized right of possession, even when it was not legally theirs. One of the largest landowners in the Verapaces, the Sappers, claimed that they had been the rightful owners of a complex of plantations since the late nineteenth century.[13] In the 1960s as the cardamom market took off, the Sappers physically claimed lowland territories for the first time.[14] A Q'eqchi' technician with a land-titling project told me that two Q'eqchi' communities on a Sapper plantation approached his nongovernmental organization (NGO) seeking a loan to buy the land they had lived on since time immemorial and as serfs since

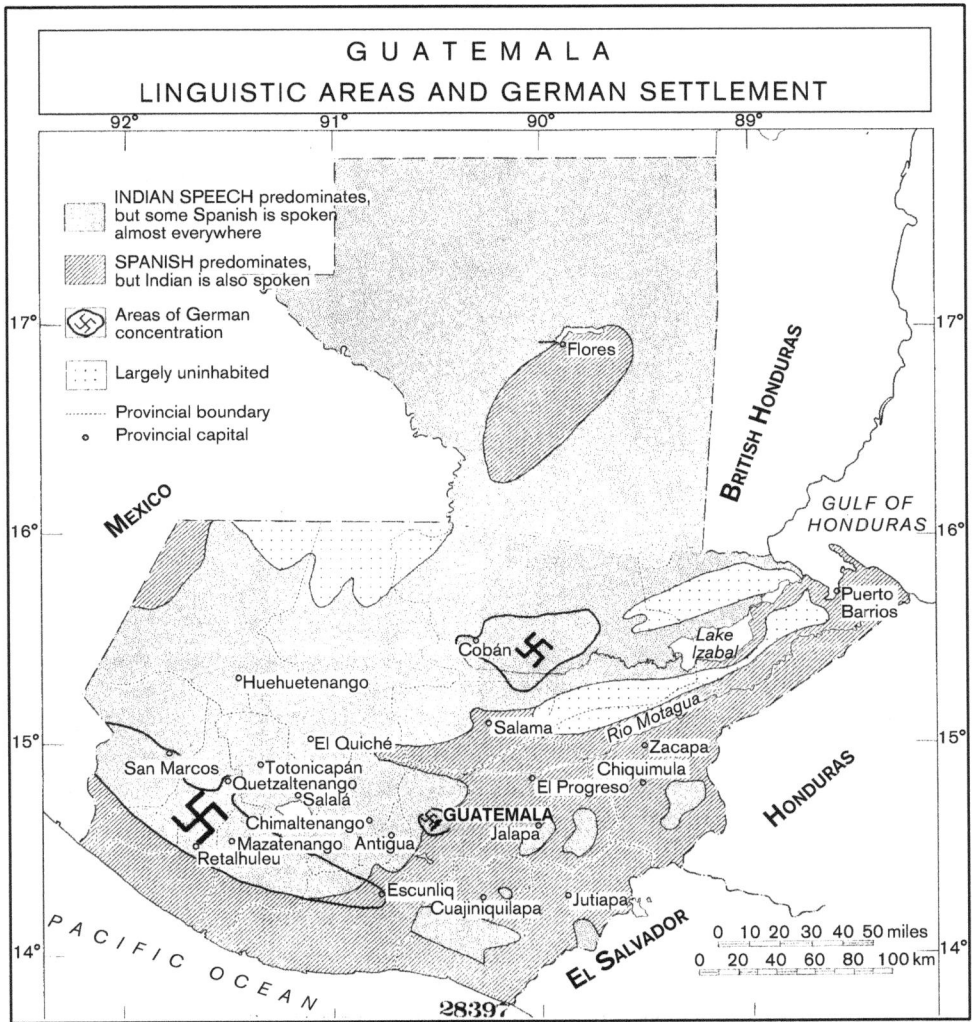

GUATEMALA
LINGUISTIC AREAS AND GERMAN SETTLEMENT

92°   91°   90°   89°

INDIAN SPEECH predominates, but some Spanish is spoken almost everywhere

SPANISH predominates, but Indian is also spoken

Areas of German concentration

Largely uninhabited

Provincial boundary
o   Provincial capital

17°   17°

MEXICO

Flores

16°   16°

BRITISH HONDURAS

GULF OF HONDURAS

Puerto Barrios

Cobán   Lake Izabal

°Huehuetenango

°Salama   Rio Motagua

15°   °El Quiché   Zacapa   15°

San Marcos   °Totonicapán   Chiquimula
°Quetzaltenango   °El Progreso°
°Salalá

Chimaltenango°   °GUATEMALA   HONDURAS
°Mazatenango Antigua   Jalapa
Retalhuleu

°Escunliq
Cuajiniquilapa   °Jutiapa

PACIFIC   0 10 20 30 40 50 miles
14°   OCEAN   EL SALVADOR   0   20   40   60   80 100 km   14°

28397

FIGURE 5. Areas of German settlement are demarcated by swastikas; the rest of the country is divided into areas where either Spanish or "Indian" is spoken or where land is "uninhabited." Based on map compiled and drawn in the Branch of Research and Analysis, U.S. Office of Special Services, 1943. (Courtesy of Earth Sciences and Map Library, UC Berkeley)

their nineteenth-century dispossession. When he looked up the property record, he discovered that the Sappers never owned the land in the first place, so he helped the community title the land in its name.[15] In cases such as these, it is not uncommon that both sides of a land conflict see their loss through the lens of racialized dispossession. While Q'eqchi's openly proclaim that the state stole their land on the basis of class and race, Germans quietly resent their World War II dispossessions.

The one continuity amid stories of dispossession is their role in producing and performing race. While my research in Sepac centered on how protected-areas creation articulates with projects of racialized dispossession, I was fascinated with what contemporary struggles signal about the reproduction of racial identities. I was captivated by the ways that Ramón Portillo both commanded scorched-earth massacres and calls on peasant organizations such as the CUC to avoid his own dispossession. The Verapaces region strips away any assumptions that Q'eqchi's need protections as a so-called minority ethnic group, as they are the majority population. Language, dress, and skin color are insufficient identifiers. While some scholars have traced the ways that some people became *ladinos* in the eyes of their neighbors when they committed horrific violence in the name of the state (Nelson, 2009; Remijnse, 2002), Indigenous men were also disproportionately drafted into violence as military or paramilitary killers. While survivors can only claim compensation for the loss of land and/or loved ones if they do not receive compensation as former paramilitaries, most Q'eqchi' men in the communities I worked with qualify for both. In other words, participating in state violence can just as easily be an act of survival as a betrayal of one's identity. That said, there is one reason left why I was confident that the Portillos are *ladinos*: they were settlers with plantation pretensions. In acting to take from others for their benefit—not just to save their lives—they became agents of the settler state.

For the central state, the liberal project of dividing up the land for modern private property did not fail; it was just incomplete. In both nineteenth-century land transfers to the Germans and civil war land transfers to homesteaders, the state presumed that it was modernizing property regimes for a modern citizen. To the extent that native sociospatial practices of hunting, gathering, and farming were recognized as "customary" (Neumann, 1998; Thompson, 1975), it was presumed that these were effectively outdated habits that would fade into the past. From archival documents to contemporary development practitioners (both Guatemalan and European), the possibility that Q'eqchi' extensive hunting and farming practices might be an effective and efficient way to manage sensitive subtropical soils was unthinkable—so much so that some laughed out loud at me when I asked (Ybarra, 2011b). To be modern is to farm using modern practices—whether state-of-the-art genetically modified seeds or state-of-the-art organic, settler assumptions that property should be held either by the state (in protected areas) or individual entrepreneurs prevail.

While the Guatemalan state treated all homesteaders as citizens who would apply for new landownership, the reality on the lowlands frontier was different. Q'eqchi's sought state recognition for lands they already knew as hunting grounds (see Chapter 4) and in other instances as home. *Ladinos* such as the Portillos sought to conquer new lands as extensively as possible, either evicting people who already lived on the land or trying to force them into plantation labor. Settler acts include the following violence: making land claims to which you have no previous relationship on the basis of paperwork, often fraudulent; attempting to force natives living on that land to work for you with little or no compensation; and demanding private property titles that impinge on others' land claims. Ultimately, like many settlers on the U.S. frontier, the Portillos' settler pretensions reaped only mixed success: they dispossessed others but did not become plantation owners. They don't see themselves as privileged because they measure privilege by what they failed to gain, not by what they stole.

From Plantation Owner to Land-Poor Ladino

Elite narratives of land loss are muted in postgenocide Guatemala, and German histories are subsumed with those of would-be *finqueros* who lost family land during the upheaval of the war. Most scholars and both truth commissions highlight the military's massive scorched-earth campaigns in condemning genocide, but elite memories challenge us to think through the implications of social revolts in the years leading up to these massacres (1960s–1970s). In terms of property regimes, many small-scale *finqueros* were pushed out of landownership, while families with more land and a greater willingness to resort to violence expanded their holdings (Huet, 2008).

Landownership among Guatemalan elites is notoriously difficult to track, but my impression is that the 1960s marked the beginning of significant change. The U.S. Agency for International Development (USAID) began to promote nontraditional agricultural exports as part of the Green Revolution, and cardamom was wildly successful in the lowlands. Putative landowners enclosed some of the best lands for cardamom production, but many also began expelling their plantation workers in fear of Indigenous revolts. Following the failed agrarian reform in the early 1950s, many elites were shaken by the eagerness with which peasants organized to claim *finquero* lands, and some expelled their serfs to keep them from claiming the land they were born on. With the Cuban Revolution just a few years later (1959), many *finqueros* became afraid that the Guatemalan Revolution might succeed. Hope for new economic opportunities articulated with racialized fears in a "fantasy of the possibility of an Indigenous revolt that would place at risk both the security they enjoy thanks to their control of the State, and the hegemonic community they imagined" (Adams and Bastos, 2003, 233).

Impending social change provoked two responses: fight or flight. Some *finqueros* allied with the army, often becoming civilian military commissioners. For

Q'eqchi' plantation workers, the relationship between the military and plantation owners was clear. As one survivor explains of a massacre, "I think it was probably ordered by the rich, because the rich thought we wanted to become owners a second time of our lands. So, because of that, what did they do? Send soldiers to kill us" (Huet, 2008, 100). In the war, many Q'eqchi's understood the army's repression as a preventative measure by *finqueros* to prevent them from becoming landowners again. The difference between "our lands" and landownership "a second time" reveals how Q'eqchi's think property relations within and beyond the settler state.

Those *finqueros* who did not fight for their plantations fled impending violence. After all, guerrillas would use high-profile murders, such as that of a *finquero* on payday in 1975 (Payeras, 1980), to announce its challenge to plantation capitalism. This not only announced to poor farmers and workers that guerrillas intended to reform land tenure by force but also warned *finqueros* that their lives were in danger. Today many *finquero* families chafe at portrayals of them as all-powerful, given that they lost their land in a context of violence. For *finqueros,* landownership is the basis of the *finquero*'s role as employer, trustee, and political power figure in local government. The potential guerrilla triumph was rife with *ladino* sorrow. When a prominent *ladino* left town in 1977, he supposedly said that "with me ends a phase in Nebaj's history. My father was the first *ladino* to arrive to the town, one son is an engineer, the other is a doctor and I, thanks be to God and to the little Indians [*inditos*], I am already rich. I am leaving. I don't want anything to do with this place" (Le Bot, 1995, 188). To save their lives, *ladinos* disengaged from plantation politics and began to reenvision their children's futures in terms of professional careers. For the landed elite, Guatemala's civil war and attendant Marxist social critiques heralded a new crisis. Not only did *finquero* families suffer death threats and land grabbing, they also suffered the indignity of knowing that retaliation against Indigenous interlopers was suddenly politically unpopular after the civil war.

POSTPLANTATION PATERNALISMS

In the first analysis of land politics on the lives of former *finqueros* after the Zapatista uprising in Chiapas, Bobrow-Strain (2007) drops tantalizing hints about social reconfigurations. Many former *finqueros* sought to use their networks in new roles, including serving as *coyotes* for people trying to migrate to the United States, smuggling goods north, lending money, and working in politics. As in Mexico, in Guatemala many families of formerly landed elites sought to reshape their networks of power to access new economic and political opportunities.[16] Many of the development professionals I worked with in Guatemala have German heritage. While some were hesitant to tell me about their family land claims at first, this seemed mostly because they wanted me to understand that most Germans in Guatemala were not Nazis, certainly not the more historic coffee families that immigrated before the 1920s. Many described their family land losses during World War II or the 1950s agrarian reform as the reason why they chose professional careers in land formalization. These development professionals, whose cadastral knowledge far outweighs mine, were often vague about how and why their families lost their land. According to Wagner (2001, 174), "rightful owners" hoped to regain their land after World War II, but the communist-influenced government did not relinquish these properties.

While the German story of dispossession is particularly stark, many elite families sent their children away to advanced schooling or abroad both to avoid potential rising insurgency violence and to prepare for professional careers that did not depend on a land base. When the peace accords negotiations brought promises of billions of dollars in aid, international organizations working on human rights, conservation, and development arrived in rural Guatemala seeking to establish projects with "local people" who were educated and computer literate. The problem with this is that Indigenous war survivors living in rural areas are the most likely to have been among the internally displaced population during the war, which forced them out of school and into deeper poverty. This helps to explain the broader pattern of why organizations such as the Project (see Chapter 2) partners with outsiders and local elites with troubling pasts of oppression—they are more likely to meet the minimum education requirements. Through both NGOs and government agencies, former *finqueros* continue to act as intermediaries for rural people, but now they focus their energies beyond the nation's capital toward foreign funders.

Postplantation paternalisms take shape in many ways and are rarely as coercive and troubling as I have argued is the case in Lake Lachuá National Park. Indeed, most of the people I have had the privilege of working with take on the very serious responsibility of trusteeship—not as domination but instead to direct and enhance rural communities' capacity for action (Li, 2007, 5). In *The Will to Improve*, Li emphasizes a Foucauldian "conduct of conduct" where the practice of development works at a distance so that people will do what they should. While Li and other critical development theorists are interested in explaining the gap between how development works in the international humanitarian imaginary and how it is received by local communities, I am interested in the people who bridge that distance and how they interpret development. Whereas Li, Wainwright, and others posit an earnest will to improve, Q'eqchi' invocations of *tenq'* (aid, help, reparations) call for gringo reciprocity for something that has already been given (see also West, 2006). In the postplantation era, *ladinos* step seamlessly into the role of trustee, where they know how the rural poor should live, what they need, and what is best for them (Li, 2007, 4). They both defuse incendiary Indigenous claims of what they are owed and offer an inventory of how gringos can help. To reflect on this, I describe at length my relationship with two different men whose fathers were plantation owners with Q'eqchi' serfs and who today see themselves of trustees of those same populations. Their role as settlers becomes normalized and noble through the paternal trusteeship relationship.

One colleague of mine from Uspantán, Mayor Victor Hugo Figueroa Pérez, explained to me that his family owned a few plantations in the Zona Reyna (northern Uspantán), but they had to relinquish them to guerrillas during the war. Although he had been to the plantations as a child (before massive violence in the mid-1970s), he had pursued a university degree in agronomy and worked in the United States for a few years, never intending to take back the land. After the civil war ended, his family sold their plantations to a group of returned refugees. I did not know that Victor had any relationship to the Zona Reyna when I first worked in Uspantán's municipal government (2004). I was pleasantly surprised that he had agreed to my proposal for community development workshops in the zone, as it implied a significant financial commitment for the cash-strapped municipal government. After we returned from one such community visit, Victor mentioned that the land used to be his family's. When I last saw him in the National Statistics Institute (Instituto Nacional de Estadística, INE) office in 2009, he was busy explaining to the director of cartography that he should remap the communities and recount the populations in the Zona Reyna, because the INE's current calculations failed to take into account all the communities that were created when *finqueros* abandoned their land during wartime violence.[17] In his role seeking development monies on their behalf, Victor did not mention that he had been a would-be *finquero*.

People in Uspantán asked Victor to run for mayor not only because of his professional qualifications but also because his father was remembered as a good *patrón* who helped people in his dual roles as landowner and mayor. Even though Victor was no longer a landowner, people wanted him as their trustee. Although he confided in me that he wanted people to take responsibility for their own development, he dealt with a never-ending queue of people asking for personal favors, both large and small. For a Peace Corps volunteer such as myself, Victor was an ideal "host country national" boss. He liked U.S. rock, understood gringo culture, and ran his office like a business, balancing the political and administrative needs of the mayoral office. His savvy made it all the more striking to me that he truly understood the kind of development that I envisioned, and he tried to accommodate my vision where possible. At the same time, he would often smile and shrug with his palms up when he explained that the people expected a different kind of development, one that entailed more responsibility than I was initially willing to shoulder.

Although some party figures asked Victor if he would be interested in a higher office, he decided to run for reelection as mayor instead. When I talked to Victor about it in 2005 (before his successful reelection campaign), he told me that Uspantán was his home and that he felt an obligation to help the people who live there. I do not believe that Victor wanted to stay in Uspantán because he enjoyed the power or the money or even because he did not want to leave home. Instead, I think Victor's noblesse oblige had roots in his *finquero* heritage. Whereas previous administrations ignored the Zona Reyna, Victor committed significant financial resources to providing services ranging from planning workshops to Q'eqchi'-speaking employees in the birth records office and even building a road that cut travel time in half. I felt like I understood Victor's commitment to the people in the Zona Reyna best when I saw how his obligations to communities of former plantation workers continued, even after they sold the land. His feat was conveying a will to improve to gringo constituents while communicating that he was taking up a responsibility to improve peoples' lives, without implying that they needed to better themselves in the process.

While I thought that some development professionals leveraged their professional roles for personal gain (see Chapter 3), many others strive to honor their families in renewed trusteeship relationships. In Victor's case, I can say unequivocally that his noblesse oblige worked to the county's benefit. Most people who are like Victor honestly want to help people, and it is important to understand that when they act as trustees in their development relationships, it is not simply because that is how they are most comfortable—it is also because their constituents (or beneficiaries) *ask* them to.

In 2008, I spent three months as a participant observer with the "land" team of New Horizons, a U.S.-based development NGO based with a Cobán office (see also Ybarra, 2011b). Alfredo, the land-conflicts program director, told me that his grandmother was Q'eqchi' and his grandfather was German. As with Ramón, I heard people refer to Alfredo as *ladino* but never to his face. Although Alfredo's family had a plantation, they lost the land due to irregularities in the cadastral process; the lawyer his grandfather hired to title the lands told him it would be costly and unnecessary to register his title.[18] Eventually the title they had was no longer sufficient, and Alfredo's grandfather lost the plantation. When I learned this, I interpreted Alfredo's decision to specialize in land administration and cadastral modernization differently, as the aim of this work is to help people legally map, title, and register their lands. In one land-conflict case, Alfredo and I spent what felt like hours arguing over the validity of a Q'eqchi' community's claim versus that of a foreign businessman. While I was unimpressed with the businessman's ream of unverified paperwork, Alfredo insisted that it was more reliable than the public records and correspondence the community was using to support its claims. Although I never asked him about it, I wondered later if my insistence that the businessman's paperwork was illegitimate reminded him of how his grandfather lost the family plantation.

Alfredo is a network hub in the Verapaces. Researchers ask him for tips on case studies, he writes and administers grants on mapping and titling lands, he is a major partner for the new mapping agency (Registro de Información Catastral) in its attempts to meet the "social" needs of its World Bank project, and he is a mediator for land conflicts. Through his family connections, Alfredo knows all the old plantation families. Through his work, he also knows most of the major peasant leaders—the National Coordinator of Peasant Organizations (Coordinadora Nacional de Organizaciones Campesinas), the CUC, Alianza Campesina—and often criticizes their actions, though he sincerely enjoys helping them resolve land conflicts.

On a number of occasions, I can recall sitting in Alfredo's office while he regaled me with tales of finding solutions to seemingly intractable conflicts between, for example, a community of demobilized paramilitaries and returned refugees who claim the same land but refuse to speak with each other. His favorite move was to schedule meetings at a hotel that miraculously had no cell phone coverage and then ask everyone to sit at the table until an arrangement was reached. He believed that people were so desperate for cell phones, food, and water that they would compromise. (People who knew Alfredo came to know the kitchen staff, as we would sneak off to the kitchen for food and phones.) Suddenly his cell phone would ring, and a peasant leader would be asking for advice on whether a potential parcel for sale had any problems (such as an invalid title or squatters claiming the land) before purchasing it for landless peasants. The importance of people such as Alfredo speaks to the continued impossibility of World Bank projects to create efficient land markets based on transparent information. If you don't know an Alfredo, you don't know what you are buying, regardless of the accuracy of maps and titles.

Alfredo is an intermediary for people who work at cross-purposes not only because of his job but also because he was born into it. As a person with German, Spanish, and Q'eqchi' heritage, Alfredo grew up in the *finquero* culture but is not a *finquero;* he grew up in Q'eqchi' culture but is not Q'eqchi'. Still, Alfredo tends to frame his own racial ambivalence (Hale, 2006) in terms of "both and," not "either or." He capitalizes on his intermediary position by being in the know and getting along with a diverse array of actors. Although I consider Alfredo a neoliberal and he probably considers me a crazy gringa socialist, we have a relationship built on respect, *micheladas,* and the mutual need that gringa researchers have for inside knowledge and that intermediaries have for prestige.

If Alfredo was an effective broker and information source to me, he was something else to rural communities. When he showed up in an SUV with a cell phone strapped to his belt, Q'eqchi' communities saw power. When he talked to them in Q'eqchi', they felt *confianza,* an immediate bond of trust. Part of the reason why Alfredo did not have a high opinion of some rural communities is that they trusted him enough to confess their weaknesses. While in a legal dispute, a community may claim to have occupied a plantation since "time immemorial" and that they are owed decades of back wages. But in Alfredo's tutelage, they would confess that some families did not move onto the land until the 1990s. They did not simply confess, however; they also asked Alfredo for guidance. More often than not,

Alfredo would advise them on their best course of action. This is why Alfredo had a stream of supplicants in the same way Victor did.

Alfredo and Victor are fluent in both neoliberal development and trusteeship. I found myself in an ethical quagmire when I tried to reconcile poor people's supplication for a relationship of trusteeship with my hopes that they would take ownership of development projects. As frustrated as I was that people expected me to contribute the most time, money, and reputation (*cuello*) for projects that benefited them, I finally realized that making people responsible for their development in microfinance and agricultural projects was unfair. In practice, rural communities do not get to choose which projects they participate in, so neither should they suffer the consequences of failures when responsibility is shared across the line of trusteeship. Rather than espousing an ideology, it seems to me that Alfredo and Victor accept neoliberal precepts as the rules of the game to work with powerful foreigners' money.

Even when they broker deals that leave rural communities ultimately responsible for debts and conflicts incurred, most development professionals who work in Guatemala consider themselves trustees. They develop relationships with communities, and most of those communities understand that if they fulfill their obligations for one project, they will be first in line to receive the next project. This is why I was not surprised that of two Q'eqchi' communities I chose to conduct three-month case studies of—both with similar histories and socioeconomic profiles—one was included in projects that multiple NGOs had on mapping, tourism, conservation, scholarship, indigenous rights, and women's rights. The other community had received no aid, apart from forensic assistance to identify and rebury loved ones from a 1980s mass grave. Projects beget projects, which belies claims that people will one day no longer need development assistance.

I have two concerns about the complicated articulation of neoliberalism and trusteeship through development projects in Guatemala. First and foremost, the displacement from *finquero*-serf to *ingeniero*-community[19] relationships strongly reproduces paternalism in these new trusteeship relationships. As I have signaled, many communities actively seek out this relationship, as they might have asked a *finquero* in the past to be their child's godfather. In the present, they ask gringas such as me to pay to paint the grade school, get computers for the junior high, and endow scholarships for our godchildren. The problem I have is that project beneficiaries seem to believe that they can bind development professionals into reciprocal relationships similar to plantation trusteeship. By and large, however, these attempts fail. For example, when a worker asks a plantation owner for a loan because he has a sick child, this increases his indebtedness to his patron. It does not necessarily mean that the worker will ever repay the debt. Everyone understands that if you are rich and you loan a poor neighbor money, she or he may not pay you back. More important, *finqueros* historically sought to bind their laborers to the fields through debt. In this history, the plantation owner did not *want* to be repaid; he wanted the laborer to die in debt. The problem with short-term projects is that communities must always pay back their debt (even if coffee plants rust and die or the cooperative's marketing plan fails). At the same time, development professionals on short-term contracts themselves often seek to declare projects successful so they can renew a contract to do the same work elsewhere rather than continue on a long-term struggle for truly sustainable development with a small number of people in a rural community.

Underneath developmental discourses, many *ladinos* seem nostalgic for past paternalistic relationships. One afternoon when I accompanied a New Horizons professional as he gave a talk on land mapping and titling, the local judge invited us to lunch in his office with other development professionals and police officers. The judge quickly directed the conversation to the scandalous way the new foreign *finqueros* were buying up land in the Polochic region for sugarcane agrofuel production. The judge asserted that traditional *ladino finqueros* worked the land and made money, but they also treated their workers well. These new *finqueros* refused to take on long-term workers, hiring people only as day laborers and refusing to let them plant crops on fallow lands. In particular, one Basque (Spanish) *finquero* refused to allow vehicles onto plantations to transport workers, forcing them to walk longer distances, and also refused to allow workers access to local water sources, forcing them to carry their own water in the intense summer heat. What was striking to me was that the *ladino* judge and police chief framed these scandals not through their professional lenses of law but instead through paternalistic plantation culture. The foreign *finqueros* were giving *ladino finqueros* a bad name, and this lack of respect for a reciprocal culture was scandalous.

My point is not just the failures of the old paternalisms but also the way that they continue to draw on settler tropes of native inferiority. Historicist views of racism posit that Indigenous people can—eventually—become civilized (Goldberg, 2002). The moment of native civilization comes into tension with the *ladino* right to rule. To paraphrase Li (2007, 14–15), if Q'eqchi's and *ladinos* are essentially the same, successful trusteeship would eventually eliminate inequalities in terms of literacy, income, and landownership. For those who cling to their settler privilege even as they deny its existence, this consigns Q'eqchi's to the back of the line in a waiting room where their number might never be called (Chakrabarty, 2008). In this way, conservation and development enfold genocide survivors into a relationship of trusteeship that elides reparations for violence.

I worry that old paternalisms reproduced in new development regimes tend to carry these self-serving biases with them. *Finqueros* see themselves as landowners (regardless of whether they mapped, titled, and registered their property with the state), whereas they see Indigenous people as "squatters" who are good as a source of labor but incapable of managing the land wisely themselves (Conklin, 1961;

Dove, 1983, 1993; Wainwright, 2008). Foreign development professionals often learn how local societies work from national development professionals. In so doing, they naturalize tropes of Q'eqchi's as "immigrants," "wood-eating termites," and "invaders," "closed off" (*cerrados*) to development and ignorant of conservation practices. This is why meddling gringos should work to fund NGOS with ethnically diverse staff; if Mayas only work as managers for "indigenous" or "human rights" projects and are relegated to low-level field positions in economic development, then international development agencies' understanding of economic development may skew toward the *finquero*'s viewpoint. In particular, I find that Mayas are underrepresented and non-Mayas are overrepresented in designing projects dealing with land tenure and conservation in the Maya Forest.

LADINOS AS CULTURAL BROKERS
Mestizaje *as a Weapon against Imperialism*

Gringos such as myself not only tend to miss the fact that many *finqueros* were dispossessed in Guatemala's revolutionary upheaval but may also be deaf to *ladinos* trying to explain why they dislike the term. (By way of comparison, much academic ink has been spilled over whether, when, and why Indigenous peoples are embracing the term *Maya*.) Some *ladinos* not only reject the name's historical origins but also honestly believe that they do not have any cultural, political, or economic power over Indigenous people.

I spent most of 2008 conducting ethnography, and the U.S. elections were a major topic of conversation. When they tired of my questions about land and conservation, my *ladino* colleagues would warn me that the United States was far too racist to elect a black president. My landlord, of German descent, told me that he was on the Left but warned me that he was afraid Barack Obama's campaign was actually a neoconservative conspiracy. Clearly, progressive U.S. citizens (including me) were being manipulated into voting for a black man so conservatives could order his assassination and plunge the country further into a security state. I protested that this seemed a bit far-fetched, but he reminded me of the assassinations of President John F. Kennedy and Dr. Martin Luther King Jr. Guatemalans' downward social comparison with the United States is a common Latin American conceit, which I usually dealt with by explicitly acknowledging that we are still racist in the United States, but a majority of us might be civilized enough to vote for a black man if he happened to be the most qualified candidate (in this, I was intentionally reworking the meaning of *civilized*). At the same time, I acknowledged that the United States was one of four countries to vote against the UN Declaration on the Rights of Indigenous Peoples in 2007.

Unlike contemporary comparisons, I never mastered the historical ones. On so many occasions that I lost track of—in cabs, buses, and coffeehouses—*ladinos* would bitterly assert that Guatemala never developed[20] because its Indigenous population survived, whereas the United States became a rich and powerful country because we systematically killed "ours" off. They expressed resentment at paternal responsibilities for a racial historic approach to dwindling racism and wishful gestures toward the classic naturalist white supremacy. Their often offensive questions point to a broader set of goals in settler colonialism. When I protested that Indigenous peoples survived and continue to exercise tribal sovereignty in the United States, *ladinos* were dismissive, claiming that their numbers were small enough that we could actually expect them to disappear—effectively, in this view, they had. It was left unsaid that one clear lesson from Guatemala's genocide was that its Indigenous peoples were survivors, perhaps even comprising the majority of the country's population. Likewise, *ladino* interlocutors were very interested in having me account for the ways that the Trail of Tears displacement led to U.S. economic development but not the ways that slavery accounts for U.S. economic development (Robinson, 2000). This parallels with a Guatemalan antiblackness that usually manifests as professed ignorance and offense but not engagement. Moreover, many *ladinos* believe that gringos have a romantic fascination with all things indigenous, seeing them as beautiful, childlike, closer to nature, and in need of our help. By contrast, they think that we despise *ladinos* or, worse, that we simply ignore them. In response to perceived gringo imperialism, *ladinos* wield discourses of *mestizaje* to decenter our simplistic racial binaries and remind us of our own cultural paternalism.

When *ladinos* take up the mantle of *mestizaje*, their argument tends to be that all Guatemalans have Spanish and Indian heritage[21] but now are a unique Guatemalan race, which can only overcome its obstacles if people put aside their ethnic and class differences and work together in alliance. This political discourse is prevalent not only in upper-class communities and the capital but also in peasant groups that accuse the Mayas' insistence on the recognition of indigenous rights as detracting from (nonindigenous) peasant rights.[22] In the biologized language of development, there is significant and unabashed slippage between "progress" and "improvement." Correspondingly, Maya unwillingness to take up the mantle of *mestizaje* is interpreted as a lack of "will to improve" on the part of project beneficiaries (Li, 2007). When this mantle is wielded against foreigners, *ladinos* tend to argue that they understand cultural politics better than international development professionals, so they are best positioned to improve "our Indians."

International Development as Brought to You by Ladinos

The idea that *mestizaje* can be a tool for people to deny their own privilege and delegitimize indigenous movements is well established (Hale, 2006; Knight, 1990), as are the ways that *ladinos* might use *mestizaje* as a national identity against foreign interlopers (Gould, 1998). A major site where *ladinos* fight for what they believe to be their rightful place is in the burgeoning development sector. Since the 1990s this has become particularly difficult, as most international development projects are geared toward truth, reconciliation, and empowerment in Indigenous communities. The primary exception to this is conservation-focused projects.

When new international agencies began working in Guatemala during the humanitarian crisis following the 1976 earthquakes, foreign donors tended to bypass traditional routes of power through local governments (Adams and Bastos, 2003), the hub of *finquero* networks. This move became increasingly significant as the presumption of political power by plantation-owning families (such as Victor's) has waned. The presence of development agencies subsided during wartime violence, partly because the military insisted that it was the hub for rural development. With the international pledge to provide $1.9 billion in development to postwar Guatemala as part of the peace accords, development agencies set up offices throughout the nation. Given the role of racism and genocide in the civil war, many development agencies brought in foreign experts to run projects and used local fieldworkers who spoke indigenous languages.

Some *ladinos* believe that they are discriminated against by foreign NGOs that want to employ only Indigenous people. One prominent *ladino* intellectual wrote that "ladinos ought to organize defensively against the offensive of the Maya ethnicity orchestrated, financed, and promoted by economists and foreign academics who do not understand our mixture and for whom we, the ladinos, are the villains in the picture" (Mario Roberto Morales in Adams, 2005, 171). Nowhere did this seem truer than development projects that sought recognition of racism and genocide. It is the simplistic war criminal/indigenous victim binary that allows the National Compensation Program (Comisión Nacional de Resarcimiento) to exclude all former paramilitaries, despite the fact that truth commission reports detailed the ways that Indigenous people were forcibly incorporated into the national genocidal project (CEH, 1999). *Ladino* privileges and resentments function somewhat like white privileges and resentments in the United States; they point to high-profile recruitment as evidence of discrimination while ignoring their continued overrepresentation in highly remunerated fields such as development.

In practice, conservation and development organizations tend to form a familiar hierarchy. New Horizons, the U.S.-based NGO I worked with for three months as a participant observer based in Cobán and traveling through lowland villages, has a foreigner in charge of its national projects; a college-educated *capitalino* runs national operations, the land-conflict project managers were both German-descended *ladinos,* and fieldworkers were Indigenous. These hierarchies also reproduce economic inequalities (Warren, 1998b, 182).

When I went out for beers with one of the project managers after a day in a rural community discussing land conflicts, I commented on how difficult managing language interpretation could be. When I saw the confusion on her face,

I explained that the fieldworker I accompanied was Maya but not Q'eqchi' Maya. (At the time I spoke as much Q'eqchi' as he did but not enough to run a multihour workshop on land-tenure regimes.) She sighed and said that it never occurred to her to ask if he spoke the language of the people she hired him to work with when she hired him. Our conversation was more than two years after she hired him and supervised his fieldwork, all without realizing that he does not speak Q'eqchi'. Likewise, my understanding is that lowlands Q'eqchi' land management and property regimes are different than those of his highland Maya community. This highlights the yawning gap between German-descended *ladinos* (as she is) and Indigenous peoples as coworkers. Finding qualified interpreters in rural villages is incredibly difficult, particularly since the project manager did not have a budget to pay interpreters (she assumed that she did not need one in all project proposals she wrote), and this usually means that training can deliver less content with fewer nuances. Rather than differentiate among twenty-one Maya peoples, non-Mayan professionals tend to assume that all fieldworkers inherently understand all rural Maya communities. This is also the information they convey in their reports to international funders, who then usually demand that these reports be translated into English. On the rare occasions that I asked why *ladinos* did not also have to undergo minimal Mayan-language training to work with a Maya population as I did (K'iche' in the Peace Corps, Q'eqchi' for my PhD),[23] responses usually deflected their own responsibilities and refocused their attentions on making fun of other gringos' poor Spanish.

When I ask about civil war violence, *ladinos* point to U.S. imperialism. While Guatemalan critiques of U.S. actions abroad are important (e.g., Grandin, 2004), they may also be a refusal of contemporary racial institutions. Even where they failed to inherit the land, *ladinos* inherit a hierarchy of racial privilege. Rather than disrupt this system as part of a postwar human rights agenda, international conservation and development are structured to value short time frames and hire formally educated professionals who offer accountability in Spanish or English. Instead of disrupt racial hierarchies, these practices help to reproduce them.

CONCLUSION: SETTLERS WITHOUT PATERNALISM

Rather than occupying a negative (not-Maya) space, the *ladino* identity inheres in two sociospatial practices. First, *ladinos* are settlers on indigenous territory. While Indigenous people also participate in homesteading programs, they tell me that they seek the most secure form of land tenure for lands they already consider home (see also Ybarra, 2011a). Community elders discuss not only trying to research land-tenure records in government offices but also walking the land and asking permission of anyone they met. By contrast, the act of seeking to dispossess people of their own land and force them to labor on it racializes the violent actor as *ladino*. Even for those *ladinos* who have failed to reap the promised benefits of free land on the supposedly empty frontier, there are still opportunities to wield racial power in acting as intermediaries between gringos and Indigenous people. Those *ladinos* with class privilege that enables education, computer literacy, and some English-speaking capabilities are most able to leverage this toward a much greater class power.

The *ladino* crisis has also provoked a crisis in postplantation paternalisms that has important implications for conservation practice. Whereas conservation practitioners often eschew agrarian histories and politics, their work shapes the horizon of possibilities in the lowlands, where the majority of territory has a protected-area status. In Chapters 1 and 2, I suggested that Indigenous peoples experience conservation's exclusions as a racial project that formalizes settler colonialism and forecloses the possibility of indigenous territorial autonomy. As long as international conservation is scaffolded in a national racial project, practitioners should expect their work to be met with fierce resistance and anger by the peoples it dispossesses.

Even those included in the sustainable development imaginary find that postplantation paternalism offers little in terms of long-term trusteeship. In an early pilot project in the late 2000s, engineers with Proyecto Ixcán arranged for Q'eqchi' rural smallholders to take out loans, which they would pay back using income from a reforestation payment for an environmental services project. When the trees died less than a year later, smallholders were shocked that the bank threatened to send them to jail if they did not pay back the loans. Ironically, I visited one Ixcán community of smallholders who thought they would earn payments for environmental services for reforestation (REDD+) but instead sold their land to a monocrop agrofuel plantation to pay back their loan debt. Former landowners were trying to rent land, as there were no jobs on the plantation. The project hailed small farmers in a relationship of trusteeship by promising that engineers would choose the best trees possible using their agroforestry training. When the engineers seemed to have chosen poorly, however, the responsibility fell squarely on the shoulders of smallholders, and the NGO did not help them negotiate with the courts. Ironically, the sustainable development project paved the way for monocrop plantations.

When I returned from a visit to one of the communities in the process of selling its land for agrofuels, I learned that some technicians I was working with in Sepac had previously worked on Proyecto Ixcán. When they told me, I asked if there was anything they could do to help the families who were losing their land. They seemed puzzled by my question and said they regretted that the project had not met its goals, but the funding had run out and the agency no longer worked in Ixcán, so there was really nothing to be done. The fact that the project did not meet its goals because it sold owners trees that died within a year was something they acknowledged but did not feel responsible for.

These same technicians expressed surprise and dismay that Sepac leaders did not want to take out loans to jump-start a new cooperative, going so far as to claim that local communities leaders lacked vision. To me, it seemed that the technicians lacked the ability to apply lessons learned from one project to the next. I cannot help but think that a *finquero* would never get away with abandoning a community like that. It is not a question of the law but rather the ways in which landed elite networks repudiate abusive behaviors, whether due to fear of labor revolts or positive pride in elite paternalism. It is precisely because these "engineers" are based hours away in the departmental capital and work on yearly contracts that they cannot afford to work with communities that are no longer part of their jobs. At the same time, reputation is crucial with community leaders who struggle with reading and filling out bank documents. Rural communities learn about land losses and have become increasingly reluctant to participate in reforestation projects and to work with those conservation technicians who leave a tidal wave of debt in their wake.

In contemporary conservation projects, it is nonindigenous peoples with better historical access to education that have become cultural brokers for conservation BINGOs such as Conservation International and the Nature Conservancy as well as USAID, which provided the majority of their seed funding to develop the national protected-areas system. This is why reforestation successes are limited to the large plantations and the highly professionalized forest cooperative intermediary in Petén, the Association of Forest Communities of Petén (Asociación de Comunidades Forestales de Petén, ACOFOP).[24] *Ladinos* perceive gringo favoritism of historically oppressed Indigenous peoples, which leads to their increased resentment toward the people they are supposed to partner with as trustees in sustainable development. In postplantation paternalism, moreover, these professionals take more short-term money and have less long-term responsibility toward rural Indigenous communities. In the event that projects fail, *ladino* cultural brokers may pathologize Indigenous communities for their foreign funders in an effort to maintain their access to project funding. Where Indigenous peoples break with the bond of trusteeship (as in Chapters 1 and 2), development professionals explain to their gringa counterparts that they should choose a more hospitable field site. For those gringo interlocutors who make the time to learn a bit of the language and ask a few questions, however, I suggest that lowland Q'eqchi's have their hands outstretched in invitation for a different kind of partnership.

Taxing the *Kaxlan*

Q'eqchi' Self-Determination within and beyond the Settler State

Colonialism produces anti-colonialism.

—DEMETRIO COJTÍ CUXIL (1997, 57)

PUBLIC PARK, PRIVATE HOTEL

In the last chapter, I posited that the *ladino* identity is performed through planta-tion pretensions and the valorization of private property, attempting once more to produce a settler frontier and extinguish Mayan territoriality. This racial territorial project entails both physical violence (scorched-earth massacres) and structural violence (creation of protected areas, denial of extant land claims). The thread of hope that runs through this book is in the unfinished nature of this colonial project and the ways that survivors take up anticolonial struggles. Many Q'eqchi's seek state recognition for their land rights, but they are often frustrated in these attempts. The case of Setzuul, a Q'eqchi' community in the Franja, exemplifies the hollow victory of obtaining formal land title but still not being able to evict their foreign invader (*kaxlan*, pronounced "kaash-lahn"). Rather than choosing between the twin poles of liberal recognition and indigenous refusal, however, I elaborate on Audra Simpson's formulation of a cartography of refusal as one that rejects the authority of the settler gaze while engaging in settler legal systems. The communi-ties I worked with do not see the need to engage in either/or strategies; rather, their lives necessitate both/and engagements with settler states to survive the present while envisioning decolonial futures. Below, I recount the history of their land struggle and look to future creative acts.

I first sought to partner with a Q'eqchi' Maya community association, Wak-liqoo, and the community of Setzuul because I was seeking a success story to use as a model for how gringos could work in solidarity with indigenous territorial struggles (as in Grandia, 2012). Instead, I found a case of settler colonialism sitting

below a thin veneer of conservation. A French man used a park-declaration process to legitimate his continued use of caves, land, and archaeological artifacts for
tourism over and against Q'eqchi' leaders' wishes, going so far as to threaten them
with violence and dispossession. More than that, the nationally famous case of
Candelaria Caves National Park shows the role of protected areas in reproducing
territoriality as a racialized identity practice. While the figure of "private property"
was powerful in the hands of a white man, it was revealed as worthless in the collective hands of an Indigenous community. The lesson this community learned
was that the rule of law and private property would not be enforced on their behalf,
evidence be damned, and that conforming to conservation respectability politics
awarded no meaningful alliances. In the wake of these events some people have
fallen into despair, while others rearticulate a radical politics of hope in imagining
collective self-determination.

In the early 2000s, the community of Setzuul joined twenty other Q'eqchi' communities in the association Wakliqoo, mapped its land claim, and obtained legal
title to community property. In 2008 in exchange for learning more about Setzuul's story, I submitted an ethnographic report to the Guatemalan Ministry of Culture and Sports (Ministerio de Cultura y Deportes, MICUDE) affirming the value
of the community's caves as a sacred place, arguing that a French tour operator
who was charging admission for on-demand Mayan religious ceremonies was profaning it. To research the report I lived in Setzuul for three months, during which
time I accompanied community leaders in their peregrinations to the capital and
attended a meeting they hosted for supporters. In addition, I interviewed neighboring community leaders and regional and national experts and obtained and
analyzed the land-tenure archives.[1]

Not long after arriving in Setzuul and moving into my quarters in the mayor's
home, I was asked to participate in a curious venture. As part of an official
MICUDE commission, I joined Setzuul leaders and MICUDE officials to demar-
cate park boundaries and demonstrate that the French-owned hotel was inside a
national park. I thought this was strange, because the French entrepreneur, Girard,
lobbied for the park's creation to legitimate the ecohotel he built next to the caves.
In other words, one of the few things that the foreign owner, the community, and
MICUDE officials agree on is that the hotel is located inside the park boundaries.
What I thought was in question was whether Girard's hotel is on land that he purchased legitimately from Q'eqchi' community members or if it is still part of Setzuul's land (now legally titled). What this venture signaled was that the park's claim
might be sufficient to evict Girard, but Setzuul's collective land title was not.

We formed a "commission": Setzuul's mayor and a motley community crew that
faded away as we walked on, two park guards,[2] and three MICUDE archaeologists
carrying a small handheld GPS unit. I leaned over to my friend Javier, who was
from Setzuul and worked for Wakliqoo, and asked, "Don't all you Wakliqoo folks

have better equipment than that?" I knew they did, because I was in the process of purchasing one significantly more sophisticated than the one we were using to complete their set. He got my joke and offered a strained smile but said that having MICUDE employees do it made it "official," as though they were disinterested parties. Just a few minutes later, Javier gave MICUDE officials advice on how to get a better reading in cloudy conditions. We could not find physical boundary markers, so we had to enter the hotel compound.

Even though Setzuul leaders had legal title to the land we were about to walk on, the mayor, Pascual, seemed nervous. I leaned over and asked him, jokingly, "Is it dangerous?" He responded, smiling but serious, "I don't think so." When I raised my eyebrow in concern, he clarified: "I don't think the German shepherds are loose today." At that point, I got nervous too. German shepherds are usually used as guard dogs by people with interests in protection, such as the military and private security firms, and those people are often poorly trained men with large guns. We lined up single-file and ducked under a barbed-wire fence, still on Setzuul's property but perhaps not safe. As we walked toward the caves (the primary site of interest from MICUDE's perspective), a security guard fired a warning shot in the distance, and I instinctively shuddered, to my embarrassment. (If anyone else did, I didn't see them.) The commission was a success in that MICUDE officials had documented that Girard was violating the law in the following ways: illegally running a tourism complex, illegally building fences, and illegally firing guns inside a national park.

Before we left I managed to snap a few hasty photos of the guards holding guns, even as they scrambled to hide them from view of the camera lens. Javier and Pascual asked me to hitch a ride to the county seat, print the pictures, and file a police report. Javier advised me that I should emphasize that the MICUDE officials and I were there when the shots were fired, noting that the police would be more concerned about one gringa than the entire village combined. I went to the police station and repeated that the picture was evidence that the park guards were violating the law against having guns in a national park. The policeman shook their heads and promised to file a report but seemed mostly confused that I was not reporting a robbery. On the ride back to Setzuul, I couldn't stop wondering: How can this happen to Guatemalan citizens on their own private property? This episode made it clear that land titles don't guarantee property claims and that citizens sometimes have fewer rights than foreigners.

The problem is that these Guatemalan citizens are Q'eqchi' Mayas, who are caught on the one hand between the promise of private property for all citizens and on the other with settler tropes of native inability to understand private property. Where postwar multiculturalism offers recognition of difference in terms of the right to language, dress, and dance, this does not extend to material property relations. The Candelaria Caves illustrate the impossibility of liberal parsing between culture and materiality, as a sacred place demonstrates the material nature of culture. This massive limestone complex is much more than an altar—the caves connect more than twenty kilometers of communities, including over twelve kilometers of underground passages that carry freshwater. The multicultural liberal state's failure is its own, however, and the loss of state recognition does not necessarily lead to a loss of indigenous identity.

Drawing on insights of indigenous studies, I develop a case study of a cluster of Q'eqchi' Maya communities that are working toward collective self-recognition. Q'eqchi' leaders mobilize both/and identities, where they seek recognition both within and beyond the settler state such that their claims to the nation-state are not symptomatic of dependence. Learning from and building on Audra Simpson's formulation of a "cartography of refusal" does not depend on Western maps or nation-state recognition. Simpson's play on words in her cartography of refusal demonstrates "the fundamentally interrupted and *interruptive* capacity of [indigenous] life within settler society" (Simpson, 2014, 33). Other scholars who have taken up this work have found it to be incredibly generative, because refusal is more than just a negation in oppositional politics—it is a redirection to other questions, other ideas, other ways of knowing, other mappings (Tuck and McKenzie, 2016). Through a series of creative acts, these communities have developed a new municipality to experiment with self-determination within and beyond the boundaries of the nation-state. In an unprecedented move, the mayor imposed a tax on extractive oil palm companies (based on trucking weight) for municipally owned and maintained roads. For some community leaders, this movement is about taxing the *kaxlan,* a term they use to critique territorial appropriations of *ladinos* and foreigners (such as Girard) alike as colonial invaders. Even as settler-state subjections increase in militarized repression and widespread rural violence, I reflect on hopes for Q'eqchi' self-determination.

LAND FOR THOSE WHO WORK IT?
RACIAL FORMATIONS IN PRIVATE PROPERTY

Guatemala's civil war was an epoch of contestation between the militarized capitalist government and the Marxist insurgency. Both before and after attempted 1950s agrarian reforms, the state upheld individual private property as the pinnacle of economic development, offering limited provisions for collective property; this was to protect supposedly precapitalist, rural, Indigenous communities that might lose their land if left to compete in the market (Ybarra, 2011b). Setzuul was one community that the state marked for communal land title during the 1970s (*patrimonio agrario colectivo,* or "collective agrarian patrimony"). The lesson that many Q'eqchi' communities learned as they lost their land through bloody and protracted struggle was that individualized private property trumps collective property. Many now seek to split up their parcels and invest their labor in their land as a performance of ownership (Ybarra, 2011a).

While liberal regimes claim universal rights of citizenship, they instead privilege white property-owning men (Appelbaum, Macpherson, and Rosemblatt, 2003). Even though liberal regimes celebrate private property as recognition of investing one's labor in land, settler colonialism is founded on the erasure of native territoriality in order to claim that the land is an empty frontier. In working through a settler rule of law, Setzuul's case devastatingly demonstrates that valid land titles in the hands of Q'eqchi's are worth less than invalid land titles in the hands of Europeans. Rather than a case of Westphalian citizenship status, nonnative claims to land by both Guatemalans and foreigners demonstrate that whiteness, with attendant expectations of civilization and funding, maintains territorial power. This is particularly stark in the case of Girard, a French student who arrived as a guest and then allied with the military and stayed as a supposed owner of their land.

During the civil war Marxist activists put forth a claim of land for those who work it, which extends into the present day with resettled refugees and cooperative ownership. As I discuss elsewhere (Ybarra, 2011b), the state property register invalidated Q'eqchi' labor by misrecognizing swidden agriculture as an inferior form of farming. While their attitudes toward land vary greatly, both Marxists and liberals viewed land justice through a framework of productivism, or an ideology that views the expansion of productive forces as a precondition for the attainment of freedom (Gilroy, 1993b, 274). Whereas the liberal project focuses on Lockean labor as liberation in a meritocracy and the Marxist project seeks labor solidarities for a social wage, both fundamentally efface the central role of territory in indigenous social reproduction. It is for this reason that *campesino* calls of "land for those who work it" (Rosset, Patel, and Courville, 2006; Wolford, 2010) does not bring together the poor as a social class and instead marks a cleavage where nonindigenous peasants collaborate in a collective project to deny indigenous pasts, presents, and futures. This is a stark legacy that shapes settler perspectives in both Marxian and postcolonial perspectives, as de la Cadena (2015, Story 2) traces in Marxist and then postcolonial intellectual Aníbal Quijano's confident declaration that there were no Indigenous leaders in Peruvian agrarian movements. Beyond failing to grapple with the complexities of spirituality in land relationships, these perspectives have occasionally been wielded to deny the identities of the people who claim their land rights as part of their identity.[3]

Setzuul's land-tenure history reveals how one Q'eqchi' community walked a tightrope between military and guerrilla politics in their efforts to make a homeland that they could pass on to their children. As with most of the Q'eqchi' people, this community's story is not one of belonging to the land since time immemorial. Rather, Q'eqchi' indigeneity is borne through repeated and ongoing racialized dispossessions where imagining a homeland is a radical act of resistance.

The only record of Q'eqchi's living on Setzuul prior to the 1970s is from sale records of a prominent German coffee family, Diesseldorff, indicating that with the land sale came eight Q'eqchi' serfs (Kit, 1998). Setzuul's founder, Sebastián, first traveled through the region with his father during the 1930s forced-labor campaigns to build state infrastructure. Later he looked for land during his seasonal travels to Petén as a rubber tapper. The civil war had already begun, and Sebastián sought to participate in the military's counterrevolutionary land-for-loyalty program when he asked the National Institute of Agrarian Transformation (Instituto para la Transformación Agraria, INTA) for permission to settle near the Candelaria River in 1970. Although Sebastián was in contact with INTA officials over the years, there is no record of any agency paperwork to process Setzuul's land title until 1978.[4] At that time, local officials informed Sebastián that he would need to measure parcels and settle families into a centralized village. He and a few others walked the land in their claim to convince settlers to centralize. Most refused, and some families even claimed that they were forming separate communities.[5]

Sebastián also denies that Setzuul had any contact with members of the Guerilla Army of the Poor (Ejército Guerrillero de los Pobres, EGP) in the 1970s. He acknowledges that the EGP was widely active in the zone but claims that when he met a guerrilla on the road one day, he lied and told the guerrilla that Setzuul wasn't organized and didn't have any committees that the EGP could talk to. The same highway that brought Sebastián to Setzuul also brought the military and guerrillas. By the 1970s, the Franja region was known as the "Generals' Strip" because retired military members received land in return for their service, and the highway was built next to an oil pipeline, which the military focused on protecting as a matter of national security.[6] For its part, the EGP was active along the highway because newly settled communities might be open to a revolutionary message. The majority of villagers were former serfs who took the risk of claiming land as their own, had some exposure to Catholic Action and liberation theology's revolutionary privileging of the poor, and sought new global opportunities such as cardamom markets.[7] There were a few folks in Setzuul, notably those who were Catholic in the 1970s, who told me that they were in regular contact with the EGP. Pascual, my host and community leader, showed me where EGP guerrillas used to camp out every so often. In Pascual's opinion, Setzuul was not affiliated with the EGP; the people didn't have problems (*cha'ajkilal*) with the EGP, but they didn't give them free food either.[8] His language indicates a significant minimizing of civil war violence: whereas others refer to this time as *rahilal* (Huet, 2008; Wilson, 1995), which translates as "time of great sadness," *cha'ajkilal* translates as something more like "time of troubles."

Most military officials received land titles in the Franja and immediately sold them, never setting foot on the land. Setzuul's troubles began when a retired presidential guard[9] officer decided to establish a cattle ranch adjacent to theirs.

Although at first some community members worked on his ranch, the relationship soured. By 1981 nobody would work on his land, and the community accused him of encroaching on their property. A lone *ladino* in a sea of Q'eqchi's, he was afraid that the EGP would kill him, so he asked the military for help. The military built a temporary post on his ranch that it staffed for about a year, during which time the military patrolled the region intensely, looking for guerrillas in the jungle.

By 1982 violence broke out, and all families abandoned their homes. Some families moved to the cattle ranch cum military post, and others sought refuge with Q'eqchi' families in nearby communities. By 1983, the army was advertising on the radio that there were free lands for (re)settlement throughout the Franja. The military directed the legislature to pass a law so that INTA could declare lands "abandoned" and rescind people's rights if they fled for extended periods during the violence, actively encouraging *ladinos* from the southern coast and the east to take over formerly indigenous property (Brett, 2007; Nelson, 1988; Padilla, 1990). When they heard that they could lose their land, most[10] Setzuul families decided to resettle under army auspices; this required them to live in a resettled, geographically centralized village and to institute their own paramilitary Civil Self-Defense Patrol (Patrulla de Autodefensa Civil, PAC).

Most community members say that violence died down by the late 1980s. Nonetheless, as Pascual explained, the community military commissioner didn't cede his role until the Guatemalan Peace Accords were signed, and he conspicuously owns the only gun that the community got to keep after the PACs disbanded. As with most war stories, I learned this in a roundabout manner. Every time I bought myself a cold Pepsi, I bought popsicles for Pascual's two grandchildren. He didn't say anything at first, but once it became clear that I considered this treat a daily necessity in hot and humid weather, Pascual suggested that he liked the other store in town with a refrigerator more. I told him that I had been to both stores, but the one I liked had better prices and a colder freezer. He laughed and said that maybe I was right, but the store I liked was run by the former military commissioner, who still kept a gun in his store. Pascual didn't shop there, and after that day I didn't either. Even today, small acts such as buying popsicles are performances of political allegiance. While such actions may seem small, in times of civil war and drug wars they signal communities of trust and distrust.

While the massacres were over by the time families resettled Setzuul in the mid-1980s, violence and fear lingered. This, then, is the context in which a French speleologist, whom I call Girard, explored the region's limestone caves in the 1970s and 1980s. When he first "discovered" the Candelaria Caves, Sebastián was his guide.[11] In 1984 and 1985, Girard paid for experts to conduct studies attesting to the caves' unique value.[12] Community members told me that he camped periodically near the caves in tents outside the community center. "He was just like you," they told me. "He said he was a researcher [*aj tz'ilok rix*], and he was going to study the caves for his thesis." Multiple interviews included pointed comments that critique the *kaxlan* perspective—arriving as a guest and then staying as an owner. This is an essential characteristic of a settler.

By the late 1980s, Girard started building his ecotourism hotel. Although he asked for permission, the community council (Comité Pro-Mejoramiento) rejected his proposal to build a home by the caves. "We thought he would take [our land] from us," a former council member bitterly noted in an interview. Eventually, about fifteen young men went to his campsite "to scare him." Nobody would tell me what specific threats they made, but subsequently Girard went to the military commissioner in Chisec to bitch and moan (*chillar*), as Sebastián explained it. Soon after, the commissioner arrived in Setzuul to inform community members that they had to let Girard live by the caves or "we will fuck you up" (*vamos a joder a ustedes*) and leave their bodies like stray dogs (*chuchos*) on the road, referencing massacres under Lucas García (1978–1982) when mutilated bodies were publicly displayed along the side of the highway to instill fear among bystanders and shame among family members who were not allowed to collect their dead. After this visit, the community military commissioner became one of Girard's employees and acted as his enforcer.[13]

The relationship between Girard and Setzuul simmered over the years. At first some community members thought that he just wanted to live in a massive house, but then they realized that he was profiting from their land as a tourist site when groups of foreigners showed up, bypassing the community completely and heading directly for what was actually a hotel. Some people worked for his hotel, but community leaders continued to pursue their land title—a process that regularly stretches over decades even when uncontested. For his part, Girard accumulated paperwork that shows his informal purchase of individuals' claims to part of the collective title. None of these purchases are legal for collective property in the process of land titling, but sometimes FONTIERRAS honors them anyway.[14] In 1996, FONTIERRAS archival records show that Girard tried to register the land as his, but the local state official informed him that this was impossible, as Setzuul's land title was already in process. It seems that Girard felt comfortable with his land claim until the civil war ended, when a civilian government in the ascendant era of the Pan-Maya movement might not uphold his claim over theirs.

It is here that Girard wielded the fatal coupling of difference and power (Gilmore, 2002; Hall, 1992): he mobilized his fear of being evicted as an illegitimate settler through racialized privilege to circumvent the normal land-titling process. With only the documentation of speleologists and Girard's proposal, the Ministry of Culture declared the Candelaria Caves Park due to its archaeological and speleological importance. In recognizing the importance of the caves to the *ancient* Mayas, however, MICUDE officials failed to carry out a site visit where they would have met *living* Mayas who could have explained the importance of the caves to their spirituality and livelihoods. It is clear that state agencies are concerned with conservation, archaeological protection, and collaborating with *kaxlan* landowners—all to the exclusion of poor, Indigenous people. It is not that Indigenous peoples are hiding or invisible, it is that the settler state does not look for them.

Whereas many Latin American peasant movements rally around the idea of land for those who work it, no amount of labor that this Q'eqchi' community could have invested in the land would have validated their property claim. At least in the case of Guatemalan cooperatives, moreover, scholars who ally with peasant activists often downplay or fail to acknowledge that there were Q'eqchi' lowlanders living on the land when they settled it. To the contrary, in an era of ascendant conservationism, staking a claim could easily be read as poor land management (i.e., deforestation), which then becomes the justification for dispossession. The community of Setzuul first tried to demonstrate, to no avail, that its members were farmers, then loyal anticommunists who patrolled against Marxist guerrillas, and finally good environmental stewards who care for the land. When all of these efforts failed, Setzuul leaders focused on their collective rights to self-determination.

THE LIMITS OF NEOLIBERAL MULTICULTURALISM AND SETTLER-STATE SUBJECTIONS

The larger project of this book looks at how settler-state subjections created the conditions of possibility for Guatemala's protected-areas system. The reasons for this are conjunctural and historical; the protected-areas system was created in 1990, but the first peace accord in which the military acknowledged the existence and rights of Indigenous peoples was not signed until five years later (see Chapter 1). Even as settler-state subjections are crucial in demarcating the possibilities for multicultural recognition, these are only one of many paths that Q'eqchi's walk to find their future. Before I offer a claim for the hope that indigenous activism brings to Guatemala, I first trace how neoliberal peace politics delimits its national horizon of possibility.

In the late twentieth century, liberalism (a belief in natural individual rights, civil liberties, and private property) experienced a resurgence under the banner of neoliberalism (Peet and Hartwick, 2009). Most poor countries underwent a reorganization of political economy: cutting state entitlements and infrastructure while simultaneously investing in short-term development projects and nongovernmental organizations (NGOs). In Latin America these initiatives had a corresponding cultural component, one that simultaneously upheld the rights and value of economically savvy men and created a slot for multicultural rights, such that nation-state "governance shapes, delimits and *produces* cultural difference rather than suppressing it" (Hale, 2005, 13). While multiculturalism offers relief from assimilation imperatives, multicultural domination works in and through the work of Indigenous people's identification, with the impossible object of an authentic self-identity (Povinelli, 2002, 6). This is a relationship of subjection laced with longing, one in which power relations impact how Indigenous peoples know themselves as subjects through the systems of meaning and control that permeate their lives (Spade, 2015, 25–26). The power of liberal multiculturalism in the context of indigenous territoriality is that it pleads with the settler state for recognition, thus reproducing the state's role as arbiter of rights (Bryan, 2012; Hale, 2002; Wainwright and Bryan, 2009). If multiculturalism menaces, it would be in the settler state's ability to induce indigenous subjections such that the loss of state recognition is akin to the loss of indigenous identity. While this grim vision may indeed occur all too often, I suggest here that indigenous alterities work both within and beyond settler states.

As Demetrio Cojtí Cuxil (1997, 57) explains in his statement "colonialism produces anti-colonialism," the Pan-Maya movement to repair and celebrate Mayan identity in Guatemala emerged from the anticolonial reaction to the settler states' most recent attempt at genocide, the civil war. In a history still shrouded in secrecy, indigenous political activists had a complicated relationship with the official revolutionary Left, which was dominated by *ladino* leadership. This split still manifests an uneasy contemporary agrarian politics whereby the isomorphism between *campesino* (peasant) and *indígena* (Indigenous person) has been undone.[15] In the western highlands, there was a complicated constellation of alliances that led to some groups splitting from the *popular* left-wing movements (including peasant groups) and reconstituting themselves as Maya, primarily through ethnolinguistic projects that allied with indigenist academics. By the late 1980s, it was clear that there was a vibrant Pan-Maya group whose primary goal was to expose the contradictions in a political system that claimed to be egalitarian but promulgated a monoethnic, monolingual Guatemalan nation (Bastos and Camus, 1993, 2003; Ba Tiul, 2007; Esquit, 2012; Warren, 1998a).

The Pan-Maya movement arguably reached its apex during the 1990s peace accords negotiations. Throughout the 1990s, Setzuul and other Q'eqchi' communities remember Pan-Maya representatives meeting with them and discussing human rights, memory, and recognition. With significant international pressure, the military agreed to the 1995 Agreement on the Identity and Rights of Indigenous Peoples, which officially recognized the existence of Maya, Xinca, and Garífuna peoples. In July 1996 Guatemala ratified Indigenous and Tribal Peoples Convention (ILO 169), which recognizes territorial rights for Indigenous peoples to reproduce their culture and way of life. In terms of implementation, however, the multicultural state has persistently sought to de-link the politics of cultural recognition from the politics of distribution—recognizing rights to speech, language, and dress while ignoring rights to collective representation and territory.

The Candelaria Caves illustrate the impossibility of liberal parsing between culture and materiality, as a sacred place demonstrates the material nature of culture. After Setzuul's attempt to harness the power of liberal private property failed, leaders took up the mantle of multiculturalism, attempting to make themselves legible as Indigenous subjects through a countermapping project. While countermapping made the conflicting claims clear, it did not convince the settler state to recognize the basis of their claims (Gordon, Gurdián, and Hale, 2003; Nietschmann, 1995; Peluso, 1995; Wainwright and Bryan, 2009). I briefly recount the ways that Q'eqchi' leaders engaged in settler-state subjections in futile efforts for multicultural recognition, and then I discuss how their current activism looks beyond the nation-state.

Western Mappings, Western Failures

In "The Territorial Turn," Karl Offen (2003) wrote about the rising phenomenon of ethnoterritorial recognition in Latin America. Most Latin American nations were founded on racialized dispossession—Indigenous peoples' territory became *tierras baldías,* or supposedly unoccupied national lands that colonial powers allocated to "productive" landowners, understood through the legitimation of European labor and the misrecognition of Indigenous labor. Over the last few decades state policies of concessioning off indigenous territories are being reversed, with nation-states recognizing African diaspora and Indigenous peoples' territorial rights. Brazil, Colombia, Ecuador, and Nicaragua have all gone beyond allocating property rights to recognizing broader principles of indigenous territoriality.

More than simply recognizing individual property claims, state recognition of territorial claims calls for an alteration of the rules (Offen, 2003). ILO 169 takes territory to mean a geographic area in which culturally differentiated peoples reproduce their way of life. In other words, indigeneity signifies a cultural condition requiring a territorial basis for its sustainability (Anderson, 2009, 151). Thus, Latin American states in the process of recognizing indigenous territoriality must rewrite their property laws and rework their definitions of citizenship.

By the 1990s, state recognition of indigenous territoriality articulated multiculturalism and environmentalism (Cárdenas, 2012; Goldman, 2005; Gordon et al., 2003; Mollett, 2011; Ng'weno, 2007; Sawyer, 2004). First, the World Bank agrees with a national government for a loan program to update cadastral registers, focusing on individualized, capitalist property. Then, the World Bank negotiates with nonstate social actors who usually make territorial claims as a legal right, a moral claim as people who are culturally different from the dominant population, and an environmental claim as a people who are stewards of the land. The World Bank then funds a two-pronged project—individual capitalist property rights for most citizens and collective property rights for African diaspora and Indigenous peoples. As with other Latin American nations, Guatemala received World Bank loans for land formalization as part of the 1990s peace accords process. Unlike other nations that also had a significant Indigenous population where the projects were rolled out, however, the 40 percent Q'eqchi' population in Petén did not trigger the Indigenous peoples' safeguards (Grünberg et al., 2012). Landed locals and mainstream environmentalists posited that Q'eqchi's were immigrants and did not require "special" consideration, and there was no consideration of them as refugees and displaced Indigenous peoples in the wake of state genocidal massacres.

To understand why lowland Mayas are regularly enunciated as Indigenous peoples without valid territorial claims, it is worth looking to the reception of international and regional indigenous countermaps. One particularly important project, sponsored by National Geographic, mapped correlations between indigenous territoriality and biodiversity, arguing that Indigenous peoples were successfully conserving endangered resources. The map sparked debate and was widely cited, and the project was repeated in 2003 (Ayres, 2003). My understanding is that both projects justified indigenous territoriality on the basis of conservation, not as an inherent right. When I asked a K'iche' Maya land activist about the importance of this project for Guatemala, he scoffed.[16] He said that when he and other consultants presented their finished map at the Guatemala City campus of the Latin American School of Social Sciences, people in the audience said that it could not be published in Guatemala because it would be taken as a territorial proposal (*propuesta*). He told me that today Guatemala is "behind" other Latin American countries because it is impossible to speak of territories, only "ethnolinguistic regions." I didn't think to ask until years later if there might not have been a territorial proposal that wasn't marked on a Western countermap.

After our interview, I cabbed to various government offices in the capital to test this assertion. At each office, including the Mayan Academy of Languages, I asked for an "ethnoterritorial" map of Guatemala. The receptionist would correct me, asking if I meant an "ethnolinguistic" map, only to then tell me they did not have one. I finally obtained a Spanish version of the map in Figure 6 (rendered in grayscale) in the Office of Bilingual Education, which stated in italics along the bottom that "this is not a territorial representation."[17] On the map, the western highland region is an orderly rainbow. The lowlands, however, are a mess. Q'eqchi' territory is the biggest, seeming to swallow up Mopan territory and overlap with Poqomchi' territory. Even stranger, Q'eqchi' territory is the only indigenous territory that is differentiated with an "expansion area." Q'eqchi' is the primary indigenous language spoken in the Maya Biosphere Reserve, but the notion of "expansion" actively undermines the territorial legitimacy that mapping might otherwise offer. This is important because it seems to reproduce the idea that Indigenous peoples can only claim land they have possessed since time immemorial. This ignores the ways that Q'eqchi's have repeatedly suffered racialized dispossession in Hispanic colonialism, liberal plantation capitalism, and modern scorched-earth massacres. Despite the fact that this temporal requirement does not exist in the framework of

FIGURE 6. Ethnolinguistic map, according to the Academia de Lenguas Mayas de Guatemala. (Blackmer Maps)

ILO 169 or the Guatemalan Constitution, state agencies and conservation BINGOs regularly use it to explain why they do not need to recognize Q'eqchi' territorial rights. Indeed, this is why the World Bank said that the Indigenous peoples' safeguard was not triggered in the land administration program (Gould, 2009). This marks the limitations of Western legibility in countermapping.

This Land Is My Land, This Land Is Your Park? Reprised

As the ethnoterritorial promise of indigenous territorial rights has not been extended to lowland Mayas, they have not sought to make their collective territoriality legible to the state. Instead, individual communities such as Setzuul partnered with powerful Western players in an effort to become legible as ecologically noble savages in need of gringo interventions (Conklin and Graham, 1995; Redford, 1991). Setzuul leaders believed that only a gringo could counteract the claims of another gringo.

Girard claims that he bought the land around the caves in the late 1980s.[18] Community members' memories of his declared intentions to buy the caves are less clear. As mentioned above, if Girard had bought two parcels from Setzuul, his purchase would not be binding under the law. Girard used this to build a hotel, and international dignitaries and national military authorities attended the inauguration. At these and other events, regional and national Guatemalan officials praised Girard's work as important economic development. Although they understood that a foreigner was profiting from their natural patrimony, they did not believe that the local Q'eqchi' community was capable of bringing in international tourism dollars as Girard did. Setzuul leaders were not informed of Girard's actions, and they did not know that their land was declared a park until it stopped their land-titling process.

After Girard's attempts to title Setzuul's land failed, he promoted the creation of a park around his hotel. A National Council of Protected Areas (Consejo Nacional de Areas Protegidas, CONAP) representative told me that he was very interested in incorporating the caves as part of the national protected-area system, but they told Girard that he would first have to resolve the "land conflict" with the Indigenous communities living there.[19] Girard's efforts met with success at MICUDE, where officials declared the park a cultural patrimony on the basis of Girard's archaeological reports of ancient Mayan artifacts. Setzuul leaders affiliated with Wakliqoo insist that the ministry's park map was sloppy because it was based on office work (*trabajo de gabinete*), not fieldwork, and that the maps are not valid because they did not walk the boundaries. Others told me that a development NGO, Talita Kumi, did arrive to measure the park boundaries, but Setzuul leaders were suspicious and refused to let the workers walk the boundaries. This points to the ways that community leaders understood that the settler state's maps were designed for their dispossession—hence their resistance to mapping (Goeman, 2013).

The common refrain in Setzuul and the other communities that found themselves mapped into a park is that it was "declared a park in secret" (*decretó al patrimonio a escondidas*). The dimensions of the newly declared cultural patrimony did not cleanly match up with Setzuul's boundaries. Instead, it traversed a longitudinal strip that encompassed the caves and overlapped with Setzuul and supposedly two other communities. In 2000 when Setzuul leaders went to check with FONTIERRAS on the status of their land title, they were informed that the price had risen from Q60 to Q400 ($50) per hectare, an increase of 667 percent. The local FONTIERRAS official suggested that he could cut them a deal if they agreed to split their land into two parts, ceding the park lands to the state. Setzuul leaders responded, "What park?"

Community leaders recall that state officials implied that Girard had legal land title[20] and that they should come to an agreement with him. They suddenly found their lot thrown together with two other communities in fighting Girard and the park.[21] Over the next year, the communities had a series of meetings with FONTIERRAS to discuss their land rights. In the most memorable meeting, FONTIERRAS and Ministry of Culture officials finally went to one of the communities in question (instead of summoning them to their office in the capital, as usual). The secretary of a neighboring community's Land Committee recalled that officials came in with a condescending attitude, telling local leaders that they didn't understand the fact of the park (*la gente no entiende*) and began a pedantic explanation of the park's boundaries. The secretary insisted that the people did understand, becoming upset just from remembering the event. In fact, they were angry that state officials treated them disrespectfully while stripping them of rights to the land they settled, suffered the war on, and planned to give to their children.

A number of people surrounded the government commission with plastic tanks that they said were full of gas, threatening to douse and burn them.[22] They did little to substantiate their threats, but they probably did not need to—the image of a horde of supposedly savage Indians threatening a few *ladinos* has been powerfully salient since the colonial period (Hale, 2006). The Ministry of Culture representative started crying, and the FONTIERRAS representative wrote out a promise to title the communities' land. A European funder of Wakliqoo told me that it was this conflict that gave the communities power to negotiate a settlement, but the FONTIERRAS representative reneged on the letter as soon as he returned to the capital. When I reviewed the FONTIERRAS file on Setzuul in 2008, it contained his subsequent written recommendation that FONTIERRAS refuse to negotiate, much less formalize land rights, with communities because they held state representatives hostage. This was the last recommendation on file.

At this point, Setzuul's history diverges from typical dispossession stories because a few powerful people intervened: three Peace Corps volunteers, one of whose father worked for the U.S. Agency for International Development (USAID); the European who today funds Wakliqoo projects; and a few urban Q'eqchi' environmentalists, who founded Wakliqoo with the help of the aforementioned foreigners. FONTIERRAS only agreed to meet again with the three communities after USAID intervened on their behalf.

USAID funded a project for a U.S. anthropologist to work with community leaders to map their land use and then develop a land-management proposal for the Ministry of Culture in exchange for finishing the land-titling process. Wakliqoo employees recall this as their first countermapping experience, one that both empowered them and trained them in skills useful to help other Q'eqchi' communities.[23] It is at this point that most observers declared success (as in Grandia, 2012, 137–138); poor Indigenous communities countermapped their land claims, and the state awarded them title. When I came to an agreement with Wakliqoo's director to take on Setzuul as a case study, this was my understanding. Although this is true, there are three key caveats to that prevent me from qualifying this as a success story.

First, when I asked Setzuul leaders what they thought about gringo characterizations of theirs as a success story (Grandia, 2009c; Stocks, 2002), they vehemently disagreed.[24] Setzuul expected, and repeatedly requested, that the state evict Girard, who was squatting on land they now own. Years later when I asked Setzuul residents why they thought Girard hadn't been evicted yet, they would laugh and say that he's white, he's French, he's rich, or he's *kaxlan*. In multiple interviews and meetings people indicated that if he were poor and Q'eqchi' like them, the state would have evicted him years ago. Today if members of Setzuul try to walk onto their land that Girard is squatting on, they risk being attacked. Even during the months when Setzuul and the hotel seem to peacefully coexist, the specter of military coercion hangs heavy through the specter of uniformed guards with guns and German shepherds. Rather than a singular moment, daily boundary practices illustrate the tenuous and unfinished experience of racialized dispossession, which threatens to encroach ever farther.

Second, during a 2008 meeting in Guatemala City, a FONTIERRAS lawyer revealed that the land agency changed its policy on their title—it will not release the titles from tutelage (*tutela del estado*). When I protested that it was legally obligated to do so once the communities finished paying for their land, the lawyer waffled and said that he would only do it if the MICUDE directed him to. Although this is a symbolic issue,[25] it makes Setzuul's victory hollow. The effect it has is to reinscribe the state's authority over the community in the figure of the Ministry of Culture. While Setzuul and Wakliqoo leaders worked very hard to develop positive relationships with MICUDE, these relationships must be continually reworked. One possible concern that Oxlajuj Ajpop (OAP), a Pan-Maya NGO based in the capital city, expressed is that each appointed minister of culture has a different vision of Mayan culture, and they were concerned that some Western-oriented archaeologists believed that only pre-Columbian cultures were "truly" Maya to the extent that they resented having to cooperate with local Indigenous communities.[26]

Most important, the weight of the settler state hangs so heavy that the fact of Setzuul's landownership and material land practices are not enough. Although it was not legally required, Setzuul's countermapping initiative included a long-term land-management plan developed by a gringo anthropologist. This reproduced the assumption that an outside expert knows more about how to manage lowlands farming than Indigenous peoples do.[27] The park declaration was focused around the ecological and archaeological value of the caves; Girard cut down trees and built a complex right next to the caves, not Setzuul community members. Nonetheless, he continues his ecotourism practice without comment, but the community has disciplined its land use to demonstrate that its members are "good" environmental subjects. In turn, this validates the idea that if Setzuul members do not act in accordance with the land-management agreement, they may be expelled as "bad" environmental subjects. It is particularly interesting that Q'eqchi' swidden agricultural practices, especially burning, are forbidden in the land-management agreement, in keeping with colonial fears of fire and in contravention to science that demonstrates that extensive land uses are appropriate for tropical lowlands (Kull, 2004; Van Ausdal, 2002; Wainwright, 2008). In effect, conservation imperatives claim to be universal but instead are racialized; while *ladino* neighbors graze cattle inside park boundaries and Girard continues to build up his ecotourism business (cut from trees inside the park, also against the law), only the Q'eqchi' community finds its land-use practices codified and disciplined. As the rules are applied disproportionately to criminalize poor, rural, and/or Indigenous communities, so too do these communities come to understand conservation as a settler practice. In other words, multicultural recognition reproduces the settler state's capacity to rescind property rights, something intolerable in indigenous ontologies.

STATE RECOGNITION SAVES LIVES

There are many land activists who are tired of seeking recognition from a state that cannot read their claims because, supposedly, they are not (yet) legible to the liberal gaze (Povinelli, 2002; Razack, 1998). I too began to think that acting as a supplicant for conditional rights that reinforce the state without demanding transformation was not worth the trouble. In walking the line between liberal legibility and radical transformation, however, a few Q'eqchi' priests with leading roles in the sacred place declaration generously shared their time with me in a key scholarly intervention. Even as the state failed to recognize Q'eqchi' territoriality, limited multicultural recognition can still save lives. One of the hardest lessons learned from genocide survivors who invited me into their lives is that Indigenous peoples can never take survival for granted. In the aftermath of massacres and and with the possibility of their future resurgence, Indigenous peoples are acutely aware that they need to seek recognition to survive. As survival is not enough, they also seek to (re)define themselves on their own terms in what some scholars have theorized as survivance (Vizenor, 1994), for themselves and for their relationships with other Indigenous peoples. Below, I recount the failures and limited futures that state recognition offered in the Candelaria Caves.

In the 2000s USAID funded the mapping and titling of the community as well as an ecotourism project, then declared success and moved on. Community members run the small tourism project, but they resent that they control less impressive cave sites and have fewer economic opportunities than Girard, who continues to profit off their land.[28] As the years drag on, the demoralizing truth has set in that state authorities (e.g., the district attorney, the Ministry of Culture, and the Land Fund) have no intention of evicting the *kaxlan* squatter. A few months before I became involved in the case, the director of Wakliqoo and Javier, a dynamic Setzuul leader who also worked on Wakliqoo's mapping team, sat down to talk about how to address Setzuul's legal problems with Girard. Setzuul needed a lawyer, but Wakliqoo didn't have any money to fund the cause. Instead, the director suggested that Javier get in touch with Amílcar Pop. The Pops are one of few Q'eqchi' families prominent on the national scene, notably for their participation in Pan-Maya political action. Amílcar was incredibly busy in his work with Rigoberta Menchú Tum[29] to create a new Maya political party, but he made time to meet with Javier and agreed to take on the nationally famous case of Setzuul. In that first meeting Javier told Amílcar about Setzuul's case, and Amílcar suggested that Javier contact the OAP and declare the Candelaria Caves a sacred place.

Around this time, Wakliqoo's director suggested that I contact Javier. I was supposed to find Javier at a meeting at a different set of caves, but when I awkwardly interrupted a blessing ceremony (one gringa, many Q'eqchi' men, and a few women sitting on the floor with small children) looking for him, he was not there.[30] Undeterred, a few days later I hopped out of a microbus in front of the big USAID sign and walked the thirty minutes to Setzuul's tourism building. I explained who I was, what information I sought, and how I thought I would use it. All the men present quickly consented to my research, and to my surprise Sebastián immediately launched into the story of how he founded Setzuul. I realized that Setzuul elders thought I intended to conduct my research over the course of a few hours, as many others have. Luckily, Javier was headed out of town after the meeting as well, and we cleared things up on the walk back to the highway.

Setzuul sought advice from a professional Maya NGO, the OAP, whose K'iche' name means "Ministry of Mayan Spirituality," on how to get the Guatemalan Ministry of Culture to declare the Candelaria Caves sacred. The OAP is a nationally known and influential NGO that has two major projects: first, to pass the Law of Sacred Places of Indigenous Peoples as mandated by the 1996 Guatemalan Peace Accords (in 2016 discussed but not voted on by the legislature), and second, to organize a national council of Mayan priests. Most Pan-Maya groups have internal power differences by class, ethnolinguistic group, and gender (Nelson, 1999; Warren, 1998b); for its part, the OAP enjoyed significant representation among K'iche's, Kaqchikeles, and Mames but had weak ties to the Q'eqchi's in 2008. OAP organizers seized this opportunity, sending out K'iche's to hold meetings in Spanish about sacred places and organize a local branch of Mayan priests. When I asked Javier about his meeting with the OAP and the requirements to get their sacred place recognized by the Ministry of Culture, he said that "It's no problem; we have it all covered except one thing." He couldn't remember what it was, so he dug his notebook out and flipped through it until he found the word: anthropology. "We need anthropology. Can you do that for us?" As I handed him a business card written in Spanish I explained that I was working on my PhD in environmental policy, science, and management but that my work was really in human geography. In a surprisingly short conversation that signaled just how often he had worked with gringos seeking research fodder, Javier quickly established that I had no skills to offer in conservation biology, that he knew more about cadastral mapping than I did,[31] and that my intention was to practice the fine art of hanging out, asking questions, taking pictures, and learning about people's relationship to the caves. He circled back to his list and asked if I could write a report that validated the claim that the caves were sacred to the Q'eqchi's. "Oh yes," I said, smiling, "that's perfect." His only request was that I include "anthropological" in the title of the report to MICUDE, which I did.

My understanding of Setzuul's plan was twofold: in Alta Verapaz, we needed to call on Q'eqchi's to come to our support and state publicly their belief that the Candelaria Caves were a sacred place; in the capital, we needed to pressure MICUDE to legally recognize our claim. Once that happened, we hoped to marshal a broad alliance (MICUDE, the OAP, regional Q'eqchi' priests, Wakliqoo, etc.) to put together a convincing campaign to show that Girard, a foreigner, was profaning a Q'eqchi' sacred place with his disrespectful behavior in imposing an entrance fee of Q30 ($3.75) on Q'eqchi's who wanted to pray in their sacred place, usually to bless seeds before planting them. The fee excluded the poorest Q'eqchi's from the site. We would seek sympathy by posing our argument as a challenge: Would you let a nonbeliever pitch a tent in your church and charge admission?

A new regional Q'eqchi' priest association, Oxlaju Aj Tz'i' (OT), quickly blossomed and became the link between the communities' land claims and Mayan spirituality. The new president of OT was a dynamic leader, having previously been an active participant in Catholic Action, an EGP guerrilla, a leader of a displaced group of Q'eqchi's successfully seeking land in Chisec after the war, and now a Mayan priest who rejected both the *ladino* Left and what he called their *kaxlan* God. On his first visit he walked authoritatively through the caves, naming formations and tapping a tall formation like a xylophone, moving his foot to the music. Finally, he settled in the middle of a large cave where he decided to have the meeting. Although Sebastián fretted that his choice would damage the caves, as he thought that letting people burn incense or fires in caves with colored formations would violate the land-management agreement, he acquiesced. The OT president gathered up the pre-Columbian ceramic shards scattered on the cave floor, then prepared a fire and lit a massive incense ball, letting the smoke billow around him, communing with the *tzuultaq'a* (pronounced "tsool-tacqk-aah").

Tzuultaq'a is a difficult word to translate, as it signals both the sacred and secular in a manner rarely encountered in the Judeo-Christian tradition. As a composite word, *tzuultaq'a* translates as "hill-valley," but more important is that it makes the landscape come to life. As Wilson (1995, 66, emphasis in original) explains, the "tzuultaq'a *is* the land, as well as being a spirit inhabiting it." *Tzuultaq'as* are at the heart of both/and binaries in Q'eqchi' lives, as hill-valley, spirit-material, man-woman. As with the expansive inclusivity in indigenous identities (see Chapter 3), these are both/and binaries that defy liberal logics of mutual exclusivity. To many Q'eqchi's, the *tzuultaq'a* is the only legitimate owner of the land, and this is funda-mentally at odds with "the 'ladino' notion of land as a material good that belongs to the State of Guatemala and that, in an arduous and expensive ritual called 'paper-work,' is converted into a commodity" (Milián, Grünberg, and Cho, 2002, 74).

When the OT president finished, he announced that the *tzuultaq'a* had made its name known in the smoke: Qana Q'ootiha', or the place where the water turns. When I told community members from Setzuul about the name, they all accepted it, nodding their approval. In a later interview I asked the president to explain the territorial reach of Qana Q'ootiha', but he declined to speculate. While he was will-ing to entertain my questions up to a point, he was careful to explain that my Western visions of fixed territorial boundaries that could be mapped simply did not apply to the *tzuultaq'a* (see also Ybarra, 2013).

People from Setzuul and two neighboring communities came together to host the first regional meeting, which was a huge success; people came from as far as Petén and both the highlands and lowlands of Alta Verapaz. They gathered flowers and avidly discussed the best arrangements to mark the four cardinal points,[32] trimmed the ecotourism center's lawn, and prepared massive quantities of food. Even I was up by 3:00 A.M., as the ad hoc meat committee decided that the vegetar-ian ethnographer should act as a participant-observer in butchering the pig. The political meeting was held for about five or six hours in the tourism reception hut, then the women led the first ceremony, a *wa'tesink,* giving food and drink to the *tzuultaq'a* to ask for a blessing and inaugurate our work. After a quick dinner break (we could not eat until after the *wa'tesink*), we all grabbed flashlights and filed into the cave. The elaborate ceremony lasted until dawn, and priests employed ancient Mayan ceramics from the caves (including the tall pot center-right at the edge of the offerings in Figure 7) and offerings including moonshine (*b'oj*), incense, and candles. The *mayejak* itself consisted of long prayers, ritual dancing, and the heal-ing of sick people.[33] I saw the Wakliqoo director around midnight, and he told me he was surprised at how many people showed up and how important the sacred place declaration was to them.

This gathering catalyzed regional organizing around the claim that Q'eqchi' spirituality is both cultural and political, as exemplified by the *tzuultaq'a*. Many lowland Q'eqchi's had completed training and now considered themselves priests

FIGURE 7. *Mayejak* and Qana' Itzam visiting in the flames. (Photograph by the author)

(*sacerdotes*), drawing on the Catholic Church's terminology as a way to signal that their learning merits respect. The priests wanted a regional organization to affiliate with, and they wanted to gather in worship together. They were also enthusiastic about affiliating with the OAP, as many were familiar with the work of influential K'iche' Maya priests on the executive council. Importantly for the Setzuul hosts, the Q'eqchi' priests were also enthusiastic about the sacred place claim and absolutely considered the caves a sacred place.[34]

While the Q'eqchi' priests asked for a written copy of my report, I was acutely aware that most of them could not read or write Spanish. As such, I spent much of my time trying to contribute through my presence at meetings, cash contributions when the hat was passed around, and printing photographs I took of people. For some people, the only photos they might have of themselves from 2008 were those that I gave to them. When I met with OT leaders and sped through a series of photos of the *mayejak* on my computer slide show that I thought would not be of much interest, they insisted that I stop and return to the photo shown in Figure 7. While I thought the picture turned out poorly due to the distorted flame, Q'eqchi' priests began talking excitedly about Qana' Itztam's visit to bless us. Where I saw a distorted flame, they saw a physical manifestation of territorial relations.

Q'eqchi' territoriality is not one where animist spirits are tethered like ropes to key spiritual sites such as caves and streams and bound by hyperlocal understandings of community and county. Instead, lowland Q'eqchi spirits traverse time and space to gossip and curse and bless them. In this case, Qana' Iztam knew the people who were seeking blessings from Qana Q'ootiha' because they were from her lands of Lanquín. In visiting to bless them in the Candelaria Caves, she was securing their relationship with Q'ootiha' and renewing their territorial ties with Lanquín. In so doing, my understanding is that the *tzuultaq'a* gave children who have never been to Lanquín claims to it as a homeland as well as claims to the land they were born on. Indigenous studies scholars have long noted that *where* matters as much as *when* in indigenous histories (Basso, 1996; Brooks, 2008; Deloria, 2003). In Q'eqchi' histories, the *where* is usually produced in the territorial relationship between two faraway places that become close through spirituality and kinship.

The Candelaria Caves were declared a sacred place, but folks in Setzuul did not experience any increased ability to control their land in the face of a foreign interloper. In 2009 and 2010, the tourism committees of Setzuul and a neighboring committee said that they might not even honor their commitment to allow Q'eqchi' priests to pray in the caves without paying a fee. When I heard this news, I visited the OT president in his community to apologize that the community I was staying with was choosing not to honor its agreement.[35] He did not accept my apology (and as it wasn't my decision to make, it wasn't really my apology to give) but instead explained to me his continued support for his Q'eqchi' brothers who turned against him, and he pointed to the successes of the campaign.

OT continues to renew limited and conditional recognition through relationships in the capital. The willingness of OT representatives to describe themselves using K'iche' terms and spirituality (as in the four cardinal points, above) garnered recognition in the form of a MICUDE-approved identification card (*carnet*). At the first meeting held in Setzuul, some Maya priests said that they suffered threats of physical violence as supposed witches, and one had been jailed. For priests who suffered taunts and threats, coming together as an organization with national recognition offered not only comfort but also possible physical protection. The president of OT told me I should not underestimate the capability of a laminated card to save lives. As frustrating as I find it that OT and Wakliqoo had translated themselves into K'iche' to become legible as Maya, I lost sight of the possibility that this was an incremental step away from *ladino* ontologies and toward recognition of rights in difference. It is only survival in the present that makes indigenous futures possible.

Q'eqchi' spiritual leaders found the ability to work within the multicultural state system to receive recognition for their dress, language, prayers, and practices empowering. OT's vision, however, was not limited to the boundaries established by multicultural recognition. Where those boundaries failed—such as in a 500-

year framework (as opposed to Q'eqchi' claims of 200 years) or in envisioning an Occidental territoriality—OT leaders did not continue to engage the multicultural state (in this case, through the Ministry of Culture). Ultimately, settler-state subjections offered individual recognition but not collective territorial recognition. For this, Q'eqchi' leaders looked beyond the settler state.

NEW HORIZONS OF HOPE IN COLLECTIVE SELF-DETERMINATION
Beyond Truth and Reconciliation to Justice

In a key intervention in indigenous studies, Coulthard (2014, 40) posits that the settler state "does not require recognition from the previously self-determining communities upon which its territorial, economic and social infrastructure is constituted." This commonsense notion does not carry over to Guatemala, where perhaps half the voting population is Indigenous. The Guatemalan settler state relies on the Mayan body to constitute the republic and also needs the figurehead to recuperate the state legitimacy that was corroded both internally and externally during the most recent genocide. While the truth and reconciliation commission failed in other ways, this marked the first moment that educated landowners, leftist peasant activists, and guerrilla revolutionaries were not allowed to speak for Indigenous peoples. Instead, Indigenous peoples had their own seat at the table (e.g., as the Coordinadora de Organizaciones del Pueblo Maya). This particular conjunctural moment is one where Maya peoples could seize power. It is for this reason that I posit that U.S. conservation activists would not have succeeded in their program to make the Maya Forest into a national protected-areas system if they had waited for democratic governance to emerge from the peace accords (see Chapter 1).

While Indigenous people speaking for themselves set an important precedent, the process remained focused on reconciliation, which Tuck and Yang (2012, 35) argue "is about rescuing settler normalcy, about rescuing a settler future." In other words, reconciliation is more about settlers making peace with themselves than with Indigenous peoples' setting a survivance agenda. Guatemala's truth and reconciliation commission allows *ladinos* to claim that racist state violence was in the past, ignoring how it reaches toward the future. While many Mayas seek reconciliation with Guatemala's past and acknowledgment of state harms, they do not agree that these ended in 1996 with the peace declaration. To truly decolonize the Guatemalan imaginary, the state would have to imagine an indigenous territoriality that does not depend on the Westphalian nation-state.

I have told the story of one community's exemplary efforts to attain recognition within the limited framework of neoliberal multiculturalism, but this is only the most recent iteration of such maneuvers. As a colonized people, Q'eqchi' lived realities transcend the fantasy of settler-state recognition (Coulthard, 2014, 23;

Fanon, 2008). In so doing, they offer a twenty-first-century Mayan territoriality that works within and beyond Guatemala. Rather than define themselves as a labor force in opposition to capitalism or seeking autonomy in a hierarchical formation that reinforces the role of the nation-state as most important and prior to indigenous nations, the Q'eqchi' territorial imaginary goes beyond the bounds of Occidental thinking.

Remembering the Maya Republic

According to Kaqchikel Maya activist and intellectual Demetrio Cojtí Cuxil, the first call for decolonization was in a manifesto by MAYAS, a western highlands activist group that imagined a "Maya Republic" that would not be subordinate to Guatemala (Cojtí Cuxil, 1997, 104). The manifesto argued that the Guatemalan national identity and boundaries are a shallow fiction that functioned only as a capitalist machine in the service of the rich. Rather than practicing wait-your-turn solidarity, in which Mayas would dutifully support *ladinos* in the Marxist revolutionary project in hopes that racism and patriarchy would eventually wane, MAYAS argued that any truly revolutionary project would question the existence of a country called Guatemala (Movimiento Indio Tojil, 1985). While the current national order thrives on uniformity, MAYAS warned the "ladino community" that imposing an assimilationist project on subjugated people inevitably leads them to resist it. They argued that

> This ethnocidal and genocidal policy, today exclusively directed against the Indian peo-
> ple [*pueblo indio*], has elevated and consolidated even more the pan-indigenous [*panin-
> diana*] consciousness of the Mayas, because they all are facing the same systematic
> extermination policy. So then, this has been and is the lived experience that has fused
> the Indian peoples into a single mighty nationality. (Movimiento Indio Tojil, 1985, 15)

In other words, the settler state's prefiguration of Maya death spurred them to come together to forge a politics of survival.

Perhaps most difficult for *ladino* Guatemalans to accept was the rejection of Westphalian borders in favor of indigenous affinities. The "single mighty national-ity" above was not a call to rewrite the Guatemalan nation but instead to decolo-nize its borders entirely in the repatriation of Maya land and life. The manifesto bluntly states that "Mayas of Guatemala consider their historical destiny to be more tied to their co-national Mayas who fell under the jurisdictions of other States than the ladino people of Guatemala" (Movimiento Indio Tojil, 1985, 20). *Ladino* Guatemalans have acute territorial anxieties; many Guatemalans reject the idea that Belize is a sovereign nation-state, and northern departments still cele-brate heroes who defended Guatemala against Mexican invaders in the nineteenth century. As hard as it may be for gringos to see, buried in Guatemalan patriotism is the colonial memory that this region was once the ruling center of Guatemala,

Belize, and Chiapas (Mexico), together with resentment that the state did not retain its territorial extent.

When Mayas reached out and affirmed their affinities across borders, this not only affirmed *ladino* fears of contemporary insurgency but also called their legitimacy as a nation into question. Why shouldn't Q'eqchi's of Belize, Guatemala, and even Mexico make a claim for a state to affirm their identity? Perhaps one indication of just how threatening this idea was is that some Mayan revolutionaries were afraid of both *ladino* insurgents and *ladino* counterinsurgents, and the leftist guerrillas even murdered some splinter Mayan organizations (Konefal, 2010, 144–146; Nelson, 1999). Intraleftist violence was very rare during the civil war, so this is an indication of how threatening some found Pan-Maya claims to be. These claims still find positive purchase among Q'eqchi's who meet in "international encounters" to compare their experiences between Belize and Guatemala.

Even the radical 1985 manifesto claimed that while an indigenous state that was separate would be ideal, it is not possible. As evidence, authors cited the cases of separatist movements in Ireland and Spain.[36] As such, even the most radical written Maya position called for a federalist solution in which the Maya Republic "would have a multinational State, as each one of the component ethnicities are also nations that would delegate part of their autonomy to the State" (Movimiento Indio Tojil, 1985). If this were the case, it is of note that the Q'eqchi' component is the one that encompasses the greatest territory and overlaps the most with the protected areas. For those familiar with contemporary Guatemalan politics, this seems entirely impractical. Nonetheless, this proposal is today within indigenous territorial rights according to international law, which calls for indigenous self-determination without dismantling the Westphalian nation-state system. Perhaps, then, it still might be possible?

In 2007, a Belizean judge became the first to apply ILO 169 in a national case that recognized Mopan and Q'eqchi' Maya land rights.[37] The meaning of the verdict is still unclear today, as Maya land activists have suffered significant oppression, including the death of a key leader. Nonetheless, this sets an important precedent at the level of the Inter-American Court of Human Rights. While Belize, as the defendant, made a key claim that Q'eqchi's are "immigrants" (from Guatemala) and cannot make time-immemorial claims to the land, the judge ruled that these claims are not relevant to applicable case law and international conventions (Grandia, 2009a; Wainwright, 2008). Given the Guatemalan Constitution's explicit recognition of the Q'eqchi's and other lowland Mayas as Indigenous peoples, this points to a clear opportunity to bring a case that might fail at the national level but could prevail in the courts. This suggests that Guatemalan multiculturalism, whether for private property or public protected areas, is much more vulnerable than it may seem. When seen from a non-Westphalian perspective, massive state repression can be read as defensiveness from a position of legal weakness.

"CAN WE TAX THE *KAXLAN*?"

In the same year that the sacred place declaration failed to ensure the community's land rights over those of the *kaxlan,* ten Setzuul community members joined a "cultural exchange," where Wakliqoo organized a bus full of Q'eqchi' leaders to visit the Miskito coast of Nicaragua. Even though they spent more time on the bus than in the community they visited, Setzuul representatives returned all smiles. We had an impromptu community meeting, where they reported back with some chagrin that they had to perform traditional songs and dances for the Miskitos, to which Setzuul youths immediately jeered and asked what "traditional" Q'eqchi' songs even were. While some of the elderly men in the crowd would have happily performed traditional dances and songs without ambivalence, these few who survived the war into old age were too weak to travel and were marginalized from exchanges that favored the ability to speak Spanish. Instead, the younger men who traveled recounted that they had only a few hours to prepare the performance, most of which was taken up deciding how to represent themselves. In recounting the story of how they decided among themselves what songs and dances were authentically Q'eqchi', Javier among the leaders seemed particularly bemused and proud. Even though just two months before he had explained to me that the community would not perform songs, dances, or rituals for ecotourism visitors because they had been lost during the war, when he recounted which songs they chose to sing for the Miskitos, the elders nodded in approval. Once settler-state subjections were not relevant, they seemed to enjoy thinking through their indigeneity in a process of mutual recognition.

The cultural exchange was eminently didactic, as the goal was to see what communities can do when states recognize the territorial nature of indigeneity. The landmark case came together when the nation-state allocated logging rights over Miskito objections. Lowland Q'eqchi's are familiar with the threat of loggers—and the roads, monoculture plantations, and cattle ranches that follow in their wake, which they regard as a tragedy.[38] That said, a key victory in the case was that the Miskitos did not win territorial autonomy in the courts subject to their performance as good environmental stewards (which can be constantly revised and assessed) but rather as inherent rights. Thus, their rights are not contingent on their actions as good environmental subjects. The other key precedent in the case is that the Miskitos are widely recognized as having mixed indigenous American and African origins, but the courts did not draw on "time immemorial" tropes in determining indigenous identities (Gordon et al., 2003). For lowlander Q'eqchi's who are often policed out of their rights to any territories as repeatedly dispossessed "immigrants," this is a great harbinger of hope.

Even as they shook their heads and pitied the Miskitos their poor soil quality, Setzuul leaders wondered out loud about the possibility of Q'eqchi' territorial autonomy. A key outcome of the ruling was that the Miskitos could choose to allow logging activities and levy a tax on the company that they could them distribute among themselves (i.e., not surrender to the central government). Within hours of the bus's return, young men who had little to do with the sacred place declaration and didn't go on the Wakliqoo trip were sweating in the high sun in the soccer field, wondering aloud what it would be like to control all of the county of Chisec or even the whole department of Alta Verapaz. "Can we tax the *kaxlan*?" one youth wondered aloud.

This daydream is of a formal expansion of existing practices throughout Guatemala. Most gringo travelers have had the experience of haggling over bus fare or other prices that seem fixed but are higher for foreigners. More formally, CONAP and other agencies charge Guatemalans a lower price of admission to parks and museums. Similarly, Setzuul leaders agreed to implement a two-tiered pricing system as part of the sacred place agreement whereby Q'eqchi' farmers seeking maize blessing would not have to pay, Q'eqchi' priests would receive a discount, and all others would pay a higher price. The key difference here is that while CONAP and other state agencies charge different prices to Guatemalans/foreigners, the Candelaria Caves communities agreed to charge different prices to Q'eqchi's/*kaxlans*. In the months I spent working with Candelaria Caves communities and the spiritual activists, they had a few working binaries: Q'eqchi'/non-Q'eqchi', Maya/non-Maya, and Indigenous/*kaxlan*. The Guatemalan/non-Guatemalan binary was simply not relevant, not discussed.[39] Likewise, taxing the *kaxlan* imagines a world where the operating governance binary is one of native/settler, not Guatemalan/foreigner. Above all, this community embraced a kind of "expansive inclusivity" (Kauanui, 2008) that would include K'iche's from Totonicapán and Coast Salish peoples of the Pacific Northwest coastal region.

That same year, Setzuul joined up with other communities' efforts to split from the county of Chisec to become a new county, Raxruhá (Figure 8).[40] At first I understood this as primarily a goal to have more voice in the national government, as county-level governments receive federal funding based on census data in ways that make them the key regional governmental players. Some of this work certainly occurred, but the Raxruhá government went beyond seeking recognition from the state as a newly legible beneficiary group or even seeking to validate Wakliqoo's campaign to create and recognize common property rights at the communal level (Ybarra, 2011b).

Over the last ten years, this region has suffered massive land conversion from subsistence crops to African palm plantations, which some decry as land grabbing (Alonso-Fradejas, 2012; Alonso-Fradejas, Alonzo, and Durr, 2008). Faced with this crisis, the Q'eqchi' mayor of Raxruhá declared a tax by weight on the transportation of African palm on county roads. The rationale was based on the national laws, which acknowledged that since county governments are responsible for road

FIGURE 8. Local leaders discuss which communities are to be included in the new county (*municipio*) of Raxruhá. (Photograph by the author)

maintenance (e.g., fixing potholes), they could charge a use fee to cover these costs. The transportation tax was unprecedented, however, and local communities and the national business community alike understood this as a claim against international resource extraction in Q'eqchi' territory. National industrial organizations—notably the Coordinating Committee for Agricultural, Commercial, Industrial and Financial Associations (Comité Coordinador de Asociaciones Agrícolas, Comerciales, Industriales y Financieras, CACIF) sued the municipality and took the case all the way to court. In cautious meetings in 2013, Q'eqchi' leaders from the region (including other mayors) discussed the promise and peril of openly challenging transnational resource extraction as Raxruhá had. The fact that

CACIF saw this case as an important precedent demonstrates just how powerful the attempt to adapt Miskito autonomy to their circumstances was. The Constitutional Court of Guatemala quickly ruled in favor of the Agro-Commerce Chamber, but national debates over extraction and land use continue to this day.

The key difference between the national debate and the lowlands debate is likewise that of Guatemalan/non-Guatemalan and Q'eqchi'/*kaxlan*. Whether through a sacred place declaration or a tax on African palm transportation, Q'eqchi' activists understand these as the defense of indigenous territory. Leftist organizations in the capital are focused on tracing the roots of transnational corporations back to the United States and the ways that capitalist extraction wreaks havoc on the environment. While Q'eqchi's also think that these are important debates, their primary focus seems to be on finding ways to live with the *kaxlan* that move from settler-state subjections to collective self-determination.

In a cartography of refusal, Q'eqchi's seek to exercise their rights within international laws and conventions, without conceding their right to collective self-determination as a people. This fundamentally would entail reshaping conservation to acknowledge the ontological relationship between humans and nonhumans in co-constitution. I believe that Q'eqchi's would understand land as an actor with agency, not as an actant. After discovering more than human theorizing of ontology, this is something that I can interpret through the voice of Subcomandante Marcos or other nonindigenous intermediaries (as in Sundberg, 2014) but much less through interviews I conducted. As the notion of the *tzuultaq'a* represents a taken-for-granted organizing principle of the world, Q'eqchi' interlocutors did not feel the need to explain to me something that they have taught their children for millennia (Todd, 2016). Instead, they asked me to keep their secrets (Ybarra, 2011a). Rather than seek liberal recognition, they look to nonhuman recognition and mutual recognition with other Indigenous peoples. A decolonial future does not require liberal maps or radical countermaps but does require the survival of a people who rethink the cartography of refusal and survival beyond this binary.

Tellingly, by 2014 the national government claimed that Raxruhá was an out-of-control municipality that needed reinforcement from the police and the army to reclaim the zone from drug traffickers. While these two events seem unrelated from a distance, Q'eqchi' leaders understand that it is narco-narratives that constrain their future possibilities, not a shallow multiculturalism. I take this challenge up in the next chapter.

5

Narco-Narratives and Twenty-First-Century Green Wars

Narcos are everywhere, or so it seems. And where narcos go, the state claims that they bring violence with them (Wright, 2011, 2012). From lurid depictions in the book Tropic of Chaos of "narco-heaven" (Parenti, 2011, 201) to policy recommendations about "narco-deforestation" in the journal *Science* (McSweeney et al., 2014), the northern triangle of Central America seems to be defined by narcos and their planes ("*narcoavionetas*"),[1] taxis ("*narcozetas*"),[2] laboratories ("*narcolaboratorios*"),[3] mansions ("*narco-mansión*"),[4] and plantations ("*narco-fincas*"). While narco-narratives do not seem related to conservation at first blush, narco-planes land on narco-plantations in protected areas, supposedly the cause of narco-deforestation. The narco associations of social ills, violence, and death map onto those living in trafficking regions.

The "narco" prefix has long captured popular imaginations, harnessing admiration, fear, and a romantic love of the rebel that inspires biographies, novels, ESPN *30 for 30* documentary movies, and in 2016 the Netflix show *Narcos* about the rise and fall of Pablo Escobar, as narrated by a gringo Drug Enforcement Administration (DEA) agent. In recent years, however, the implications have shifted: whereas Guatemala used to be understood as "untouchable narcostate" (Smyth, 2005), now it is a "failing narcostate."[5] More ominously, security experts such as former military officer and director of the Office of National Drug Control Policy Barry McCaffrey increasingly decry "narco-terrorism."[6] They call for using the mechanisms and means of the war on terror designed for Iraq and Afghanistan in Latin America, as figures as prominent as 2017 U.S. homeland security secretary John Kelly collapse "transnational criminal organizations, drug trafficking organizations, and violent extremist organizations" when referring to Central America

(Kelly, 2014; Ybarra, 2016). When applied to drug trafficking corridors in Central America, they frame protected areas as the battleground for green wars.

The call to violence is clear in the presumptive conjoining of two social wars: the war on drugs and the war on terror. Whereas post-2001 security experts have tended to think about terror in terms of the proliferation of radical Islamist calls to bring heretical nation-states to their knees, General McCaffrey's 2008 report does not assert any link between antistate organized terror and drug trafficking. Rather, he justifies his use of "narco-terrorism" because everyday people are terrorized by violence. While I think he is correct about the fears and difficulties many people experience in navigating their lives through illicit networks that work in and through violence, this misrepresents illicit networks. Drug traffickers do not have a political agenda to overthrow the nation-state for an alternative ideology; rather, they use state apparatuses to their own ends (Lunstrum and Ybarra, in press; Nordstrom, 2004).

These calls for violent action in the name of security, both in Guatemala and the United States, are increasingly answered with violence. Over the last decade, the "narco" prefix became commonplace in newspapers and everyday speech. When I conducted interviews in 2012 about state evictions of communities during states of emergency, I was surprised to hear development and conservation professionals casually refer to them as "narco-peasants." These are not peasants who farm marijuana or coca, and nobody claimed they were. More insidiously and harder to disprove, they claimed that these were peasants who were guilty by their association with narcos. Most important, some of these professionals were hired to improve the livelihoods of those same communities they cast aspersions on. As discussed in Chapter 3, nongovernmental organization intermediaries play a key role in making Q'eqchi' speakers legible to state and media actors. While some family networks still garner favor with patriarchal relationships, they are increasingly punctuated by fear of rape, torture, and assassination.

Drug trafficking is very real along the Mexican-Guatemalan border, as is its violence. More than two-thirds of all cocaine trafficked to the United States passes through Guatemalan territory (Martínez, 2016; Smyth, 2005). Likewise, Central America has some of the highest death rates in the world, higher than Iraq or Afghanistan (UNODC, 2013). While the highest homicide rates are undoubtedly in major cities (such as Guatemala City and San Pedro Sula, Honduras), if one accounts for population densities it becomes clear that border departments are not living in pastoral peace. In Guatemala, this has a striking parallel with civil war violence: while not recognized as a focal point, the Franja Transversal del Norte accounts for 39 percent of known massacre sites (MAGA, 2012).

Key interventions on necropolitics and social death inform my analysis of cartel politics in twenty-first-century green wars. First, Mbembe's work on necropolitics takes Foucault's biopolitics to the postcolony to reveal how the spectacle of violent death shapes the horizons of possibility for those people it makes live

(Foucault, 2003; Mbembe, 1992, 2003). In this, I draw on the insights of works that think about populations posited as less than human, particularly African diaspora peoples in the afterlives of slavery, in terms of the ways that the white settler state posits a supposedly universal humanity that consigns people to lives without liberty (Hartman, 1997; Patterson, 1982; Silva, 2007; Spade, 2015). Likewise, Wright (2012) and Osorno (2012) develop a theory of narco-politics in dialogue with necropolitics, one where the death of the Other gives life to the state. In this, the state feeds on the life of so-called narcos while arguing that their deaths do not merit investigation. The view from Guatemala unsettles the notion that any single organization is responsible for narco-politics. Instead, the articulation of conservation, drug wars, and border threats in Guatemala's Maya Forest demonstrates the porous networks that traffic relationships back and forth between licit and illicit economies as well as state and nonstate actors. In other words, Indigenous peoples framed as narco-peasants suffer violence from two sets of actors: first, illicit actors who use spectacle violence to keep people silent to save their lives, and second, state actors who punish them for keeping silent and accuse them of narco-collaboration. The territorial nature of Q'eqchi' struggles seems to mean that U.S.-based actors are very interested in keeping drugs and migrants south of their border without regard to the implications for justice struggles in Guatemala.

I draw on Cacho's (2012) analytic of racialized rightlessness to grapple with how the racialized narco-peasant is, by definition, unable to follow the law. This is key to understanding why settler rationalities attribute violent spatial practices not to their own oppression but instead to the Q'eqchi's pathological need to migrate. Silva (2007, 265) suggests that the association of criminalization and material economic dispossession has become the twenty-first-century signifier of the racial subaltern. In postwar Guatemala, narco-narratives work to shape the urban poor and the rural Indigenous alike as peoples who are worth more in death than in life. Civil war counterinsurgency sought insurgents, drug war policing seeks narcos, and green war conservation seeks park invaders—all three social wars operate on a racialized terrain that disproportionately limits indigenous life chances. Limited life chances manifest in three distinct but articulated ways. First, life chances are limited in the public health sense, where Indigenous peoples are more likely to suffer malnutrition, low literacy rates, and shorter life spans (see also Gilmore, 2002). Second, life chances are limited in the ways that Indigenous peoples are read as the affectable subject, one who cannot be rational or give informed consent (Hartman, 1997; Silva, 2007). Third, building out from these insights, I argue that racialized rightlessness limits indigenous life chances by individualization. In treating lowland Q'eqchi's as narco-peasants, state and nonstate agents refuse to recognize them as a broader indigenous body politic.

The latter is a particularly urgent question in the Maya Forest, where Q'eqchi' Mayas are often framed as land-hungry farmers or "narco" collaborators rather than rights-bearing Indigenous peoples. For those of us seeking to understand where criminalization and brute violence come from, we must look to the "security gaze," to the "moral panics" that serve to rationalize states of exception and presumptively criminalize entire peoples (Cohen, 2002; Gilmore, 2002; Hall et al., 1978; Wright, 2011, 2012). While the meanings of difference change in context, deep-seated fears lead people, institutions, and armies to act in violence as a matter of their own security against the unknown Other who is too close for comfort. In this, Q'eqchi's come to be defined by their supposed aberration from the national body politic, racializing indigeneity to a characteristic of the (individualized) Other. In this third and most important valence, the settler state not only strips Indigenous peoples of their territorial rights but also strips them of their territorial identities. The liberal relationship to land recognizes only its productive value, such that subsistence farming does not make sense—unless one is also part of a valuable trafficking network. For Q'eqchi's who knowingly risk losing their lives and livelihoods in subsistence farming (as with the man on the cover of this book) because it is part of who they are and what they want to pass on to their children, to be right in their relationship with the *tzuultaq'a* is unthinkable and then becomes less possible in narco-politics.

This chapter traces the history of narco-politics to reveal how rural communities in the Maya Forest have become vulnerable to accusations that they are narcos. Narco-narratives draw on older imaginaries that serve to systematically oppress Indigenous peoples (Devine, 2014; Sundberg, 1999), but these older narratives are freighted with new meanings in twenty-first-century green wars. The reframing of *environmental criminals* as part of *organized crime* links them with sophisticated weapons, paramilitary skills, and/or terrorist affiliations. Narco-narratives facilitate a material politics of subjection only because the massive rise in cartel economies and politics along the Mexican-Guatemalan border seem to legitimate concomitant green wars. Specifically, the rise of the Zetas cartel reshaped the scale of trafficking through Guatemala and expanded the horizon of illicit violence. As such, I first trace what is different about cartel territoriality after the Zetas. I use the analytic of green wars to think through what is at stake in the articulation of drug wars and conservation in contemporary remilitarization of the Maya Forest. In so doing, I draw on postcolonial complements to biopolitics as necropolitics and narco-politics as well as insights from scholars who think through the relationship between racial subjection and drug war policing in the United States. Finally, I ask what this means for Maya territoriality in and against the settler state.

THE RISE OF THE ZETAS
AND CARTEL TERRITORIALITY

Some of the same territorial logics are at work for traffickers as those of counterinsurgency and protected-areas policies (Peluso and Vandergeest, 2001, 2011). The

Maya Forest encompasses the borderlands between Mexico, Belize, and Guatemala (see Figure 1). Large highways paved for timber and oil trafficking are used as landing strips for small planes, where drugs are carried across a border or two. Likewise, migrants have been increasingly forced through the forest, as Mexican migration authorities have made crossing through traditional routes more dangerous.[7] Smugglers, traffickers, and cartel bosses tend to live in the east (the Oriente) or the capital city—their homes and offices are rarely disturbed. Instead, state violence is largely visited in the rural lowlands in the name of fighting drug traffickers, even though all parties involved know that the men who run the operations will not be present. For this reason, narco-narratives rationalize state violence in the lowlands—the DEA and Kaibiles (Guatemalan special forces, similar to U.S. Green Berets) are not out to protect the scarlet macaw (recall Chapter 1), but they are the primary state agents present in the protected areas that house them.

Traffickers have long played an important role in Guatemala's economy, but their presence and politics have undergone a remarkable shift since the 1990s. Most smugglers (*transportistas*) emerged to facilitate illicit markets during the Cold War. One of the first major smuggling rings was set up around the international illicit cheese market, which continues today (Ayuso, 2012; Martínez, 2016). Over the next few decades, this smuggling network specialized in goods that were difficult to obtain and would increase one's power and prestige, ranging from specialty foods to specialty guns. As they dominated territorial control, smuggling networks were tightly intertwined with armed forces personnel, whose networks spanned beyond enlistment dates and eventually permeated the civil police system (Peacock and Beltrán, 2002).

In the 1990s, the U.S. DEA was relatively successful in closing key South American trafficking corridors. This was due to a shift in attention from Cold War to drug war politics, notably through U.S. engagement in Plan Colombia, which was meant to punish traffickers and provide economic alternatives to poor farmers. Drug trafficking flows were not stopped or slowed—they were just rerouted. Colombian cartels looked increasingly to the Northern Triangle: Guatemala, El Salvador, and Honduras. During this same decade, the Zetas emerged as the paramilitary enforcement arm of the Sinaloa cartel. The bold rise of the Zetas took Mexico by storm. In the late 1990s, banners draped across roads (*narcomantas*) were Zetas's calling cards that both threatened local communities and invited Mexican soldiers to leave behind the sad world of eating ramen in the barracks for the best food the world has to offer (Osorno, 2012, 16). By 2000, Zetas kingpin Osiel Cárdenas Guillén created a massive training camp where Kaibiles came to Mexico to hold annual training sessions for new recruits (Osorno, 2012). Drawing on Mexican and Guatemalan special forces training, this new enforcement wing reshaped cartel politics toward meticulous intelligence gathering on the one hand and violence as spectacle on the other. Even as this information became widely known, funding for military special forces continued to rise in Mexico and Guatemala.

Over time, Guatemalan family-based *transportista* traffickers developed relationships with the Zetas (ICG, 2011). Some prominent traffickers saw themselves as patriarchs, investing in key licit economies such as bus lines and sponsoring community groups such as soccer teams. Nonetheless, by the late 2000s *transportista* alliances with Mexican-based cartels brought a rise in intelligence activities and violent spectacle murders.[8] When the Zetas broke away from the Gulf cartel and expanded their influence into the Guatemalan lowlands, violent turf wars shook the nation. In 2011 Zetas killed twenty-seven farmworkers on the Los Cocos plantation in Petén, allegedly because the plantation owner stole a drug shipment. As with the Dos Erres massacre committed nearby in 1982, Kaibiles led the brutal killings.[9] As mentioned in Chapter 2, the Zetas also ran training camps on the Guatemalan side of the border. There have been multiple drug trafficking arrests of active-duty Kaibiles; they are labeled "deserters" only after their arrest (Smyth, 2005). While successive administrations declared that military sweeps and calls for states of siege (*estados de sitio*) in Alta Verapaz, Petén, and Huehuetenango have been successful against the cartels, the relative calm that returned to Alta Verapaz seems to be due to the Zetas winning the cartel war, not because the state vanquished drug traffickers.

Twenty-first-century drug war transformations reshaped both trafficking flows and a broader narco-territoriality. While I follow Wright (2011) in calling this phenomenon narco-politics, it bears mentioning that most cartel economies have mushroomed over time such that illicit networks include facilitating the trafficking of drugs, guns, and migrants as well as extortion, fraud, robbery, and money laundering, often through prestigious legitimate businesses such as cattle ranching and oil palm plantations.[10] In Mexico and Guatemala, it seems probable that everyday extortion and migrant kidnapping for ransom garner drug trafficking organizations more money than drug trafficking does.[11] Rather than changing the nomenclature or analysis of these networks, enforcement agencies instead have used the diversity of illicit activities to their advantage. In this new regime, a narco does not have to be related to narcotics. To paraphrase Ahmed (2016), this means that the could-be narco easily becomes the might-as-well-be narco.

Rather than claiming sovereignty over the state, narco-politics today involves regulating a milieu (Foucault, 2003, 29), establishing circulations of people and merchandise along set yet flexible territorial networks. As Osorno (2012, 20) explains, "the Zetas' business is not drugs, but the business of controlling who can traffic in its territory." Rather than trafficking drugs and people, the Zetas operate like a franchise, authorizing the use of their name and relationships along specific territorial networks and capitalizing on name-brand recognition. Part of this power comes from the value added in engaging in illicit activities across national borders. In other words, as state security forces make it increasingly dangerous to cross nation-state borders, they raise both the risks to migrants and the rewards to cartels who control them. While the Foucauldian milieu helps focus our attentions on the ways that Zetas regulate territorial flows of populations, it is racialized rightlessness that explains how state-sanctioned actors shape what kinds of lives are possible for those who live in the Maya Forest.

What Has Transformed: How Nation-States
Imagine Borders as Threats

When the Central Intelligence Agency fomented the 1954 coup in Guatemala, sparking massive militarization and genocide, it was in the name of U.S. national security to keep the threat of communism from creeping north. At the time, the U.S. national security imaginary used the domino theory of communism to turn leftist Latin American governments into a geopolitical threat. This led the United States to displace its securitization onto borders farther south. While in the late 1970s the United States cut military aid to Guatemala due to human rights violations, U.S. agencies continued to develop security collaborations. As early as the 1980s, the drug war was an "easier sell" to Congress than the Cold War (Weld, 2014, 144), such that it became the rationale for funding the militarization of police in programs including the U.S. Criminal Investigations Training Assistance Program (ICITAP).

Illicit networks reveal the myth of the container state, in which ethnicities and economies emerge from one national identity that maps naturally onto Westphalian territorial boundaries (Agnew, 2003; Elden, 2010). In the Latin American version, the container state is a milieu in which the mestizo citizen is formed, and anyone who does not conform to the *ladino* national identity is not a loyal citizen. It is only in this context that we can properly understand the central role of U.S. state agents, Mexican border agents, and regional organizations (the United States Southern Command, which current White House chief of staff John Kelly formerly headed) in the production of the borderlands as a threat to the heart of the nation. While supposedly the DEA only works in the United States, agents perform key job duties internationally, where they are effectively exempted from following either U.S. or host country laws when they conduct operations (Paley, 2014). The premise of "domestic" U.S. agencies working in Mexico and Central America seems to be that they are working abroad in a temporary suspension of normal activities until these putatively weak states can effectively control their own national borders. During Operation Martillo in 2012,[12] the Guatemalan government gave U.S. personnel permission to carry arms; import and export goods without inspection or taxation by the Guatemalan government; freely transit into, out of, and throughout the country without interference by the Guatemalan government; and make free and unlimited use of radio frequencies. Crucially, U.S.

soldiers and contractors were granted immunity from prosecution in Guatemala should injury or death result from the operation (Paley, 2014). Thus, while antinarcotics operations are meant to reassert nation-state boundaries in a performance that stages "weak states" as coherent and fixed in bounded spaces, the insecurities that spark these operations demonstrates the fallibility of state-centric boundaries. In supposedly shoring up Guatemala's borders from external threats, U.S. security sovereign transgressions revealed their weakness.

What do the Guatemalan military and state protected-area agencies have in common? As I argue elsewhere (Lunstrum and Ybarra, in press; Ybarra, 2016), both attempt to territorialize Westphalian container states, even as the continued need for their work stems from the impossibility of ever sealing the border. Both utilize crisis narratives to represent frontiers as a threat and create an impetus for (re)militarization, and both follow logics that claim to implement regional or even global political projects but through the performance of nation-state boundaries. Territorialization, or the writing of new spatial relations, produces cultural imaginaries that produce different categories of rights-bearing peoples in the same space—in other words, social hierarchies (Mbembe, 2003, 25–26). Much of Guatemala's protected-areas system, particularly the Maya Biosphere Reserve, contain "blind passes" through which traffickers bring illicit people, drugs, and natural resources without submitting to state checkpoints (Galemba, 2012). The articulation of blind passes with parks produces them as sites that threaten sovereignty. Whereas indigenous territorial claims in the center of Guatemala are read as calls for multicultural recognition, on the borderlands state security forces read them as disloyalty.

GREEN WARS

For over three decades, Guatemalans survived civil war and dreamed of a return to democracy. Over years of peace negotiations and implementation, guerrillas and paramilitaries alike demobilized, policing and prosecution were overhauled from the top down, and the constitution was rewritten. For many rural communities, though, reforms took place in the capital, and "human rights" was a spectacle of foreign observation that came once a year in a blue and white United Nations jeep and spoke poor Spanish (no indigenous languages). The grind of daily life returned to danger far too quickly, and people who reclaimed their land rarely enjoyed tenure security. To underscore the point, communities in protected areas often only see a state human rights observer (from the Procuraduría de Derechos Humanos) when he comes to oversee their eviction by the state—the premise being that an eviction from their territory, livelihoods, and homes is not violent if the weapons carried are not used against them.

In both the Cold War and the drug war, Guatemalan securitization constructs a fear of outsiders who perniciously infiltrate state governments and turn them against national interests. State institutions mobilize fears of faraway jungles into interagency collaboration for raids by the Kaibil special forces. Whereas the United States feared that leftist political ideologies would make their way north in the Cold War, securitization today crystallizes around fears of illicit peoples moving north—bringing criminal tendencies, drugs, and deadly viruses (Zika, Ebola) with them to U.S. soil. Rather than hold security professionals accountable for outrageous and unproven statements, as with John Kelly's blatant fearmongering of Ebola-infected migrants carrying the disease from Central America to the United States, they are celebrated and promoted.[13]

The Guatemalan government declared states of emergency to carry out military campaigns unhindered by habeas corpus protections, first in Alta Verapaz (*estado de sitio*, December 2010 until February 2011) and then in Petén (*estado de sitio*, May to August 2011), immediately followed by a 30-day *estado de alarma*. While neighboring El Salvador targeted urban violence, the Guatemalan military instead targeted the northern lowlands with the supposed goal of rooting out traffickers. This is notable because both countries suffer disproportionate violence in urban areas, with illicit trafficking concentrated in rural areas. This is because the Guatemalan trope of the narco-peasant builds on sedimented histories that pose political contestation over land grabbing as criminal acts, articulating with new dangers of cartel politics to transform border threats. In these states of emergency and beyond, Guatemalan, U.S., and Mexican security forces posit rural inhabitants as criminal narcos to justify their territorial sweeps.[14]

States of emergency all too quickly become normal social phenomena that limit political possibilities for oppressed people (Benjamin, 1968). While key interventions in philosophy and political science draw on the World War II Holocaust as a new phenomenon, looking beyond Occidentalism reveals that colonies were laboratories of subjection long before liberal governments learned to work on their own citizens as an abstracted population. Foucault said little about how practices of liberal government would determine which populations to make live and even less about which to let die (Li, 2010, 66). In this regard, politics as a "work of death" (Mbembe, 2003) is a corrective complement to Foucauldian biopolitics, one that links state formations to subject formations (Wright, 2011, 726). Instead of a steady move away from the spectacle of death (Foucault, 1991), Latin American counterinsurgency and illicit criminal organizations have each leveraged the power of torture and the spectacle of living in pain.

The basis of the right to make live is also the right to kill (as distinct from simply letting die), which relies on states of exception, appeals to emergency, and fictionalized notions of the enemy (Mbembe, 2003, 16). As the difference between declared states of emergency and de facto militarization has blurred, so has the rationale for impinging on the right to have rights. Rodriguez (2006, 19) notes that where the state has come to rely on the pageantry of crisis to produce society, it has also reconstructed the political and cultural fabric of policing, incarceration, and punishment. In this regard Guatemala breaks significantly with U.S. policing. Guatemala eschews the death penalty, but its jails are significantly more dangerous than the United States for those who are incarcerated. Like the United States, however, wealthy and white lives are valued more in policing practices than the lives of poor and Indigenous people. Rather than a politics of entitlement and empowerment, violent spectacles and escalating homicide rates naturalize the role of U.S. and Guatemalan state forces in securing the rural countryside.

Narco-Politics as Social Death: Who Must Live, and Whose Life Is Worthless

In Foucault's work on liberal government practices, he points to a key distinction: treating a crime as a social problem for repair and treating crime as a problem of prevention. In focusing on preventing crime, liberal states produced an isomorphism between the act of crime and the person who commits a crime (a criminal), effectively assuming recidivism (Foucault, 2008, 250–254).[15] His key insight into government is to point to the link between regimes of truth and criminalization:

> The veridictional question at the very heart of modern penal practice, even to the extent of creating difficulties for its jurisdiction, [was] the question of truth addressed to the criminal: Who are you? When penal practice replaced the question: "What have you done?" with the question: "Who are you?" you see the jurisdictional function of the penal system being transformed, or doubled, or possibly undermined, by the question of veridiction. (Foucault, 2008, 34–35)

In this way, the work of the justice system is not to prove culpability for specific crimes and seek corrections on that basis. Instead, criminal justice moves beyond the realm of investigations and trials to a state formation that seeks to find criminals who harm society and remove them—in emergencies by any means necessary and perhaps before emergencies to prevent them (e.g., *estado de prevención*). The use of the "narco" prefix works only through drug war regimes of truth: narcos need not deal in drugs, just be affiliated with someone else who associated with drug trafficking organizations. In this case "being a narco" is being associated with a network that deals in drugs—along with cheese, guns, and migrants—and "narco-activity" is anything that narcos do. This is how a farmer who plants beans and maize can become a "narco-peasant," even if he himself has never seen illicit drugs, much less profited from them.

State-sanctioned violence operates in and through the assumption that criminal acts, or association with others who commit criminal acts, signal pathologies that shape who to let die and who to make live. Crimes are not necessarily things that all people find morally reprehensible (these change with time, place, and circumstance) but rather those acts that are legally inscribed as unlawful. When people who commit unlawful acts are understood to do so inherently, they become unlawful people. As Cacho (2012, 82) notes, this "not only forecloses empathy but does so through producing people and places always already subject to a form of discrimination believed to be both legitimate and deserved [from the viewpoint of those in power]." In this regime of truth, a criminal is someone whose relative visibility as a state enemy inversely reflects their structural powerlessness (Gilmore, 2004, 267). This is why FONTIERRAS agents viewed a French ecotourism operator's land invasion as legitimate—if not actually legal—while the Q'eqchi' residents who sought to protect their land from him were read as conflictive hostage takers (see Chapter 4). The continued impunity of the powerful together with increased criminalization of the poor demonstrates the relevance of U.S. ethnic studies critiques in Guatemala.

Narco-narratives ask if someone was living inside a protected area or traveling along the border, and narco-narratives tell the story: Everyone knows it's dangerous there because the cartels run that park, so only a person affiliated with a cartel would dare go there. Without a different epistemological framework, it is beyond the realm of possibility that returned refugees who are homeless and harassed can move into parks because they have nowhere else to go is. In narco-narratives, anyone who dies in putative drug wars must be implicated in illegal activities that justify the person's death post hoc.[16] When state and media representations claim that "drug violence is the killing of criminals by other criminals" (Wright, 2011, 720), this allows the living to tell themselves that those who died deserved it and, by extension, that if they are innocent they can still survive. While narco-narratives would seem to affect only putative narcos, these narratives create "systems of meaning and control—the ways we understand our own bodies, the things we believe about ourselves and our relationships with other people and with institutions, and the ways we imagine change and transformation" (Spade, 2015, 25). Q'eqchi' youths try to strike a balance between wearing T-shirts and shoes that indicate a relationship to wealth to generate valuable social relations, but not so much wealth that neighbors think they are involved in illicit activities or, worse, that they are vulnerable to kidnapping. Increasing criminalization also increases state-sanctioned violence. Narco-narratives offer rationalizations, but the social distribution of death is shaped by the contours of stereotypes of place, gender, and ethnicity. A *ladino* driving through Laguna del Tigre National Park in an expensive SUV emblazoned with the logo of an oil company is not a criminal, but a Q'eqchi' farmer walking in the same park is a narco-peasant.

Narco-narratives normalize emergencies in which so-called narcos have no rights and the rest of us hope that we are not mistaken for narcos. Whereas country-to-country combat makes it seem that the line between their side and ours is clear, social wars blur the lines. If you fight a phenomenon, how do you know what you're fighting for, whom you are fighting, and when you have won? Despite their seeming confusion, the power in these ideas comes from the ideological place that these liminal imaginaries occupy as "*not war* but also *not political*" (Moodie, 2010, 5). Drug wars, green wars, and terror wars work to pit loyal citizens against kidnappers and thugs, arguing that they are lazy and violent and take advantage of the rest of us. The threat narratives that underpin social wars foreclose the possibility of making rights claims that transform who "we" are. Once an authority figure claims that you are holding hostages for money, not because foreign conservation BINGOs stole your land during the war, no one listens to you (see Chapter 1). Civil war violence set the stage for green war violence because racialization produced the internal fission of society into binary oppositions (*ladino*/Maya), a means of creating internal enemies against whom society must defend itself (Foucault, 2003; Schirmer, 1998; Stoler, 1995, 59). Civil war counterinsurgency sought communists, drug war policing seeks narcos, and green war conservation seeks park invaders— all three social wars operate on a racialized terrain that disproportionately limits indigenous life chances. At the same time, each of these wars racializes indigeneity to a characterization of the Other that belies centuries of negotiation over place, language, dress, and genealogy.

States emerge through the reciprocal relationship of the reproduction of life through death, including their meanings and representations. Rather than pinpointing errors in policing that can be fixed while maintaining institutional structures, the articulation of all three reveals that they work as regimes of truth— empirical evidence that disproves allegations about insurgents, narcos, and invaders does little to reshape cultural and material practices that have already been imperiously inscribed as social truths. It is this insight that links ideas about biopolitics with those of necropolitics, where the reassuring spectacle of another's death reproduces one's life (Mbembe, 2003). At its root, the biopolitical management of populations at a distance is predicated on the fearful reasoning of the would-be survivor:

> My killing those supposedly racially not like me secures the projection of my racial being; but in predicating my security on a foundation that motivates a counter-killing equally racially predicated, my security is coterminously and at the deepest level an insecurity. Security through the destruction of those not (like) me is tantamount to the insecurity and ultimately threat and fear of death of the self-denying secure. (Goldberg, 2009, 27)

It is worth recalling that land politics in rural Guatemala are shaped by survival tactics. In targeting those "supposedly not racially like me," their destruction affirms both their racialization as subhuman and my life as human (Goldberg, 2009, 27; Wolfe, 2008, 111). As Hall (1996, 244) cogently explains, political positionalities and their frontier effects are not given—rather, they are made and remade. Outright racism in civil war military violence shaped a context in which Indigenous activists speak openly of racial profiling in policing and *ladinos* deny the existence of race. In my fieldwork I found this to be common among neighbors, project technicians, and project beneficiaries and in dialogue between state agents with the power to recognize land tenure and land title claimants.

In postwar Guatemala, narco-narratives work to shape the urban poor and the rural Indigenous alike as peoples who are worth more in death than in life. In the crisis of meaning that violence conceives, territoriality of nations and corporeality of people are key mechanisms for reorganizing body politics and producing new national imaginaries in states of emergency (Coronil and Skurski, 2006a, 84). The lowlands as Maya Forest has the affective achievement of becoming a place to be feared due to its long-standing history as a borderlands site of death, disease, and suspect citizens who might betray the Guatemalan nation for Belizean or Mexican affiliation. In the present context, lack of collaboration with conservation's dispossession is read as a lack of loyalty to the national climate change mitigation project. This lack of loyalty, partnered with the productive unknown of the frontier, makes lowland Mayas particularly vulnerable to narco-narratives that criminalize all individuals without recognizing them as Indigenous peoples.

STATES OF EMERGENCY

The driving force that makes racism into the "fatal coupling of difference and power" is "the fear—the terrifying, internal fear—of living with *difference*" (Hall, 1992, 17). While the meanings of difference change in context, deep-seated fears lead people, institutions, and armies to act in violence as a matter of their own security against the unknown Other who is too close for comfort. For those of us seeking to understand where criminalization and the violence it authorizes come from, we must look to the "security gaze," to the "moral panics" that serve to rationalize states of exception and presumptively criminalize whole peoples (Ferradás, 2004; Gilmore, 2002; Hall et al., 1978; Wright, 2012). To the extent that security is also understood as "the ability to protect oneself" (Burrell, 2010, 96), it forces us to ask whose security is at stake when we speak about security (Mutimer, 1999), who is silenced in the attribution of guilt and who is the culprit in the security gaze (Ferradás, 2004), and what violence is authorized in the name of "citizen security." The latter is an urgent question in the Maya Forest, where land-tenure roundtables funded to promote citizen security and conflict resolution become a place where Q'eqchi' Mayas are often framed as land-hungry farmers or narco-collaborators rather than rights-bearing Indigenous peoples.

When presidents declare states of emergency, they roll out high-profile drug war campaigns that promise results to beleaguered citizens and friends to the north. Even if the state has the best of intentions, professional drug traffickers are likely to have access to customized SUVs, guns, and insider information that allows them to evade capture. In many cases, state agents know perfectly well the names, addresses, and phone numbers of major drug kingpins. This is so blatant that when I was conducting fieldwork in 2008, police arrested the son and wife of a major drug trafficker, holding both in custody and executing a search warrant at his home. In response, Cobán radio stations were engulfed in paid advertisements that warned that he would order the mass murder of everyone in the city if they were not released within a day. Along with Cobaneros, I bought food, water, and batteries and then returned to sit at home with the lights out. The next day, the police released his wife and son without charging them with a crime. Perhaps five days after the city had returned to normal, I received a travel warning from the U.S. State Department about potential safety concerns in the city. Nobody was subsequently arrested.

Instead of going after the trafficking kingpin who took to the radio to threaten the lives of both police and citizens in Cobán, the military targeted the northern lowlands, reopening military bases that were closed at the end of the civil war and basing Green Battalions there (Ybarra, 2012). As Oscar Martínez (2016, 66) explains, "international organizations have pumped Guatemala with money intended to protect forested areas and archaeological sites. How does the state show the donors they're tough? By targeting the weakest, and accusing them of being narco-traffickers, which makes the state look even stronger." While the relationship between state security forces and drug trafficking organizations is a mix of coercion and collaboration, they neither fear nor have reason to collaborate with poor and/or Indigenous peoples.

When park guards tried to arrest men planting maize in 2008 (see Chapter 2), there were just a few park guards and police, which led to a standoff between many families (men, women, and children) and a few state agents. While the state agents were held hostage for grueling hours, the outcome of the case was that some of the men were arrested and sentenced, but nobody was hurt. By contrast, when the Ministry of Defense declared an *estado de sitio* to root out top Zetas leaders in 2011, there was a massive show of force against the same men illegally growing maize in the park. The National Council of Protected Areas (Consejo Nacional de Areas Protegidas, CONAP) obtained an order of eviction, but the army-police-CONAP joint task force primarily consisted of soldiers who engaged in violence against men, women, and children armed only with machetes, one of whom was shot. After all of that, the army found no drugs or evidence of trafficking activities and arrested four people—the same number as in 2008 but with more injuries. As in 2008, landless farmers were injured, but security forces were not.

As is usually the case, only men were arrested. This allows CONAP, the Guatemalan Division of Nature Protection of the National Civil Police (División de Protección a la Naturaleza de la Policía Nacional Civil, DIPRONA), and the army to argue that the men are dangerous, even though the arrests harm entire families. Children and women are often present and participate in farming, and they often also try to shield men from state violence. At the least, they bear witness to conflicts and arrests. The man who was shot did not receive medical treatment until he was taken to jail in Cobán, more than a four-hour drive over an unpaved road. He can walk but only with a noticeable limp. He can no longer farm, so his children have taken over his plot in the park. When I showed a picture of his injury to a conference of academics studying archaeology, planning, and conservation in the region, there was an audible gasp in the room, and many people looked away. Nobody asked questions after my presentation, and a good friend chastised me because the image of someone who suffered violence was "too much." I believe that it was "too much" precisely because the people whose work informs and is in turn enabled by this violence rarely have to face it.

When the four men were arrested in 2011, the army took them to the Cobán departmental Court of Narco-Activity and Crimes against the Environment. Not only is a farmer caught planting beans processed through the same court as a Zetas hit man, but the state then uses these arrests as evidence of the success of the *estado de sitio* to root out drug traffickers. Meanwhile, entire families strive to raise the money for release on bail, equivalent to about one month's work, and manage the time-consuming and dangerous travel to bail him out.

The narco and nature exceptions for these two kinds of crimes were written into law during the 1990s peace processes. Even in the reform of the Penal Procedures Code (Decreto 51-92, Código Proceso Penal), however, the law repeatedly offers a single exception to protections for lengthy prison sentences: if the crime is of the type specified in the Law against Narco-Activity (Decreto 48-92, Ley contra la Narcoactividad). When the Guatemalan government later passed a law against organized crime (Decreto 21-2006, Ley contra la Delincuencia Organizada), it used the 1992 definitions of narco-activity as its foundation.

Likewise, the district criminal court was supposed to be split up into civil, penal, narco-activity, and environmental cases. The law explains that "the judges of narco-activity will know specifically about crimes related to trafficking, ownership, production and processing of drugs, pharmaceuticals or narcotics and related crimes. The judges of crimes against the environment will know about crimes against the environment." The lack of specificity in the latter as compared to the former demonstrates the ways that drug trafficking was understood as a primary postwar concern. In response, the judicial branch of government then declared that all departmental courts would "be transformed" by changing their names and specifying new competencies (Corte Suprema de Justicia Acuerdo No. 8-94), but I know of no training or advisory support for the narco-activity law until the Mérida and Central America Regional Security Initiative programs.[17] It is impossible to know whether and to what extent the narco provisions in the 1990s laws were truly supposed to be exceptional, but this exception is redefining normal life.

Exceptional budgets for policing during states of emergency are increasingly institutionalized in the Maya Forest. In 2012, the Guatemalan Congress officially approved a loan for a project to create the System of Vigilance and Protection of the Guatemalan Biosphere, which strengthens the institutionalization of the Jungle Special Operations Brigade. As this is the first legislative approval of remilitarization since the 1996 Guatemalan Peace Accords dictated its dismantling, it is worth examining Decree 28-2012 at length:

> The Guatemalan Republic has registered in recent years an increase in illicit activities in its territory, especially where the State has no presence, Alta and Baja Verapaz and Petén in the north of the country. This circumstance has allowed for a high level of natural-resource depredation, due to problems related with the increasingly high levels of international drug trafficking; due to organized crime, the scourge of poverty amongst the majority of the population and the institutional weakness of state agencies responsible for safeguarding sovereignty and security, which has a strong impact on economic, social and environmental issues.

This institutionalization follows on the heels of actions where successive presidents declared martial law in the Maya Forest, stripping residents of freedom of assembly, giving police and soldiers the right to search and arrest without a warrant, and censoring press coverage of these activities. Former military officer Otto Pérez Molina was elected president in 2012 after campaigning to bring back iron-fisted justice (*mano dura*). This law demonstrates congressional approval for remilitarizing border regions "where the State has no presence," bringing together claims of conservation with "sovereignty and security." Whereas Álvaro Colom began assembling "green forces," Pérez Molina expanded their reach, renaming them roving brigades as part of the System of Vigilance and Protection of the Guatemalan Biosphere and equipping them with planes, ships, and guns (Decree 28-2012). To the best of my knowledge, there are currently three major roving brigades: the Jungle Special Operations brigade Víctor Augusto Quilo Ayuso, based out of La Libertad, Petén; the High Mountain Brigade on the northwestern border with Mexico in San Marcos; and the Military Police brigade General Héctor Alejandro Gramajo Morales,[18] in San Juan Sacatepéquez. As of August 2014, the fourth brigade will be an extension of the Jungle Special Operations brigade into Alta and Baja Verapaz. A state functionary explained that people in Alta and Baja Verapaz are "accustomed to not having authority" and that if left unchecked these locations "would be converted into a drug trafficking corridor that starts in Izabal, arrives in El Quiché and Huehuetenango to penetrate Mexico" (Anonymous, 2014).

Whereas the first two roving special operations brigades are arguably responses to the nexus of deforestation and drug trafficking, the third brigade reveals the disjuncture between U.S. funding for "citizen security" and Guatemalan implementation for "safeguarding sovereignty and security." San Juan Sacatepéquez was not listed as a problem site for intervention in the 2012 law because it is not along Guatemala's northern border, it does not have a significant drug trafficking problem, and the Guatemalan legislature does not list this as a place where "the State has no presence." Rather, it was the site of massive peaceful protests against natural resource extraction by the Cementos Progreso company. The demonstrations were met with police and military violence. In September 2014 the Defense Ministry declared martial law (*estado de prevención*), and the role of the new brigade is to bring "security" where rural citizens protesting environmental degradation supposedly are the root cause of insecurity that threatens state sovereignty.

In this logic, military brigades, with international assistance, use violence against citizens in the name of "citizen security." Pérez Molina is one person whose ideologies weave these seemingly disparate threads together; for most Guatemalans, there is no contradiction that he was a military commander who ran a major scorched-earth military campaign and as president advocated for illicit drug decriminalization. Unfortunately, the contradictions of killing people in the name of safety are thoroughly in keeping with historical patterns. As shown above, the institutional mechanisms for *mano dura* drug war justice were created during peace processes meant to bring an end to Guatemala's civil war. While many people call for *mano dura* justice in the face of daily insecurity, it is also because they hope that they will not be subjected to it.

In Guatemala's Maya Forest, legal exceptions for drug wars and crimes against the environment are the real states of emergency that shape people's daily lives. While green wars authorize roving jungle brigades to combat "a high level of natural-resource depredation, due to the problems related with the increasingly high levels of international drug trafficking" (Decree 28-2012), U.S. and Guatemalan funding is geared toward guaranteeing safety and sovereignty through militarized violence. The effect of the twenty-first-century green wars has been to subject indigenous territorial claims to narco-narratives, interpellating all communities that contest the legitimacy of protected areas into putative narcos. While military actions occasionally work to protect capitalist interests (including water and oil extraction) to the exclusion of conservation, international conservationists seem to accept these because they do not challenge the rationale for protected areas created during a civil war. These inconsistent principles of collaboration corrode conservation's legitimacy for rural communities, whose members see themselves as fighting an alliance of transnational capitalist extraction, conservationist landgrabbing, and state repression.

The articulation of green security and drug wars in the Maya Forest has the effect of rendering all park invaders as criminals, as if by nature. The interpellation of rural Q'eqchi' territoriality as criminality, to the extent that the settler state succeeds in its genocidal goals, limits Q'eqchi' life chances. First, as individuals and communities, Q'eqchi's in protected areas experience structural state violence in the denial of basic services (including running water, electricity, and public schools), state-led dispossession, and state-sanctioned private violence against "conflictive" communities. Second, as a population, Q'eqchi's are subjected to social death, one where they are rendered incapable of rational thought but punished for bad actions anyway. Paradoxically, this means that the systemic and institutionalized nature of racial violence renders its perpetrators irresponsible (Goldberg, 2002), as these communities are seen as experiencing property and economic opportunities—as well as their loss—less than settler communities. This is why in the Los Cocos massacre and a score of other massacres that did not receive national media attention, state officials point to the actions of victims to justify their death and do not seem to inquire more deeply. Third and most important, racialized rightlessness limits indigenous life chances by severing the conceptual relationship between Indigenous peoples and their territory. U.S., European, and Guatemalan conservation and development professionals all act as though the project of racialized dispossession has already succeeded and they are now migrants whose land ties have been severed. Their proposals, plans, and projects that start from this assumption collectively work to make it true, and the developmental work to see a series of disconnected communities instead of recognizing an indigenous body politic limits Q'eqchi' life chances. As long as conservation BINGOs fund sustainable development and the United States funds anti-immigration and anti-trafficking enforcement, there is no need to examine who may live and who must die in the Maya Forest.

Even in the cases of state agents who view them as narcos or of academics and development professionals who simply gasp and look away from the violence they suffer, Q'eqchi's do not define themselves by their (in)visibility as an Other. Instead, they reimagine a territoriality beyond the bounds of the Westphalian nation-state. While Q'eqchi' ontologies and mutual recognitions of indigenous sovereignty are crucial, communities also come together to save their lands. For example, Setzuul (see Chapter 4) seeks state recognition from FONTIERRAS without accepting its paternalistic role as the arbiter of property. While national laws say that only FONTIERRAS administrators have the right to exclude someone from the community whose name is on the title, they learned about ILO 169 and decided to administer their land according to "custom." When someone abandoned the land and attempted to sell it to a *kaxlan* (nonindigenous) outsider, community leaders decided to make his return impossible. According to the customary logic of swidden agriculture, planters' rights establish that anyone else who attempts to take over the land is a usurper. In order to avoid individualized legal battles, community leaders planted maize together, thereby establishing the entire community as the responsible party for the actions. The choice to plant maize invokes its sacred role in feeding the community, and its low value (as opposed to cardamom and papaya) serves as a political statement that the community is making a claim not about money but instead about land and Q'eqchi' belonging. This is a cartography of refusal—even as their actions engage with settler logics and property laws, they do so to demonstrate the refusal to subsume Q'eqchi' territoriality to them. In the conclusion, I outline a call for decolonization.

Conclusion

Decolonizing the Maya Forest, and Beyond

For a people to survive in struggle it must be on its own terms: the collective wisdom which is a synthesis of culture and the experience of that struggle.
—CEDRIC ROBINSON (2000, XXXIV)

Under the Spanish, the Germans, and then the *ladinos,* Guatemala's Maya Forest has experienced waves of settler colonialism that construct Indigenous peoples as the Other to its imagined loyal citizen. In this imaginary, nature is both a threat as a jungle that threatens to swallow up humanity and a promise to separate wilderness from civilization. From the Yellowstone fortress model through to the present day, white wilderness imaginaries place civilization in cities, nature in uninhabited forests, and Indigenous peoples as disappeared and dead. In addition to separating the worker from his means of production, racialized dispossession seeks to strip Indigenous peoples of their relationship to territory and each other. Rather than shrug off racialized dispossession as a regrettable historical past, civil war survivors insist that dispossession is their present way of life and also insist on their future. They call for collective self-determination as both justice and survival (Tuhiwai Smith, 2012; Vizenor, 1994).

I use the analytic of green wars to highlight how nature and narco exceptions to postgenocidal policing have reshaped the social distribution of death in the Maya Forest. It is often unclear whether murderers are traffickers, state forces, or some combination thereof, and this is part of what bestows spectacle violence with the power to inspire fear. In this context, rural Guatemalans agree to "let" narco-peasants die in a violent spectacle in the hopes that this will allow bystanders to live (Goldberg, 2009; Mbembe, 2003). Settler colonialism is not an event to remember on Columbus Day but rather a continuous set of state structures. National independence freed elites from the Spanish, but they repeatedly strove to dispossess Indigenous peoples of their territories and reproduce inequalities founded on racism. Today, the U.S. and Guatemalan state agencies use drug war states of emergency to rationalize territorial sweeps and indigenous subjection. While I hope that the primary contribution of this book is to call attention to the ways that global conservation is implemented with material and epistemic violence in settler colonies, I want to go a step further and return to the idea of decolonizing the Maya Forest. Even as I mourn the ways that violent pasts presage a dark present, I am reminded that many of my friends have high hopes for their children's indigenous futures.

NEW HOPE?

In August 2011, the Guatemalan government made international headlines for one of the communities it evicted during the Petén state of siege. This group called itself the "Agro-Ecological Community" of Nueva Esperanza (New Hope) and had already been evicted twice before but had nowhere else to go after Hurricane Mitch. Evictions are not particularly notable, whether from protected areas or private property, and this one had no more than 100 soldiers, 5 army officials, representatives from the National Council of Protected Areas (Consejo Nacional de Areas Protegidas, CONAP), the judge, and the national police, to evict a community of perhaps 300 people.

In a press release written in an attempt to clear the matter up, the Ministry of Defense and CONAP referred to Nueva Esperanza as a settlement (*asentimiento*) that was peacefully evicted.[1] The only irregularity apparent from the Defense Ministry's statement is that an observer from the Procuraduría de Derechos Humanos is usually present in the normal course of evictions but was not in this case. This was just one instance of what had been more than a year of evictions over two states of siege. The interior minister of Guatemala explained that the families of Nueva Esperanza were evicted because they were involved in drug trafficking (Paley, 2012). People living in and near the park know that it is a trafficking corridor, but it strains the imagination to believe that men, women, children, and elderly grandparents would live without access to roads, running water, or electricity if they had access to cartel money.

This time, however, eviction as usual became an international incident because families fled the military and headed north into Mexico, effectively internationalizing the park problem. Amid the outcry over the treatment of innocent families, I was confused. While all the cases I chose from for this book have families that claimed historical ties to the land, in this case no family claimed that it had settled before 2000, ten years after Sierra de Lacandón National Park was founded.[2] This is a classic "park invader" story, but that was not the focus of media attention. Instead of a peaceful eviction, families described fleeing when they heard gunfire, then hiding in the jungle as they watched the military douse their homes with gasoline and burn them down (Paley, 2012). These eviction experiences are consistent with those I shared in the introduction, Chapter 2, and Chapter 5. A report I have been able to find of subsequent land use is a plan to use the building that formerly housed their informal school as a joint operations center for CONAP, police, and military patrols. According to a local newspaper, the community buildings were razed, and the government dedicated more than $1 million to building a new operations center with an Inter-American Development Bank loan.[3]

Nueva Esperanza was the first community to seek refuge in Mexico since the end of the civil war. According to the Mexican National Migration Institute (INM), asylum was not possible because this was an "agrarian conflict" due to "landlessness." Instead, the INM called this a "humanitarian rescue" and asked the Guatemalan government to cooperate with a "repatriation" plan (Mayorga, 2012). I want to ask if perhaps, despite the massive show of force involved in evictions, the joint operation's shameful aftermath and the Defense Ministry's scramble to legitimize its actions in both Guatemala and Mexico might point to a key weakness in green wars. Unlike the Centro Campesino community also in the Sierra de Lacandón National Park (Corzo Márquez, 1999) or communities with claims in Lake Lachuá National Park (see Chapter 2), community leaders had no property claims to the land they lived on. They moved onto the land after it became a national park, they did not have permission through a usufruct agreement with CONAP, and they had no history of titling, registering, or paying land taxes in a core protected area. Nonetheless, the interior minister did not use the protected-areas laws as a justification for evicting poor and Indigenous farmers from their homes and burning down subsistence crops. Once it became obvious that there was no evidence to support the claim that Nueva Esperanza was a drug trafficking outpost, the legitimacy of property claims mattered less than the reality of a community displaced. Official rationalizations reveal a weakness when it comes to legitimizing violence against land activists. State officials appear acutely aware that national protected areas might not have passed if subjected to democratic processes, so they do not use those legal means as their public rationales.

Once media reports reveal men as community leaders, fathers, and brothers and narco-narratives recede, so too does public legitimacy for dispossession. This case demonstrates the possibility that most Guatemalans do not accept on the face of it that protected areas are a public good that justifies army eviction of very poor rural families. While CONAP officials argued that the reason why they collaborate with the military in patrolling and eviction is for their own safety, CONAP officials' collaboration with state security forces also provides a broader rationalization of securing the land against so-called narcos. When the public sees not a narco but instead a woman carrying only a *comal* to make tortillas in her hands and a child on her back, CONAP needs more than the law on its side. Legally, the police could have arrested all the families in Nueva Esperanza for trespassing in the core zone of a national park. Instead, the Mexican state and peasant leaders negotiated with the Guatemalan Secretariat of Agrarian Affairs (Secretaría de Asuntos Agrarios, SAA) for approximately 810 hectares of land as well as shelter and basic food aid for six months or until the first harvest (SAA, 2014). This is not a lot of land, and one community leader claimed that they were "negotiating on their knees" from Mexico (Mayorga, 2012), but it is still more land than Q'eqchi' communities that have longer documented histories—but do not receive international media attention—are able to negotiate.

This negotiation allowed the Defense Ministry to claim that this was an exceptional eviction and use the resettlement as a way to dodge responsibility for countless other evicted communities during the same states of emergency. At its root, negotiating on a community-by-community basis with the state and agreeing on resettlement in unfamiliar and inferior lands serves to reproduce the legitimacy of the protected-areas system and efface Indigenous communities' affective ties to territory. That said, this exception calls into question the legitimacy of the laws that allow for repeated army evictions in protected areas.

The case of Nueva Esperanza is instructive primarily because of the surprising strength of telling the same story to a new audience. When the eviction became an international humanitarian problem, narco-narratives were no longer enough without some kind of empirical backing. As is usually the case, state agencies had no evidence of drug trafficking activity. This suggests that international courts might serve as a way to nudge public discourse away from narco-narratives and toward indigenous livelihoods. While it seems probable to me that the Spanish-speaking capabilities of Nueva Esperanza were key to their ability to question the Guatemalan state narrative, this nonetheless points to possibilities for political openings. In recent years, many *ladinos* chafed at their international image as brutes who abuse poor Maya victims and resent human rights interventions on that basis (see Chapter 3). Might solidarity gringos be willing to trade the fighter planes that narco-narratives demand for imagining Maya territoriality as a creative act?

I wonder if, like Mexicans who have taken up the #yamecanse cry in the wake of the Ayoztinapa massacre of high school youths (unsolved to date but widely understood as an act of state violence), Guatemalans have tired of *mano dura* law and are more open to seeking state formations that affirm the rights of their Indigenous majority. For example, even Nobel laureate Rigoberta Menchú Tum argued in the 1990s that the Guatemalan courts would not be willing to put former dictators on trial in their own country. In the 2000s, they did just that. As of 2016, it appears that former dictators such as Ríos Montt can escape trial only through dementia, not impunity. (By way of comparison, former dictator Augusto Pinochet received a similar reprieve, but this was from the British courts, as Chile failed to hold him accountable for his actions.) In the summer of 2015, Guatemalans who either hadn't been told or simply didn't believe that it was supposed to be impossible for them to successfully call for the arrest of a president while in office did just that under the cry #RenunciaYa ("resign now") and #YaNoTengoPresidente ("I don't have a president anymore," disavowing then-president Otto Pérez Molina). Instead, Vice President Roxana Baldetti resigned as a scapegoat in the corruption investigation.[4]

In the first attempt to strip Pérez Molina of his immunity against criminal prosecution, not enough legislators attended to reach a quorum. In response, an estimated 100,000 people took to the streets on August 27, 2015, to demand that the president leave office. When I arrived in front of the National Palace after ten o'clock at night, Constitution Square had the air of a party that wouldn't stop. While normally the square cleared out at nightfall due to fears of violent crime,[5] families with children and folks young and old stood around watching the band, just not yet ready to go home. They arrived the next day and the next, sporting the blue and white colors of Guatemalan pride and demanding that their nation deserved better. On September 1, Amílcar Pop called legislators to a vote. When some people threatened legislators, others made a human chain to protect their path into the Congreso de la República and threw white roses as a gesture of peace. Even as journalists and activists took to Twitter to report the location of every legislator who ate lunch in fancy restaurants instead of showing up to vote, this time Congress revoked Pérez Molina's immunity with a vote of 132 to 0. He was arrested and in 2017 is on trial. This offers hope for a new generation of justice.

Mostly unremarked was the prominent role of the sole Q'eqchi' legislator in bringing the sitting president to his knees. Months before the #RenunciaYa movement was viral, lawyer and legislator Amílcar Pop dared to call the Guatemalan Congress to effectively vote the movement's president into jail. For the first time in history, Guatemalans have a leader who both calls for popular anticorruption measures and advocates for indigenous territorial rights. His leadership offers promise in demonstrating that a call for Q'eqchi' territoriality is not anti-Guatemalan. Rather, it is a call to transform the nation into a more just version of itself. Instead of an easy long-term relationship, Pop's work engages in a series of "contingent collaborations" between national human rights projects and Q'eqchi' territoriality (Tuck and McKenzie, 2016).

In 2017, the Goldman Environmental Foundation awarded Rodrigo Tot the Central and South American Environmentalist Prize for protecting Q'eqchi' lands against a rapacious nickel mining company. While his and other communities had secured land rights, the pages in the General Property Register that noted this were simply ripped out. In 2011, he won a landmark case before the Constitutional Court of Guatemala to have their collective property rights recognized. Five years later, two of Tot's sons were murdered and a third was severely injured under suspicious circumstances, the Guatemalan government has failed to enforce the ruling, and the mining company still seeks expansion. Together with Defensoría Q'eqchi', Tot and these communities continue to fight for their survival.

Accountability Starts at Home

Solidarity is an uneasy, reserved, and unsettled matter that neither reconciles present grievances nor forecloses future conflicts.
—TUCK AND YANG (2012, 3)

I am writing in English because I hope that English speakers in the United States will use this book as an opportunity to think through their relationships to people they do not know and perhaps have never thought much about until now. There are three key arenas for intervention where I think we can work to support indigenous territoriality and a socially just conservation. Gringos cannot decolonize Guatemala for Maya peoples, but we can tear down institutions and ideas that make their decolonizing activism more difficult. Decolonization does not prematurely signify the end of colonialism but instead signifies the ongoing project of resistance that persists in the midst of exploitation (Coulthard, 2014; Fanon, 2004 [1961]; Lowe, 1996). As is often the case, our work begins at home.

Gringo good intentions in Guatemala can amount to little more than buying Maya handicrafts to take home as souvenirs of the weeks when we opened our eyes to poverty and worked side by side with community members to build a school with a sustainable foundation of plastic bottles. Even here, gringos see only what we look for: many U.S. youths do not bother to ask if the Guatemalan school year is the same as ours (it is not) and thus fail to notice that kids are pulled out of school to work with them on a project that is supposed to promote education. Even more insulting, we gringos seem to have a habit of lecturing *ladinos* that they should stop violating human rights of the Mayas—when *ladinos* themselves are often poor and have already heard the lecture. I too express myself through gringo good intentions because they are tangible and can build fulfilling relationships (Ybarra, 2014). I too seek to call the *ladino* state to task. This is where the work begins, though, not where it ends.

Those travelers who want to learn about the difficult history of genocide during the civil war and the resilience of Indigenous peoples must do the same homework in their own backyards. Indeed, it is questioning whose homelands we inhabit. Many U.S. and Canadian citizens often fail to recognize that we are settlers encroaching on indigenous territory or think of it as a problem relegated to the past. Those of us with settler citizen privilege must support Indigenous peoples in the United States and the reinstatement of tribal recognition and territoriality.[6] Most important, settler citizens must advocate for the U.S. government to ratify international conventions. While President Barack Obama announced U.S. state endorsement of the UN Declaration on the Rights of Indigenous Peoples in 2010 the United States has yet to ratify important legal conventions such as ILO 169. If the United States actively supports ILO 169 and seeks recognition with settler colonialism in our present, this could create enormous political pressure on countries, including Guatemala, to follow suit. Likewise, our failure to do so supports the corresponding failure of Guatemala to do so.

Most international conservation organizations working in Latin America are based in Washington, D.C., and work with funds from the U.S. government (such as the U.S. Agency for International Development) and major donors (such as Harrison Ford). U.S. environmentalists need to rethink our own responsibilities in global conservation, beginning with Conservation International, the Nature Conservancy, and the World Wild Fund for Nature. A simplistic perpetrator perspective would seek out individual people, getting rid of so-called bad apples in conservation and development. This move, however, would act as though it is not the case that international monies facilitate violence as collaboration between conservation and state security forces. In other words, international conservationists can only disavow responsibility for state-related violence to the extent that they also disavow the legitimacy of an undemocratic protected-areas system. Instead, it seems that repression begets repression, and the net effect of zero-tolerance deforestation strategies may reproduce more deforestation, narco or otherwise (see also Zilberg, 2011, 18). Institutional transformation can only start with recognition that conservation's accountability problems are systemic. To the extent that U.S. conservation organizations disavow one person or one program, they can reasonably expect that Guatemalan citizens will scoff at these halfhearted efforts in the same way they did when the president had the vice president resign but claimed that the rest of his administration was not corrupt. We would do well to remember that his attempts at scapegoating were met with even more people calling him to account.

The need for accountability at home only grows in the face of increased anthropogenic climate change. Rather than seek to mitigate climate change through reforesting someone else's backyard, as in the REDD+ strategy, U.S. citizens must acknowledge that offsetting represents a threat to rural livelihoods and people who are, in their majority, poor and indigenous in Latin America (De Schutter, 2011). Rather than take advantage of the ways that the settler colonial state refuses to acknowledge their territorial rights and offset our own responsibility, we should ask tough questions about our own energy use, which is the highest per capita in the world. In 2016, I was privileged to join a group led by Got Green Seattle, which both rejected Washington state's move to internationalize offsets and called for a just transition to cleaner economies. As the Just Transition Assembly includes people of color, Indigenous peoples, and people with close family ties to Mexico, and the Philippines the work of imagining a clean economy at home that doesn't offset our pollution afar is precisely what diverse communities are doing right now. This level of accountability is simply necessary once an environmental organization places the people most affected by climate change at the center of the agenda—in the United States, this invariably means that folks with transnational ties easily reject offsetting responsibility to their cousins' homes. At the same time, movements such as RED-OIL and #NODAPL demonstrate that Indigenous peoples are not waiting for settlers to save them from people like us.

Some of the most important, creative movements that achieve much with little money are those movements led by Indigenous peoples and people of color. The movement against the Dakota Access Pipeline (#NODAPL) is led by the Standing Rock Sioux, and allies are those the tribe is generous enough to allow in. As I have described in this book, I think that the most important example for Q'eqchi' land activists is that of the Miskitos in Nicaragua or indigenous communal property structures (*ejidos*) in Mexico. I believe that the most important thing people such as myself can do is to facilitate their encounters, dialogue, and relationships without expecting a seat at the table in return. I should note that I don't generally think of myself as a powerful person, but more times than I believed were possible I found that a nice dress, a printed business card, and a light-skinned face served to get my friends in the door to visit mayors, judges, and national agency heads. This means awkwardly stepping up where it shouldn't be necessary and then taking a step back and letting those who can best represent their communities do that work.

Finally, U.S. agencies are implicated in both Cold War and drug war violence in Guatemala. As of December 2014, the "humanitarian crisis" of increased immigrants from Central America, including both accompanied and unaccompanied minors, has led El Salvador, Guatemala, and Honduras to propose a thumbnail sketch of a plan titled "Alliance for Prosperity," which posits further infrastructure development and debt to jump-start national economies, with relatively little attention to social safety nets.[7] Meanwhile, the United States appears to continue to fund the consolidation of Mexico's interior southern border through the Mérida Initiative and the Central America Regional Security Initiative. In other words, U.S. taxpayers are footing the bill for some of Guatemala's remilitarization and Mexico's border violence. Moreover, U.S. state agents, including the Drug Enforcement Administration, are playing an active role in policing other nations' territories without accountability mechanisms—at home and abroad. Before we teach other countries how to manage the rule of law and guarantee citizen security, perhaps we need our own national conversation about how and why black and brown lives matter. If we in the United States reformed our systems of incarceration and detention, this would have a massive cascading effect for Latinxs on both sides of the border. Given that an estimated 10–15 percent of Guatemala's gross domestic product comes from international remittances (Cohn, Gonzalez-Barrera, and Cuddington, 2013),[8] moving from a model of social death to social reproduction would allow transnational communities to support themselves. Likewise, Indigenous peoples in diaspora could participate in decolonizing processes and imagining collective self-determination in Guatemala.

While many of us seek truth and reconciliation, the painful reality is that reconciliation is more about settlers making peace with themselves. Instead, we must understand our role in mutually implicated histories that articulate imperialism and settler colonialism. Indigenous futures require "an intergenerational connection to an individual and collective sense of presence and resistance in personal experience and the word, or language, particularly through stories" (Vizenor et al., 2014, 107), pointing toward indigenous futures. In this context solidarity cannot offer closure or even necessarily good feelings. Rather, solidarity is a drawn-out painful experience that offers neither pat answers for current issues or ways to avoid future problems. Instead, true relationships of solidarity acknowledge unequal power relations and also acknowledge that no small acts can ameliorate their effects. Most important, calls to decolonization sometimes feel like they blame us (the settler us) for harms we have not caused and ask us to give what we have not offered. The work of solidarity demands that settlers move from a notion of giving up what we think is ours. Instead, we must begin to understand that the land is not ours in the first place and take up the task of giving back what was stolen on our behalf.

NOTES

INTRODUCTION

1. Reducing emissions from deforestation and forest degradation (REDD+) is a mechanism approved by the United Nations Framework Convention on Climate Change whereby local landowners receive incentive payments for reforestation and avoid deforestation on their land.

2. Small-scale farming practiced on shallow tropical soils. Lowlands farmers prefer to rotate land use on a sixteen-year cycle between different crops and fallow.

3. The literal translation into Q'eqchi' of the term protected area (*k'olb'il na'aej*) was not widely used until the 1990s.

4. Their existence was not acknowledged in any Project documentation I reviewed. They participated in roundtable conflict negotiations, but I was told that those records no longer existed.

5. *Aj rub'el pim,* or "people of the bush," the Q'eqchi' term for guerrillas.

6. In a subsequent interview with a Lake Lachuá park guard, he confirmed that the park director signed the agreement. Furthermore, he claimed that he denounced the agreement in the capital as a "crime." While the agreement did not break a law, he successfully sparked a political backlash that prevented Quixpur's landownership recognition.

7. I refer to these as Indigenous peoples (*pueblos*), not groups, because peoples are recognized in international law as having the right to self-determination (Tuhiwai Smith, 2012, 118–119). Failure to recognize Indigenous peoples as a collectivity is an act of settler-state violence. While I draw on works that discuss federally recognized tribes or bands, neither of these terms is appropriate for Guatemala; for some Indigenous peoples, they are offensive. I use the term *communities* to refer to groups of people who live on shared land and whom the nation-state recognizes as *aldeas* or *caseríos,* even when they do not agree themselves that they are a community (see Chapter 2).

8. Due to agricultural inability to treat the Panama disease on banana plantations, the United Fruit Company and others held large swaths of land in reserve.

9. Many of the original guerrilla fighters had trained at the Politécnica and/or had been enlisted in the army.

10. Grandin's portrayal of the 1978 Panzós massacre repeatedly calls Q'eqchi' land activists "peasants," even while acknowledging that they questioned the rights of the liberal state to grant land rights, invoked "millenarian" spirituality, and were stigmatized for "witchcraft." A close read of memories from communist informants reveals a divide between *ladinos* who wanted to focus on labor rights and Q'eqchi's who used rituals and language to critique the titling system for private land (see Chapter 5).

11. For example, by directing census takers to label anyone who speaks Spanish as *ladino,* this prominent K'iche' scholar would be classified as *ladino* due to his ability to speak Spanish.

12. The 1992 protests did not address the antiblackness in *mestizaje* discourses. In 2015, the Mexican census added the ability to self-identify as Afro-Mexican for the first time after decades of activism.

13. In the lowlands, these occurred in a series of military campaigns including those through the Usumacinta River cooperatives in Petén through present-day Sierra Lacandón National Park, northern Cobán through present-day Lake Lachuá National Park (see Chapter 4), Chisec cooperatives, and subsequent development poles through present-day Candelaria Caves National Park (Ybarra, 2011, 2013; see also Chapter 6).

14. Guatemala and Belize are still embroiled in a territorial dispute, and some Guatemalans do not recognize Belize's existence as a sovereign nation.

15. This was the basis for the World Bank's Land Administration Program I, as Grandia (2006, 2009c, 2012) and Gould (2006, 2009, 2014) examine in detail.

16. *Ladinos* were granted individual holdings, up to one *caballería* (forty-five hectares) in Petén, whereas Indigenous communities were granted private community titles that only allowed for smaller family plots. In postwar land-formalization projects, the state has increasingly pushed for individualized private land titles.

17. I first heard this in my work with the women's political participation in Uspantán, El Quiché, in 2004. It is of note that I regularly heard this from *ladinos* but not from K'iche's.

18. The current president is reported to have strong ties to military leadership, but the role of his administration in remilitarization is not yet clear as the book goes to press.

19. I do not use terms such as *green counterinsurgency, ecotourism counterinsurgency* (Devine, 2014), or *ecoterrorism* because these imply the existence of "insurgents" or "terrorists," which I argue serve to criminalize land activists.

20. Audra Simpson (2014) uses this term in the introduction of *Mohawk Interruptus* but does not return to it.

21. Latinx refers to all people with Latin American heritage within and beyond the United States. While commonly written as "Latino," I use the "x" on the end to signal a politics that does not adhere to gender binaries. In Spanish, "a" or "o" appended to a word gives it feminine/masculine signifiers, whereas the "x" derives from Mayan languages and is not gendered.

22. For example, in 2003 I worked with the Nahualá municipal government at the same time as a young woman who was completing an internship for her architecture degree at the national university, Universidad de San Carlos. When she shaved her head and began to incorporate K'iche' clothes (*traje*) into her wardrobe, everyone in town decided that she was the gringa volunteer and I was the *capitalina* intern, despite my protests to the contrary.

23. I use Americas to refer to North, Central, and South America.

24. This was demonstrated at length in a presentation I gave at the national University of San Carlos in Guatemala City in September 2016. I continue to use this term because it most accurately describes what I learned from Q'eqchi' intellectuals and also because non-indigenous student and faculty objections were about negative connotations, not whether the theoretical application was accurate.

25. I have conducted case studies that focus on the International Union for Conservation of Nature, the Nature Conservancy, and the World Wildlife Fund for Nature.

CHAPTER 1. MAKING THE MAYA FOREST

1. This was more than ten years before the hostage situations described in the introduction and Chapter 2. In addition to CI documents, I also draw on first-person accounts from Liza Grandia (2009, 2012) and Jim Nations (2006).

2. The government of Guatemala signed a US$22 million loan contract with the Inter-American Development Bank for Project GU-L1014, titled "Establishing Cadastral Registry and Strengthening Legal Certainty Protected Areas" in 2011. As of 2017, the project is in implementation phase.

3. I did not interview anyone who admitted to participating in this action. My assertion is based on conversations with conservation professionals who have worked to develop relationships with these same community members over subsequent decades.

4. Grandia continues to work with the spin-off organization Pro-Petén in promoting cultural heritage, environmental, and reproductive health education. Pro-Petén is no longer affiliated with CI, as she explains in Grandia (2009b).

5. Colonization is generally understood as the "conquest, inhabitation, possession, and control of a territory by an external power" (Smith and Katz, 1993). In Guatemala and other Latin American nations, however, the extension of a newly designated "agricultural frontier" happened via a process commonly understood as "colonization."

6. E.5.1 Franja Transversal (1975–1986), Latin American History and Culture: Series 5: Civil War, Society and Political Transition in Guatemala: The Guatemala News and Information Bureau Archive, 1963–2000, Centro de Investigaciones Regionales de Mesoamérica Archives. The list of target departments also includes counties with significant Kaqchikel and Tz'utujil populations. It is also of note that Ch'orti's who suffered early in civil war massacres were then recruited—as *ladinos*—to join agricultural cooperatives (Casolo, 2011).

7. Claims were similarly made about the East, which is similarly placed in the shadow of the western highlands (Casolo, 2011).

8. Many parents have told me in firm Spanish that they want their children to grow up Q'eqchi' but particularly read Spanish in order to defend themselves against fraud (*para que puedan defenderse* is a common phrase.)

9. Guayo is reluctant to admit engaging in traditional animist practices, as he has embraced evangelical Christianity. He believes that worshipping the caves made God angry, and this is why the *kaxlans* evicted his family from Lanquín.

10. I capitalize this in quoting directly from military planning documents for the Franja Transversal del Norte. At the same time, scholars of ethnicity and identity in Guatemala regularly write about a singular national Guatemalan project (e.g., Taracena Arriola, 2004).

11. Ibid.

12. Lucas García's regime tended to leave bodies by the side of the road as a warning to other potential dissidents, and people were not allowed to bury their loved ones after massacres (for an example, see Ybarra, 2011). Nonetheless, Ríos Montt's administration (1982–1983) committed the most killings (Ball, Kobrak, and Spirer, 1999).

13. As of 2017, it seems unlikely that Pérez Molina will stand trial for his role in the Ixil Triangle massacres but probable that he will stand trial for participating in a graft scheme while president.

14. Colección de Documentos IGE, Colección CIRMA, Centro de Investigaciones Regionales de Mesoamérica Archives.

15. As Morrissey (1978) describes, they were bitter because of the joint decision of the Catholic Church and INTA to cut plot sizes and essentially double the population living on the land while promised projects and land titles still hadn't materialized.

16. Schirmer's (1998) penetrating analysis shows how the peace processes have largely followed the military's stated plan.

17. In gross monthly estimations, violent deaths in the countryside were higher under Ríos Montt than his predecessor, Lucas García, peaking in July 1982 (Ball et al., 1999).

18. At the time of publication, Russell Mittermeier was the president of CI. Myers was a research fellow with CI.

19. Norman B. Schwartz, personal communication, August 16, 2012.

20. Prensa Libre, http://www.prensalibre.com/infografia/AREAS-PROTEGIDAS_PREFIL20130421_0003.pdf, accessed May 25, 2013.

CHAPTER 2. WE DIDN'T INVADE THE PARK

1. For this case study, I consulted with the land archives at the FONTIERRAS offices in Ixcán, El Quiché, Cobán, Alta Verapaz, and Guatemala City, each of which had a partial file. I also looked at Project records and the INAB Archive in Guatemala City. Many community members also provided me with copies of land titles and *actas* that document meeting minutes and agreements signed by military and/or park officials.

2. In Q'eqchi', the word *lachúa* means "stinky," referring to the lake's sulfur smell. The official park name places an accent on the last syllable, suggesting that those who formally declared the national park did not know how to correctly pronounce the Q'eqchi' word.

3. Lake Lachuá is recognized as a site of international importance according to the Ramsar Convention on Wetlands. The threats are mentioned on the information page "Eco-Región Lachuá," Ramsar Sites Information Service, May 25, 2006, https://rsis.ramsar.org/ris/1623.

4. The Spanish term *hermanos* could be interpreted as meaning "brothers and sisters." My translation genders this male because the majority of forest technicians and other workers who bunked at the Project were men.

5. To the best of my knowledge, women have never been named in the warrants. They participate in farming inside park boundaries and in taking hostages, but it seems that both park guards and invaders see their presence as one that serves to mitigate violent escalations. National news coverage rarely mentions the presence of women and children when it covers hostage situations.

6. Their descendants explained that this was so the entire plantation would be passed down to the eldest son rather than split up into smaller plots.

7. They are considered "evangelical" in Guatemala, shorthand for Protestants whom military dictators considered exceptionally loyal (Garrard-Burnett, 2010).

8. "Entrance fees" have a murky legal history in colonization zones. The first settlers sometimes charged new families fees to pay for existing physical improvements (such as a road) or legal fees that other community members had already invested. By all accounts, Sepac's "entrance fees" were unusually high.

9. I was unable to reach them for interviews, so my analysis is based only on the plans, falsified titles, and other peoples' interpretations of their actions.

10. The EGP was a Marxist guerrilla organization that fought the army and worked for the revolution. While there were probably fewer than 10,000 guerrillas in the entire country, the EGP had significant influence in this region.

11. I found corresponding evidence in maps of the "reserve area" north of the park and bordering Mexico in the park's archives in undated park plans.

12. This policy radically shifted by the early 1980s, and cooperatives in the northern lowlands were targeted for counterinsurgency violence.

13. At the time, there was no standard Q'eqchi' word. Today, this is commonly rendered as k'olb'il na'ajej, or "protected place."

14. This classification was generally reserved for Indigenous communities (Ybarra, 2011b).

15. Much of the food aid came through Public Law 480, whereby the United States gives away excess surplus grain to countries in need as part of the Farm Bill.

16. This was the case in interviews I conducted with survivors in this development pole as well as with two others in Chisec, Alta Verapaz. Rather than international assistance, food-for-work programs are often seen as a means for coercing starving people because of this military history.

17. Hunting and fishing were prohibited, but almost everyone ignored or disputed the park's restrictions.

18. With the Project's introduction of new crops and reforestation incentives, rental prices have increased 150–400 percent from 2000 until 2008, when I conducted fieldwork.

19. The Guatemalan state never had treaties with Indigenous peoples, so it does not use the common U.S. instrument of blood quantum to determine tribal belonging (on this, see Kauanui, 2008; Simpson, 2014).

20. Instead, they claim that the only other community with a similar history in Lake Lachuá National Park is Quixpur (see the introduction).

21. As of 2009, the conflict negotiator works as a community liaison for an oil company.

22. I went with a rather larger group of "park invaders." While I took photographs and learned immensely from the tour, it also seems possible that they used my presence as a way to tend their crops without interference from park guards and police.

CHAPTER 3. RETHINKING LADINOS AS SETTLERS

1. I also verified these histories with archival evidence, truth commission reports, and interviews nearby community members.

2. As of 2017, it seems likely that his age and ailing health will delay the trial indefinitely. By way of comparison, the British courts made a similar determination for former Chilean dictator Augusto Pinochet because domestic prosecutors were unwilling and/or unable to do so.

3. This is in keeping with international law, but former military dictator Ríos Montt and other Guatemalans previously invoked it as a legal defense.

4. I conducted interviews before this historic ruling, which is one reason why I have erred on the side of caution in confidentiality.

5. This is in contrast to other Mayan languages and seems to be due to the articulation of Q'eqchi' and German social relations.

6. Whereas Hale (2006) frames a rejection of *ladino* identity as a reaction to the Pan-Maya movement, he places less emphasis on disavowal of responsibility for racist violence.

7. He has worked for a number of agencies over the years I have known him, most of which are NGOs with U.S. and European funding.

8. My working assumption was that the CUC would not knowingly represent people who committed genocide, although this may have been incorrect.

9. The language teacher is from another community that is not in the lowlands, and he did not personally know the Candelaria Caves communities.

10. Casaús Arzú argues that European elites consolidated their identities as creoles (*criollos*) as a claim to racial purity against both Indigenous and African heritage. Many Germans, however, married into Q'eqchi' families and would sometimes formally recognize their children.

11. This was partially due to the role of K'iche' leaders signaling Q'eqchi's as troublesome, in keeping with their historical territorial disputes.

12. While these are widely known as Japanese internment camps, the World War II camps run by the U.S. Department of Justice and the U.S. Army also had a small number of Germans and Italians.

13. Rights claims were traced from fathers to legitimate sons. I also interviewed people who claimed to have Sapper heritage, but they had Q'eqchi' mothers and tended to identify as Q'eqchi' or German Q'eqchi' without making land claims.

14. USAID promoted cardamom as a nontraditional agricultural export beginning in the 1960s. Today it is the third most expensive spice in the world, notable for its use in masala chai tea.

15. This is how he presented the story to me in a 2008 interview, but the Sapper family company was still suing for compensation in 2009.

16. My impression is that so-called traditional Peteneros similarly work disproportionately as conservation and development professionals in Petén.

17. The INE's population census data is used to determine how much money the central government allocates to municipal governments.

18. This is usually the case when someone else has already registered a competing land claim.

19. Literally "engineer," a common term of respect that people use for development professionals that does not always signal degree attainment.

20. The two most common verbs they used were *desarrollar* and *superar.*

21. This conveniently makes all Europeans "Spanish" and ignores African heritage entirely.

22. This led to the Coordinadora Nacional Indígena y Campesina splitting off from the historic peasant organization, CUC.

23. Mayan-language training is unfortunately relatively rare among would-be ethnographers in geography but is often required in cultural anthropology programs.

24. ACOFOP's impressive success (Gómez and Méndez, 2005) might be difficult to replicate because it is land extensive, benefits few people, and required significant long-term foreign funding.

CHAPTER 4. TAXING THE *KAXLAN*

1. I intended to ask the French tour operator for an interview but decided not to contact him due to concerns for my own safety. I toured the cave complex and ate a meal at the hotel, but I used a pseudonym and did not identify myself as a researcher.

2. MICUDE was the park guards' official employer. They were also Q'eqchi' Mayas and members of either Setzuul or its neighboring community. Thus, they had both personal and professional interests in resolving the land conflict.

3. While I did not work closely with peasant organizations, Velázquez Nimatuj (2008) and others have engaged in critical analysis in the role of Indigenous peoples in Guatemalan peasant movements and institutions.

4. In an interview, Sebastián said that he thought that officials did not start to document his claim because he does not know how to read and write. Perhaps a legacy of this is that he and other community elders would watch carefully to ensure that I took notes during our interviews, occasionally saying things like "write that down" while pointing at my notebook.

5. Sebastián denies that other communities existed, but other village members said that they only joined Setzuul after they were displaced in the war.

6. Not coincidentally, President Lucas García also accumulated significant landholdings near the highway/pipeline nexus.

7. Cardamom is one of the most important cash crops for small farmers, who can sell this spice for consumption in the Middle East or for Starbucks chai tea lattes. As with coffee roasters, it is the middlemen who dry the cardamom that have the highest profit margins.

8. At the time, the military considered selling food to EGP members a crime meriting extrajudicial killing, and failing to report EGP presence to the army also brought significant suspicion. A military slogan was "For the guerrilla, neither bread nor tortilla" (Remijnse, 2002).

9. Estado Mayor Presidencial was an entity notorious for committing political assassinations and was dissolved as part of the peace accords.

10. Sebastián and others asserted that all the members of new Setzuul were the same as old Setzuul, but I interviewed a few people who arrived and paid an entrance fee to take over someone else's parcel in 1984. It is not legal to do so after INTA conducts a household

census during the land-titling process, but it is common practice and is perceived as legitimate relative to how high the "fee" is.

11. For about two decades he claimed in written materials to have "discovered" the Candelaria Caves, but on a tour in 2009 a guide explained that the local population had always used the caves, although Girard was able to explore further than they had because he brought spelunking equipment.

12. To the best of my knowledge, Girard does not have a degree in either speleology or archaeology.

13. I spoke informally with him multiple times, but he declined to participate in an interview.

14. According to the law, claimants may not sell their land claims and do not legally own any particular parcel and instead have an equal share (*partes alícuotas*) in communal property. The only event in which FONTIERRAS allows names to be substituted during the titling process should be if an owner dies, in which case the rights pass to his heirs.

15. While landless groups that claim to be genocide survivors in Sepac are affiliated with the Coordinadora Nacional Indígena y Campesina and CUC, a group that strives to bring together indigenous and peasant platforms, Setzuul did not have a relationship with any peasant organization.

16. Personal communication, July 27, 2011.

17. The Spanish version is titled "Ethno-Linguistic Map of Guatemala." I do not know why "Ethno" was dropped in the English version.

18. If one actually compares the two parcels that he says he bought with the land area he fenced in, it is clear that he has encroached on caves that he does not claim to have purchased.

19. The CONAP representative's framing elided acknowledgment that Girard hoped to use protected-area status to settle the land conflict. At the same time, CONAP's reluctance to declare a protected area demonstrates that the parks agency has learned valuable lessons about declaring protected areas where Indigenous peoples live.

20. Girard did not and does not have de jure land rights, but *ladino* state agencies have de facto recognized his claims since the late 1980s.

21. There were also a few cattle ranchers who had significantly deforested land inside the new park. They evinced no interest in the park and refused to participate in management plans, and they were not concerned that anyone would restrict their land use. They were correct; the Ministry of Culture and CONAP regularly restrict land use in protected areas by communities while leaving massive cattle ranches untouched because they are "private property," as though private community property is "public."

22. Community members and affiliated groups today claim that the tanks were empty. When I asked a Ministry of Culture representative, he declined to speculate.

23. This empowerment also had the unintended effect of exacerbating existing inequities by rewarding younger Spanish-speaking educated Q'eqchi' men (such as Javier) while effacing traditional, often monolingual, authorities from political territorial processes (such as Pascual).

24. In 2008 I asked the Setzuul community mayor and his family and Wakliqoo's executive director about this, and I had extended conversations with Javier in 2011 and 2012 after

he left Wakliqoo. Likewise, friends at other development organizations familiar with the community described it as "troubled," not a model for success.

25. The question of state tutelage normally matters only in a land sale, and Setzuul has vowed not to sell its land.

26. I found this to be true of some MICUDE employees and appointees but not others.

27. Wakliqoo and its primary European funder also believe this. When I suggested to the European leader of the organization based in Chisec that swidden practices are not harmful if extensive, he laughed and called me naive.

28. Since 2008, a *ladino* has also purchased and developed substantial landholdings as an ecotourism complex, increasing competition for Candelaria Caves ecotourists.

29. Winner of the 1992 Nobel Peace Prize and presidential candidate during the case study period.

30. I later found out that he was ill with malaria.

31. I intended to offer my assistance in mapping skills and equipment, but it was clear that Wakliqoo needed equipment, not gringo expertise. While I eventually helped Wakliqoo obtain some equipment, it was not until a few months after I finished my fieldwork (still in 2008). When I arrived in the office with the equipment, Wakliqoo employees were clearly surprised and told me that the executive director told everyone that I would not keep my promise. I was angry and disappointed at the time, but this was a reasonable assumption based on his past gringo experiences.

32. Q'eqchi' spiritual practice has not historically included the four-points ritual, but they did this with K'iche' visitors from the OAP.

33. When I later had an opportunity to ask what ailed the sick people, the symptoms they described sounded like what Western medicine would describe as post-traumatic stress, depression, and anxiety. A major function of the healing ceremony is to bring that person back into the fold of her or his community.

34. The case of the Candelaria Caves revealed important cleavages between generalizations of a Pan-Maya cosmovision and Q'eqchi' spirituality. Whereas prayers at a national level tend to be conducted in K'iche' and reference a global *nim ajaw* (great god), Q'eqchi's do not employ this language, and their spiritual relationships are territorialized rather than global. The *tzuultaq'a*, which was key to Setzuul's sacred place claim, is territorialized as the true owner of a place, especially wild animals and the land. Q'eqchi's develop a relationship with the *tzuultaq'a* through planting cycles and prayer. If they pray at a general level, it tends to be to thirteen *tzuultaq'as*, a figurative device that invokes Q'eqchi' territory at a regional level but not the nation of Guatemala and certainly not the world (many authors list the thirteen *tzuultaq'as*, but those that are named sometimes change when invoked in spiritual practice). Some Q'eqchi's have adapted in an attempt to share in the Pan-Maya movement, invoking a *nim ajaw* and learning to call themselves *aj q'ij* (in K'iche') to represent themselves as Maya brothers. This work is not easy or natural.

35. I felt that leaders made promises that we could not keep and that my work was supposed to make those promises possible. I never heard anybody say anything that I thought would create unreasonable expectations, but it was clear that some people had high hopes that our work did not realize. I did my best to manage their expectations, but this does little to ameliorate the daily injustice they live.

36. Three decades later, Wakliqoo brought Basque activists to Chisec to discuss territorial autonomy. A regional government official described them to me as "ETA" and "terrorists." He acknowledged that they did not claim to be either of these but only after I repeatedly asked him to clarify (interview, September 2016).

37. This recognition is in direct contrast to the identity parsing that conservationists used to police all but one Maya people out of their rights in the Mexican Maya Forest.

38. While some men from Setzuul and other nearby communities did work on African palm plantations, this was understood to be economically and socially shameful.

39. This was also true for people such as OAP representatives, who doubted whether I should be allowed to observe meetings about important community decisions. When they objected to my presence it was as a *kaxlan*—the only nonindigenous person present.

40. The director of Wakliqoo decided to use the association as a vehicle to campaign for mayor of Chisec. Accordingly, Setzuul and other communities whose members would become voters in Raxruhá ceased to benefit from Wakliqoo's support. The director has since run unsuccessfully for mayor in the last two elections.

CHAPTER 5. NACRO-NARRATIVES

1. Gustavo Gorriti, "Entre el macartismo y los narcovuelos," *Plaza Pública,* July 24, 2013, http://www.plazapublica.com.gt/content/entre-el-macartismo-y-los-narcovuelos.

2. Clare O'Neill McClaskey, "Over 150 'Narcotaxis' Operate in Mexican State Capital," *InSight Crime,* July 30, 2013, http://www.insightcrime.org/news-briefs/guerrero-taxi-drivers-demand-action-on-narcotaxis.

3. "Desmantelan tres narcolaboratorios," *Siglo XXI,* http://www.s21.com.gt/nacionales /2013/07/24/desmantelan-tres-narcolaboratorios.

4. Anonymous, "Narcomansión," *Siglo XXI,* http://www.s21.com.gt/nacionales/2013/07 /21/narcomansion.

5. "Guatemala and Organised Crime: Reaching the Untouchables," *The Economist,* March 11, 2010, http://www.economist.com/world/americas/PrinterFriendly.cfm?story_id=15663302. See also H. Brands, *Crime, Violence and the Crisis in Guatemala: A Case Study in the Erosion of the State,* Strategic Studies Institute, May 2010, http://www.strategicstudiesinstitute.army .mil/pdffiles/PUB986.pdf.

6. B. R. McCaffrey, "After Action Report: Visit Mexico 5–7 December 2008," Council on Hemispheric Affairs, January 16, 2009, http://www.coha.org/after-action-report%E2% 80%94general-barry-r-mccaffrey-usa-ret/.

7. This follows a similar pattern of migration rerouting through the dangerous Sonoran Desert on the U.S.-Mexican border.

8. These include massacres, *feminicidio* (violent killing and display of a woman's corpse designed to shame her femininity), and beheadings. In the latter case, heads have been left in the central town plaza separate from the body, sometimes with explicit warnings in the form of graffiti or messages to the press.

9. Tim Padgett, "Guatemala's Kaibiles: A Notorious Commando Unit Wrapped up in Central America's Drug war," *Time,* July 14, 2011, http://world.time.com/2011/07/14 /guatemalas-Kaibil-terror-from-dictators-to-drug-cartels/.

10. Land-extensive legitimate businesses serve multiple functions: protected territory for trafficking, legitimate business, money laundering opportunities, and social prestige.

11. This suggests that drug decriminalization would not cripple the financial well-being of drug trafficking organizations.

12. The Spanish term *martillo* means "hammer."

13. Mark Thompson, "General: Expect 'Mass Migration' to U.S. if Ebola Comes to Central America." *Time,* October 9, 2014, http://time.com/3486009/marine-general-john-kelly-ebola-migration/, accessed August 14, 2017.

14. My thinking on states of emergency owes a debt to scholars including Carl Schmitt and Giorgio Agamben, but I use the term primarily as a direct translation from the Spanish. While the Occidental approach privileges liberal individualism and democracy in siting sovereignty (Agamben, 1998; Schmitt, 1985), my analysis draws on postcolonial works that center the role of difference and violence in state formations and social relations (Coulthard, 2014; Fanon, 2008; Gilroy, 1993a; Mbembe, 2003). As Simpson (2014) notes, Agamben's reading of the World War II camp is neither innovative nor exceptional when read against a longer history of settler colonialism.

15. Foucault also claims that (all) societies originally viewed this as a problem of "individual correction" rather than a social good, and he further errs by globally claiming that restorative justice no longer exists. These assumptions are untrue for many Indigenous peoples.

16. Narco-narratives rarely represent women and children, because only male figures are represented as having the agency to kill. This renders the deaths of women and children unspoken and unseen.

17. In contrast, international institutions devoted significant energy to revamping civil laws and civil courts as part of the peace processes in the 1980s and 1990s.

18. Named for the former defense minister. A U.S. civil court found him guilty of massacring Q'anjob'al Mayas as well as kidnapping and torturing a nun, Dianna Ortiz, in 1995.

CONCLUSION

1. Departamento de la Prensa, Ministerio de la Defensa Nacional, "Communicado de Prensa No. 22-cl-2011," 2011, accessed May 27, 2013, www.mindef.mil.gt/noticias/PDF/comunicados/comunicado 22.pdf.

2. Families settled Nueva Esperanza in a *zona intangible,* the core of the park where homesteading, hunting, fishing, and planting crops are prohibited.

3. Iván Medrano, "Centro Protegerá Reserva," *Nuestro Diario,* 2011, accessed December 30, 2014, http://digital.nuestrodiario.com/Olive/ODE/NuestroDiario/LandingPage/Landing Page.aspx?href=Ro5ELzIwMTQvMTAvMTc.&pageno=NjA.&entity=QXIwNjAwMA..&view=ZW50aXR5,.

4. In ways reminiscent of the memory of Augusto Pinochet in Chile, citizens seem more outraged over allegations that their president participated in a graft scheme than allegations that he led a military genocide campaign.

5. In the summer of 2016, this was a refreshingly untrue statement. I walked through Constitution Square after dark in the company of skateboarders, break-dancers, and regular

folk walking home carrying groceries. Likewise, official statistics reflected a significant (perhaps 30 percent) drop in homicide rates.

6. I live and work on Duwamish territory. The Duwamish tribal government is currently struggling for federal recognition, which settler courts ironically denied them because they do not have a land base.

7. In 2017, it is unclear what the U.S. stance will be toward the Alliance for Prosperity under the Donald Trump administration.

8. The World Bank estimates monies that international migrants send to their home country via formal channels (such as banks) at 10 percent; "informal" remittances would increase this figure by 50 percent.

GLOSSARY OF TERMS AND ACRONYMS

baldío	"Wastelands" from Spanish colonialism; refers to any parcel that has not been and is not in the process of being legally mapped and titled through the Guatemalan government (whether public or private), without regard to actual settlement.
BINGOs	Refers to "big international nongovernment organizations," commonly identified as Conservation International, the Nature Conservancy, and the World Wild Fund for Nature in the conservation sector (Brockington, Duffy, and Igoe, 2008).
COCODE (Consejo Comunitario de Desarrollo)	Community Development Council. Created as part of democratic decentralization in postwar development, councils consist of usually twelve members who represent the community's interests, potentially managing funds for projects.
CONAP (Consejo Nacional de Areas Protegidas)	National Council of Protected Areas, Guatemala's national park administration, created in 1990.
DEA (Drug Enforcement Administration)	The U.S. DEA collaborates with Latin American states for intelligence and operations, occasionally including boots on the ground.
DIPRONA (División de Protección a la Naturaleza de la Policía Nacional Civil)	The Guatemalan Division of Nature Protection of the National Civil Police accompanies park guards on patrols and during raids of human settlements in core protected areas.

EGP (Ejército Guerrillero de los Pobres)

Guerrilla Army of the Poor; Marxist guerrilla group active in the Franja Transversal del Norte in the 1970s and 1980s.

FONTIERRAS (Fondo de Tierras)

Guatemalan Land Fund created in the 1990s to facilitate loans for land purchases. FONTIERRAS assumed all land titling responsibilities from the previous state agencies: FYDEP in the Petén Department and INTA in the rest of the country.

FYDEP (Empresa Nacional de Fomento y Desarrollo Económico de Petén)

Company for the Promotion and Development of Petén, a land agency run by the military from the 1960s through the 1980s. Today, FONTIERRAS has taken over the role of allocating and titling land.

gringo

Latin American term for a person from the United States, although this is often employed for any foreigner who appears to be of European descent; as Nelson (1999) details, the term can be dismissive, offensive, and/or affectionate.

ILO 169 (International Labour Organization Convention No. 169 concerning Indigenous and Tribal Peoples in Independent Countries)

Advocates for the rights of Indigenous groups to develop their own ethnic and cultural characteristics; to protect their cultural and spiritual practices and sites; and to gain recognition of their customary laws and land tenure systems. Guatemala ratified this legally binding international treaty, but Indigenous activists argue that laws and practices do not comply with ILO 169.

INAB (Instituto Nacional de Bosques)

National Forestry Institute, which created and controlled protected areas (including Lake Lachuá) until CONAP was created in 1990. Most INAB offices today focus on issuing timber permits and enforcing laws against forest fires.

INTA (Instituto Nacional de Transformación Agraria)

The National Institute of Agrarian Transformation, charged with land titling throughout the nation, with special focus on newly colonized lands. During the 1990s peace accords process, a new state agency, FONTIERRAS, was created to take over this work.

Kaibil

The Guatemalan special forces unit with required training based out of southern Petén. The name of the unit is appropriated from Kayb'il B'alam (Kaibil Balam), a Mam Maya Indigenous leader who fought the Spanish invasion.

kaxlan ("kaash-lahn," Q'eqchi')

Originally meaning "Spanish invader," today Mayas use this term to describe anyone "foreign," including gringos, Spaniards, and nonindigenous Guatemalans.

ladino (Spanish)	Under colonial Spain, a *ladino* was a non-Spaniard (Indigenous and/or African) who spoke Castilian Spanish, often taking on an intermediary social position between colonizers and colonized. Today the term is widely used to refer to any nonindigenous person, although many find this term pejorative, calling themselves mestizo or rejecting any ethnic identity (see Chapter 3).
Latinx (English/Spanish)	Refers to all people with Latin American heritage within and beyond the United States. While commonly written as "Latino," I use the "x" on the end to signal a politics that does not adhere to gender binaries (signaled as a/o in Spanish, as feminine/masculine signifiers) unless referring to a specifically gendered individual.
mano dura (Spanish)	Literally "iron fist"; refers to militarized policing with strong law enforcement discretion and weak due process guarantees.
Mayas	Approximately twenty-one peoples, of which Q'eqchi' is one, whose origin predates the Spanish invasion that are legally recognized in the Guatemalan Constitution. As they are differentiated ethnolinguistically, the number of Maya peoples estimated ranges from twenty to twenty-three, depending on the status of dialects within a language. Maya peoples are generally treated as a "minority" ethnicity but are 40–60 percent of Guatemala's population.
mestizo	Ethnoracial term that denotes a mix of Spanish and Indigenous heritage. In rejecting the term *ladino,* some Guatemalans today call themselves mestizo in association with the positive connotation of the Mexican "cosmic race," together the best of Spanish and Indigenous for a singular national identity. In recent decades, this ideology has been widely critiqued for denial of African diaspora heritage in Latin America as well as for the appropriation of indigenous culture that recognizes a folkloric past while denying the possibility of indigenous futures.
MICUDE (Ministerio de Cultura y Deportes)	Guatemalan Ministry of Culture and Sports, which controls protected areas that are declared cultural patrimonies, including those of archaeological importance (see Chapter 4).
OAP (Oxlajuj Ajpop)	K'iche' for "Ministry of Mayan Culture." This Guatemalan nongovernmental organization works for recognition of Mayan spiritual places and practices at the national level (see Chapter 4).

PAC (Patrullas de Autodefensa Civil)	Civil Self-Defense Patrols, community-level paramilitary militias during the civil war. All men and boys living in rural communities had to participate in PACs, whose activities ranged from irregular patrols to committing massacres.
Q'eqchi' (also Q'eqchi' Maya; spelled Kekchi in Belize)	Of the Mayas, Q'eqchi's have the second-largest population and cover the most Guatemalan territory (as well as part of Belize). Nonetheless, Q'eqchi's are socially marginalized to a greater extent than other Maya peoples; many scholars account for this with the fact that they are 90 percent monolingual, often excluding them from political conversations held in Spanish.
SAA (Secretaría de Asuntos Agrarios)	Secretariat of Agrarian Affairs, charged with mediating land conflicts when there are disputes over boundaries, titling, and/or ownership.
tzuultaq'a ("tsool-tacqk-aah")	A Q'eqchi' term that literally translates as "hill-valley," *tzuultaq'a* refers to the spirit that makes the landscape come alive and is the ultimate owner of any given place. Q'eqchi's ask for permission from the *tzuultaq'a* to hunt, plant, and live where they live (see Chapter 4).
United Nations Declaration on the Rights of Indigenous Peoples (UNDRIP)	Adopted by the UN General Assembly in 2007, declared the legal rights of Indigenous peoples to live free of discrimination and to exercise self-determination. Guatemala was one of 143 countries that voted in favor of the Declaration; the United States was one of 4 countries that voted against it, although in 2010 President Obama endorsed it. UNDRIP is not legally binding.
Victims' Committee (Comité de Víctimas)	Communities wishing to participate in the United Nations–sponsored National Reparations Program must form a committee to put together the paperwork to document family members killed or disappeared during the civil war, violence suffered, and homes lost. As of 2017, some verified victims still had not received reparations payments from massacres in the early 1980s.

REFERENCES

Adams, AE (2001). The transformation of the *tzuultaq'a:* Jorge Ubico, Protestants and other Verapaz Maya at the crossroads of community, state and transnational interests. *Journal of Latin American Anthropology* 6: 198–233.

Adams, RN (2005). The evolution of racism in Guatemala: Hegemony, science, and antihegemony. *Histories of Anthropology Annual* 1: 132–180.

Adams, RN, and Bastos, S (2003). *Las relaciones étnicas en Guatemala, 1944-2000.* Antigua, Guatemala: Centro de Investigaciones Regionales de Mesoamérica.

Agamben, G (1998). *Homo sacer: Sovereign power and bare life.* Stanford, CA: Stanford University Press.

Agnew, J (2003). *Geopolitics: Re-visioning world politics.* Abingdon, UK: Routledge.

Aguirre Beltrán, G (1979). *Regions of refuge.* Washington, DC: Society for Applied Anthropology.

Ahmed, S (2016). "Bogus." Feminist Killjoys, https://feministkilljoys.com/2016/10/27 /bogus/. Accessed October 27, 2016.

Alonso-Fradejas, A (2012). Land control-grabbing in Guatemala: The political economy of contemporary agrarian change. *Canadian Journal of Development Studies* 33: 509–528.

——— (2015). Anything but a story foretold: Multiple politics of resistance to the agrarian extractivist project in Guatemala. *Journal of Peasant Studies*: 1–27.

Alonso-Fradejas, A, Alonzo, F, and Durr, J (2008). Caña de azúcar y palma africana: Comestibles para un nuevo ciclo de acumulación y dominio en Guatemala. Ciudad de Guatemala: Instituto de Estudios Agrarios y Rurales, Coordinación de ONG y Cooperativas.

Anderson, B (1991). *Imagined communities: Reflections on the origin and spread of nationalism.* Revised ed. New York: Verso.

Anderson, M (2009). *Black and indigenous: Garifuna activism and consumer culture in Honduras.* Minneapolis: University of Minnesota Press.

Anonymous (2014). "Desplegarán PNC y Ejército en las Verapaces." Prensa Libre, http://www
.prensalibre.com/noticias/justicia/policias-retenidos-verapaces-mauricio_lopez-Reten-
cion_de_policias-Raxruha-Alta_Verapaz_0_1195080599.html. Accessed September 8,
2014.

Anzaldúa, G (2012). *Borderlands/La Frontera: The new mestiza.* 4th ed. San Francisco: Aunt
Lute Books.

Appelbaum, NP, Macpherson, AS, and Rosemblatt, KA (2003). Racial nations. In NP
Appelbaum, AS Macpherson, and KA Rosemblatt (eds.), *Race and nation in modern
Latin America* (pp. 1–31). Chapel Hill: University of North Carolina.

Arias, O, and Nations, JD (1992). A call for Central American peace parks. In S Annis (ed.),
Poverty, natural resources, and public policy in Central America (pp. 43–58). Oxford, UK:
Transaction Publishers.

Ayres, E (2003). *Mapping the nature of biodiversity.* Washington, DC: World Watch.

Ayuso, T (2012). "Central America: The downward spiral of the Northern Triangle." http://
www.noria-research.com/wp-content/uploads/2012/07/Tomas-pour-PDF.pdf. Accessed
August 3, 2013.

Ball, P, Kobrak, P, and Spirer, H (1999). *State violence in Guatemala: A quantitative reflec-
tion.* Washington, DC: American Association for the Advancement of Science.

Bang, M, Medin, D, Washinawatok, K, et al. (2010). Innovations in culturally based science
education through partnerships and community. In *New Science of Learning* (pp. 569–
592). New York: Springer.

Basso, KH (1996). *Wisdom sits in places: Landscape and language among the Western Apache.*
Albuquerque: University of New Mexico Press.

Bastos, S, and Camus, M (1993). *Quebrando el silencio: Organizaciones del pueblo maya y sus
demandas (1986–1992).* Ciudad de Guatemala: Facultad Latinoamericano de Ciencias
Sociales.

——— (2003). *Entre el Mecapal y el Cielo: Desarrollo del moviemiento Maya de Guatemala.*
Guatemala: Facultad Latinoamericano de Ciencias Sociales, Guatemala y Cholsamaj.

Ba Tiul, KM (2007). Movimiento Winaq, la controversia: Ni a la izquierda ni a la derecha.
Izquierdas y construcción de orden democrático en Guatemala. Working paper of the
seminar "Left and Building Democratic Order in Guatemala," organized by FLACSO
Guatemala and the Friedrich Ebert Foundation.

Benjamin, W (1968). *Illuminations.* New York: Random House.

Bianet Castellanos, M (in press). Introduction: Settler colonialism in Latin America. *American Quarterly* 69(4).

Black, G (1984). *Garrison Guatemala.* New York: Monthly Review Press.

Bobrow-Strain, A (2007). *Intimate enemies: Landowners, power and violence in Chiapas.*
Durham, NC: Duke University Press.

Bocarejo, D, and Ojeda, D (2016). Violence and conservation: Beyond unintended consequences and unfortunate coincidences. *Geoforum* 69: 176–183.

Borras, SM, Hall, R, Scoones, I, et al. (2011). Towards a better understanding of global land
grabbing: an editorial introduction. *Journal of Peasant Studies* 38: 209–216.

Borras, SM, Franco, JC, Gómez, S, et al. (2012). Land grabbing in Latin America and the
Caribbean. *Journal of Peasant Studies* 39: 845–872.

Brett, R (2007). *Una Guerra sin Batallas: Del odio, la violencia y el miedo en el Ixcán y el Ixil, 1972–1983*. Ciudad de Guatemala: F&G Editores.

Brockett, CD (1998). *Land, power and poverty: Agrarian transformation and political conflict in Central America*. Boulder, CO: Westview.

Brockington, D, Duffy, R, and Igoe, J (2008). *Nature unbound: Conservation, capitalism, and the future of protected areas*. London: Earthscan.

Brooks, LT (2008). *The common pot: The recovery of native space in the Northeast*. Minneapolis: University of Minnesota Press.

Bryan, J (2012). Rethinking territory: Social justice and neoliberalism in Latin America's territorial turn. *Geography Compass* 6: 215–226.

Burgos-Debray, E (ed.) (1984). *I, Rigoberta Menchú: An Indian woman in Guatemala*, London: Verso.

Burrell, JL (2010). In and out of rights: Security, migration, and human rights talk in postwar Guatemala. *Journal of Latin American and Caribbean Anthropology* 15: 90–115.

———— (2013). *Maya after war: Conflict, power, and politics in Guatemala*. Austin: University of Texas Press.

Büscher, B, and Ramutsindela, M (2016). Green violence: Rhino poaching and the war to save Southern Africa's peace parks. *African Affairs* 115: 1–22.

Cacho, LM (2012). *Social death: Racialized rightlessness and the criminalization of the unprotected*. New York: New York University Press.

Cárdenas, R (2012). Green multiculturalism: Articulations of ethnic and environmental politics in a Colombian 'black community'. *Journal of Peasant Studies* 39: 309–333.

Carroll, C (2015). *Roots of our renewal: Ethnobotany and Cherokee environmental governance*. Minneapolis: University of Minnesota Press.

Casasola, O (1968). *Grandezas y Miserias del Petén*. Guatemala City: n.p.

Casaús Arzú, ME (2010). *Guatemala: Linaje y racismo; revisada y ampliada* (4th ed.). Guatemala City: F&G Editores.

Casolo, JJ (2011). Unthinkable rebellion and the praxis of the possible: Ch'orti' Campesin@ struggles in Guatemala's Eastern Highlands. PhD dissertation, University of California–Berkeley.

Castillo, G, and Martoccia, H (2011). "*Kaibiles* dan entrenamiento militar a *Zetas* en Guatemala." *La Jornada*, http://www.jornada.unam.mx/2011/04/07/politica/009n1pol. Accessed August 5, 2015.

CEH (1999). "Guatemala: Memoria del silencio." Comisión para el Esclarecimiento Histórico, http://shr.aaas.org/guatemala/ceh/mds/spanish/toc.html. Accessed January 4, 2011.

Chakrabarty, D (2008). *Provincializing Europe: Postcolonial thought and historical difference*. Princeton, NJ: Princeton University Press.

Chapin, M (2004). A challenge to conservationists. *World Watch Magazine* (pp. 17–31).

Cohen, S (2002). *Folk devils and moral panics: The creation of the mods and rockers*. London: Routledge.

Cohn, DV, Gonzalez-Barrera, A, and Cuddington, D (2013). "Remittances to Latin America recover—but not to Mexico." Pew Research Center, http://www.pewhispanic.org/2013/11/15/remittances-to-latin-america-recover-but-not-to-mexico/. Accessed July 21, 2015.

Cojtí Cuxil, D (1992). Problemas de 'la identidad nacional' Guatemalteca. In D Rodríguez Guaján (ed.), *Cultura Maya y Políticas de Desarrollo* (pp. 116–133). Guatemala: Coordinadora Cakchiquel de Desarrollo Integral.

—— (1996). The politics of Maya revindication. In EF Fischer and R McKenna Brown (eds.), *Maya cultural activism in Guatemala* (pp. 19–50). Austin: University of Texas Press.

—— (1997). *El movimiento Maya (en Guatemala) = Ri Maya' moloj pa Iximulew.* Guatemala City: Editorial Cholsamaj.

—— (2004). Heterofobia y racismo guatemalteco: Perfil y estado actual. In C Arenas Bianchi, CR Hale, and G Palma Murga (eds.), *Racismo en Guatemala? Abriendo el debate sobre el tema tabú* (pp. 193–216). Guatemala: Asociación para el Avance de las Ciencias Sociales en Guatemala.

—— (2007). Indigenous nations in Guatemalan democracy and the state: A tentative assessment. *Social Analysis: The International Journal of Social and Cultural Practice* 51: 124–147.

Comisión Interministerial (1980). *Volumen I: Problemas y Potencialidades de la Franja Transversal del Norte.* Guatemala: Secretaría General del Consejo Nacional de Planificación Económica, Gobierno de Guatemala.

Conklin, BA, and Graham, LR (1995). The shifting middle ground: Amazonian Indians and eco-politics. *American Anthropologist* 97: 695–710.

Conklin, HC (1961). The study of shifting cultivation. *Current Anthropology* 2: 27–61.

Conservation International (1997). "Protecting a fragile planet: 1997 annual report." Conservation International, http://www.conservation.org/Documents/CI_Annual_Report_1997.pdf.

Coronil, F (1997). *The magical state: Nature, money and modernity in Venezuela.* Chicago: University of Chicago Press.

—— (2008). Elephants in the Americas? Latin American postcolonial studies and global decolonization. In M Moraña, E Dussel, and C Jáuregui (eds.), *Coloniality at large: Latin America and the postcolonial debate* (pp. 396–416). Durham, NC: Duke University Press.

Coronil, F, and Skurski, J (2006a). Dismembering and remembering the nation: The semantics of political violence in Venezuela. In F Coronil and J Skurski (eds.), *States of violence* (pp. 83–152). Ann Arbor: University of Michigan Press.

—— (eds.) (2006b). *States of violence.* Ann Arbor: University of Michigan Press.

Corzo Márquez, AR (1999). Vida, migración, tragedia. *Delaware Review of Latin American Studies* 1, http://www.udel.edu/LAS/vol1Corzo.html.

Coulthard, GS (2010). Place against empire: Understanding indigenous anti-colonialism. *Affinities: A Journal of Radical Theory, Culture, and Action* 4: 79–83.

—— (2014). *Red skin, White masks: Rejecting the colonial politics of recognition.* Minneapolis: University of Minnesota Press.

Craib, RB (2004). *Cartographic Mexico: A history of state fixations and fugitive landscapes.* Durham, NC: Duke University Press.

Crampton, J (2007). Maps, race and Foucault: Eugenics and territorialization following World War I. In J Crampton and S Elden (eds.), *Space, knowledge and power: Foucault and geography* (pp. 223–244). Burlington, VT: Ashcroft.

Cronon, W (1983). *Changes in the land: Indians, colonists and the ecology of New England.* New York: Hill and Wang.

———— (1995a). The trouble with wilderness: Or, getting back to the wrong nature. In W Cronon (ed.), *Uncommon ground: Toward reinventing nature* (pp. 69–90). New York: Norton.

———— (ed.) (1995b). *Uncommon ground: Toward reinventing nature.* New York: Norton.

Danner, M (1994). *The massacre at El Mozote: A parable of the Cold War.* New York: Vintage Books.

De Angelis, M (2001). Marx and primitive accumulation: The continuous character of capital's enclosures. *The Commoner* 2: 1–22.

De la Cadena, M (2015). *Earth beings: Ecologies of practice across Andean worlds.* Durham, NC: Duke University Press.

Deloria, V (1998). *Playing Indian.* New Haven, CT: Yale University Press.

———— (2003). *God is red: A native view of religion.* Golden, CO: Fulcrum Publishing.

Deloria, V, Jr., and Wildcat, DR (2001). *Power and place: Indian education in America.* Golden, CO: Fulcrum Publishing.

Denevan, W (1992). The pristine myth: The landscape of the Americas in 1492. *Annals of the Association of American Geographers* 82: 369–385.

De Schutter, O (2011). How not to think of land-grabbing: Three critiques of large-scale investments in farmland. *Journal of Peasant Studies* 38: 249–279.

Devine, J (2014). Counterinsurgency ecotourism in Guatemala's Maya Biosphere Reserve. *Environment and Planning D: Society and Space* 32: 984–1001.

Dove, MR (1983). Theories of swidden agriculture, and the political economy of ignorance. *Agroforestry Systems* 1: 85–99.

———— (1993). A revisionist view of tropical deforestation and development. *Environmental Conservation* 20: 17–24.

Dowie, M (2011). *Conservation refugees: The hundred-year conflict between global conservation and native peoples.* Cambridge, MA: MIT Press.

Du Bois, WEB (2007). *Darkwater: Voices from within the veil.* New York: Oxford University Press.

Duffy, R (2016). War, by conservation. *Geoforum* 69: 238–248.

Dunlap, A, and Fairhead, J (2014). The militarisation and marketisation of nature: An alternative lens to 'climate-conflict'. *Geopolitics*: 1–25.

Dussell, ED (1995). *The invention of the Americas: Eclipse of the "other" and the myth of modernity.* New York: Continuum.

Elden, S (2009). *Terror and territory: The spatial extent of sovereignty.* Minneapolis: University of Minnesota Press.

———— (2010). Land, terrain, territory. *Progress in Human Geography* 34: 799–817.

Esquit, E (2012). Nationalist contradictions: Pan-Mayanism, representations of the past, and the reproduction of inequalities in Guatemala. In FE Mallon (ed.), *Decolonizing native histories: Collaboration, knowledge, and language in the Americas* (pp. 196–218). Durham, NC: Duke University Press.

Euraque, DA, Gould, JL, and Hale, CR (eds.) (2004). *Memorias del Mestizaje: Cultura política en Centroamérica de 1920 al presente.* Guatemala: Centro de Investigaciones Regionales de Mesoamérica.

Fairhead, J, Leach, M, and Scoones, I (2012). Green grabbing: A new appropriation of nature? *Journal of Peasant Studies* 39: 237–261.

Falla, R (1993). *Masacres de la selva: Ixcán, Guatemala, 1975–1982*. Guatemala: Editorial Universitaria.

Fanon, F (2004 [1961]). *The wretched of the Earth*. New York: Grove.

——— (2008). *Black skin, white Masks*. New York: Grove.

Farnham, TJ (2007). *Saving nature's legacy: Origins of the idea of biological diversity*. New Haven, CT: Yale University Press.

Ferguson, J (2015). *Give a man a fish: Reflections on the new politics of distribution*. Durham, NC: Duke University Press.

Ferradás, C (2004). Environment, security, and terrorism in the trinational frontier of the Southern Cone. *Identities* 11: 417–442.

Fledderjohn, DC, and Thompson, DC (1982). Final report: Northern transversal strip land resettlement project. AID Project No. 520-0233-Small Farmer Development, Agricultural Cooperative Development International and US Agency for International Development.

Foucault, M (1978). *The history of sexuality*, Vol. 1, *An introduction*. New York: Vintage Books.

——— (1991). *Discipline and punish: The birth of the prison*. New York: Vintage Books.

——— (2003). *Society must be defended: Lectures at the Collége de France, 1975–1976*. New York: Picador.

——— (2008). *The birth of biopolitics: Lectures at the College of France, 1978–79*. New York: Palgrave Macmillan.

Galemba, RB (2012). Remapping the border: Taxation, territory, and (trans)national identity at the Mexico-Guatemala border. *Environment and Planning D: Society and Space* 30: 822–841.

Garrard-Burnett, V (2010). *Terror in the land of the Holy Spirit: Guatemala under General Efraín Ríos Montt, 1982–1983*. Oxford: Oxford University Press.

Gibson-Graham, JK (2006). *The end of capitalism (as we knew it): A feminist critique of political economy* (2nd ed.). Oxford, UK: Blackwell.

Gill, L (2004). *The School of the Americas: Military and political violence in the Americas*. Durham, NC: Duke University Press.

Gilmore, RW (2002). Fatal couplings of power and difference: Notes on racism and geography. *Professional Geographer* 54: 15–24.

——— (2004). Race and globalization. In RJ Johnston, PL Taylor, and MJ Watts (eds.), *Geographies of global change: Remapping the world* (2nd ed., pp. 261–274). Malden, MA: Wiley.

——— (2007). *Golden gulag: Prisons, surplus, crisis, and opposition in globalizing California*. Berkeley: University of California Press.

Gilroy, P (1993a). *The black Atlantic: Modernity and double consciousness*. Cambridge, MA: Harvard University Press.

——— (1993b). One nation under a groove: The cultural politics of "race" and racism in Britain. In DT Goldberg (ed.), *Anatomy of racism* (pp. 263–282). Minneapolis: University of Minnesota Press.

Gleijeses, P (1991). *Shattered Hope: The Guatemalan revolution and the United States*. Princeton, NJ: Princeton University Press.

Gobierno de Guatemala (1964). *Ante-Proyecto de Desarrollo Integral Sebol—Chinaja*. Ciudad de Guatemala: Secretaría de Planificación y Programación de la Presidencia Centro de Documentación 0001181.

———— (1985). *Polos de Desarrollo*. Ciudad de Guatemala: Editorial del Ejército.

Goeman, M (2013). *Mark my words: Native women mapping our nations*. Minneapolis: University of Minnesota Press.

Goldberg, DT (2002). *The racial state*. Malden, MA: Blackwell.

———— (2009). *The threat of race: Reflections on racial neoliberalism*. Malden, MA: Wiley-Blackwell.

Goldman, M (2005). *Imperial nature: The World Bank and struggles for social justice in the age of globalization*. New Haven, CT: Yale University Press.

Gómez, I, and Méndez, VE (2005). *Association of Forest Communities of Petén, Guatemala (ACOFOP): Context, accomplishments and challenges*. Bogor Barat, Indonesia: Center for International Forestry Research.

González Ponciano, JR (2004). La visible invisibilidad de blancura y el ladino como no blanco en Guatemala. In DA Euraque, JL Gould, and CR Hale (eds.), *Memorias del Mestizaje: Cultura política en Centroamérica de 1920 al presente* (pp. 111–132). Guatemala: Centro de Investigaciones Regionales de Mesoamérica.

Gordillo, G (2004). *Landscapes of devils: Tensions of place and memory in the Argentinean Chaco*. Durham, NC: Duke University Press.

Gordon, ET; Gurdián, GC, and Hale, CR (2003). Rights, resources and the social memory of struggle: Reflections on a study of indigenous and black community land rights on Nicaragua's Atlantic coast. *Human Organization* 62: 369–381.

Gott, R (2007). Latin America as a white settler society. *Bulletin of Latin American Research* 26: 269–289.

Gould, JL (1998). *To die in this way: Nicaraguan Indians and the myth of mestizaje*. Durham, NC: Duke University Press.

Gould, KA (2006). Land regularization on agricultural frontiers: The case of Northwestern Peten, Guatemala. *Land Use Policy* 23: 395–407.

———— (2009). Marking land, producing markets: The making of a rural Guatemalan land market. *Geography* (pp. 227). PhD dissertation, University of British Columbia, Vancouver.

———— (2014). Everyday expertise: Land regularization and the conditions for land grabs in Petén, Guatemala. *Environment and Planning A* 46: 2353–2368.

Gould, KA, Carter, DR, and Shrestha, RK (2006). Extra-legal land market dynamics on a Guatemalan agricultural frontier: Implications for neoliberal land policies. *Land Use Policy* 23: 408–420.

Graham, R (ed.) (1990). *The idea of race in Latin America, 1870–1940*. Austin: University of Texas Press.

Grandia, L (2006). Unsettling: Land dispossession and enduring inequity for the Q'eqchi' Maya in the Guatemalan and Belizean frontier colonization process. PhD dissertation, University of California–Berkeley.

———— (2009a). Milpa matters: The Maya community of Toledo versus the government of Belize. In BR Johnston and S Slyomovics (eds.), *Waging war, making peace: Reparations and human rights* (pp. 153–181). Walnut Creek, CA: Left Coast Press.

———— (2009b). Silent spring in the land of eternal spring: The germination of a conservation conflict. *Current Conservation* 3: 10–13.

———— (2009c). *Tz'aptz'ooqeb': El despojo recurrente al pueblo q'eqchi'*. Guatemala: Asociación para el Avance de las Ciencias Sociales en Guatemala.

———— (2012). *Enclosed: Conservation, cattle, and commerce among the Q'eqchi' Maya low-landers.* Seattle: University of Washington Press.

Grandin, G (2000). *The blood of Guatemala: A history of race and nation.* Chapel Hill: Duke University Press.

———— (2004). *The last colonial massacre: Latin America and the Cold War.* Chicago: University of Chicago Press.

———— (2005). The instruction of great catastrophe: Truth commissions, national history, and state formation in Argentina, Chile, and Guatemala. *American Historical Review* 110: 46–67.

Gregory, D (2004). *The colonial present: Afghanistan, Palestine, Iraq.* Malden, MA: Blackwell.

Grünberg, G (2003). *Tierras y territorios indígenas en Guatemala.* Guatemala: FLACSCO, MINUGUA, CONTIERRA.

Grünberg, J, Grandia, L, Milián, B, et al. (2012). *Tierra e Igualdad: Desafíos para la Administración de Tierras en Petén, Guatemala.* Guatemala City: Fondo Fiduciario para el Desarrollo Ambiental y Socialmente Sostenible (TFESSD) de los Gobiernos de Noruega y Finlandia con el Departamento de Agricultura y Desarrollo Rural para América Latina y el Caribe (LCSAR) del Banco Mundial.

Gudmundson, L (2010). What difference did color make? Blacks in the 'white towns' of western Nicaragua in the 1880s. In L Gudmundson and J Wolfe (eds.), *Blacks and blackness in Central America: Between race and place* (pp. 209–245). Durham, NC: Duke University Press.

Gudmundson, L, and Wolfe, J (eds.) (2010a). *Blacks and blackness in Central America: Between race and place:* Durham, NC: Duke University Press.

———— (2010b). Introduction. In L Gudmundson and J Wolfe (eds.), *Blacks and blackness in Central America: Between race and place* (pp. 1–23). Durham, NC: Duke University Press.

Hale, CR (2002). Does multiculturalism menace? Governance, cultural rights and the politics of identity in Guatemala. *Journal of Latin American Studies* 34: 485–524.

———— (2005). Neoliberal multiculturalism. *PoLAR: Political and Legal Anthropology Review* 28: 10–28.

———— (2006). *Más que un Indio (More than an Indian): Racial ambivalence and neoliberal multiculturalism in Guatemala.* Santa Fe: School of American Research Press.

Hall, S (1992). Race, culture, and communications: Looking backward and forward at cultural studies. *Rethinking Marxism* 5: 10–18.

———— (1995). Fantasy, identity, politics. In E Carter, J Donald, and J Squires (eds.), *Cultural remix: Theories of politics and the popular* (pp. 63–72). London: Lawrence & Wishart.

———— (1996). When was the 'post-colonial'? Thinking at the limit. In I Chambers and L Curti (eds.), *The post-colonial question: Common skies, divided horizons* (pp. 242–260). New York: Routledge.

Hall, S, Critcher, C, Jefferson, T, et al. (2013). *Policing the crisis: Mugging, the state and law and order* (35th anniversary ed.). New York: Palgrave Macmillan.

Harris, CI (1993). Whiteness as property. *Harvard Law Review* 106: 1707–1791.

Hart, G (2002). *Disabling globalization: Places of power in post-apartheid South Africa.* Berkeley: University of California Press.

Hartman, SV (1997). *Scenes of subjection: Terror, slavery, and self-making in nineteenth-century America.* Oxford: Oxford University Press.

Harvey, N (2001). Globalisation and resistance in post–Cold War Mexico: Difference, citizenship and biodiversity conflicts in Chiapas. *Third World Quarterly* 22: 1045–1061.

Hecht, SB, and Cockburn, A (1989). *The fate of the forest: Developers, destroyers and defenders of the Amazon.* New York: Harper Perennial.

HoSang, DM, LaBennett, O, and Pulido, L (eds.) (2012). *Racial formation in the twenty-first century.* Berkeley: University of California Press.

Huet, A (2008). *Nos Salvó la Sagrada Selva: La memoria de veinte comunidades q'eqchi'es que sobrevivieron al genocidio.* Cobán, Guatemala: ADICI Wakliiqo/Maya Na'oj.

Hurtado Paz y Paz, L (2008). *Dinámicas Agrarias y Reproducción Campesina en la Globalización: El caso de Alta Verapaz, 1970–2007.* Guatemala: F&G Editores.

ICG (2011). "Guatemala: Drug trafficking and violence." International Crisis Group, http://www.crisisgroup.org/en/regions/latin-america-caribbean/guatemala/139-guatemala-drug-trafficking-and-violence.aspx. Accessed October 11, 2011.

IDS (1961). *The Sebol Project: A proposed extension of the rural development program in Guatemala.* Dirección General de Asuntos Agrarios, Guatemala: International Development Services and U.S. Operations Mission to Guatemala.

INAB (2003). *Plan Maestro 2004–2009, Parque Nacional Laguna Lachuá, Cobán, Alta Verapaz.* Guatemala: Proyecto Laguna Lachuá, Unión Mundial para la Naturaleza (IUCN), Embajada Real de los Países Bajos, Instituto Nacional de Bosques (INAB).

IUCN and INAB (1997). *Diagnóstico General de las Comunidades Colindantes con el Parque Nacional Laguna Lachuá.* Guatemala: Union Mundial para la Naturaleza (IUCN) and Instituto Nacional de Bosques (INAB).

Jacoby, K (2001). *Crimes against nature: Squatters, poachers, thieves, and the hidden history of American conservation.* Berkeley: University of California Press.

——— (2008). *Shadows at dawn: A borderlands massacre and the violence of history.* New York: Penguin.

Jones, JR (1990). *Colonization and environment: Land settlement projects in Central America.* Tokyo: United Nations University Press.

Kauanui, JK (2008). *Hawaiian blood: Colonialism and the politics of sovereignty and indigeneity.* Durham, NC: Duke University Press.

Kelly, AB (2011). Conservation practice as primitive accumulation. *Journal of Peasant Studies* 38: 683–701.

Kelly, AB, and Ybarra, M (2016). Green security in protected areas. *Geoforum* 69: 171–175.

Kelly, JF (2014). "SOUTHCOM chief: Central America drug war a dire threat to U.S. national security." http://www.militarytimes.com/article/20140708/NEWS01/307080064/SOUTHCOM-chief-Central-America-drug-war-dire-threat-U-S-national-security. Accessed September 1, 2014.

King, A (1974). *Cobán and the Verapaz: History and cultural process in northern Guatemala.* New Orleans: Middle American Research Institute, Tulane University.

Kit, WA (1998). *Costumbre,* conflict and consensus: Kekchí-*finquero* discourse in the Alta Verapaz, Guatemala, 1880–1930. PhD dissertation, Tulane University.

Knight, A (1990). Racism, revolution and *Indigenismo:* Mexico, 1910–1940. In R Graham (ed.), *The idea of race in Latin America, 1870–1940* (pp. 71–113). Austin: University of Texas Press.

Konefal, B (2010). *For every Indio who falls: A history of Maya activism in Guatemala, 1960–1990.* Albuquerque: University of New Mexico Press.

Kosek, J (2006). *Understories: The political life of forests in northern New Mexico.* Durham, NC: Duke University Press.

Kull, C (2004). *Isle of fire: The political ecology of landscape burning in Madagascar.* Chicago: University of Chicago Press.

Laclau, E, and Mouffe, C (2014). *Hegemony and socialist strategy: Towards a radical democratic politics* (2nd ed.). London: Verso.

LaFeber, W (1993). *Inevitable revolutions: The United States in Central America.* New York: Norton.

Le Bot, Y (1995). *La Guerra en Tierras Mayas: Comunidad, violencia, y modernidad en Guatemala (1970–1992).* Mexico City: Fondo de Cultura Económica.

Li, TM (2007). *The will to Improve: Governmentality, development and the practice of politics.* Durham, NC: Duke University Press.

——— (2010). To make live or let die? Rural dispossession and the protection of surplus populations. *Antipode* 41: 66–93.

Loperena, C (2017). Settler violence? Race and emergent frontiers of progress in Honduras. *American Quarterly* 69(4).

Lovell, GW, and Lutz, C (1995). *Demography and empire: A guide to the population history of Spanish Central America, 1500–1821.* Boulder, CO: Westview.

Lowe, L (1996). *Immigrant acts: On Asian American cultural politics.* Durham, NC: Duke University Press.

Lunstrum, E (2014). Green militarization: Anti-poaching efforts and the spatial contours of Kruger National Park. *Annals of the Association of American Geographers* 104: 816–832.

Lunstrum, E, and Ybarra, M (in press). Deploying difference: Security threat narratives and displacement from protected areas. *Conservation and Society.*

MAGA (2012). "2013." Ministerio de Agricultura de Guatemala (MAGA), http://web.maga .gob.gt/wp-content/blogs.dir/13/files/2013/widget/public/franja_transversal.pdf. Accessed April 13, 2017.

Manz, B (1988). *Refugees of a hidden war: The aftermath of counterinsurgency in Guatemala.* Albany: State University of New York Press.

——— (2004). *Paradise in ashes: A Guatemalan journey of courage, terror and hope.* Berkeley: University of California Press.

Martínez, O (2016). *A history of violence: Living and dying in Central America.* New York: Verso Books.

Martínez Peláez, S (2009). *La Patria del Criollo: An interpretation of colonial Guatemala.* Durham, NC: Duke University Press.

Mayorga, JP (2012). "Guatemala pide que se investiguen abusos de México contra refugiados." CNN México, http://mexico.cnn.com/nacional/2012/01/12/guatemala-pide-que-se-investiguen-abusos-de-mexico-contra-refugiados. Accessed August 24, 2015.

Mbembe, A (1992). The banality of power and the aesthetics of vulgarity in the postcolony. *Public Culture* 4: 1–30.

——— (2003). Necropolitics. *Public Culture* 15: 11–40.

McAllister, C, and Nelson, DM (2013). Aftermath: Harvests of violence and histories of the future. In C McAllister and DM Nelson (eds.), *War by other means: Aftermath in postgenocide Guatemala* (pp. 1–48). Durham, NC: Duke University Press.

McCreery, D (1994). *Rural Guatemala, 1760–1940.* Stanford, CA: Stanford University Press.

McSweeney, K, Nielsen, EA, Taylor, MJ, et al. (2014). Drug policy as conservation policy: Narco-deforestation. *Science* 343: 489–490.

Menjívar, C, and Rodriguez, N (2005). *When states kill: Latin America, the U.S., and technologies of terror*. Austin: University of Texas Press.

Middleton, ER (2011). *Trust in the land: New directions in tribal conservation*. Tucson: University of Arizona Press.

——— (2010). A political ecology of healing. *Journal of Political Ecology* 17: 1–28.

——— (2015). Jahát Jatítotodom*: Toward an indigenous political ecology. In RL Bryant (ed.), *The international handbook of political ecology* (pp. 561–576). Northmpton, MA: Edward Elgar Publishing.

Mignolo, WD (2007). Introduction: Coloniality of power and de-colonial thinking. *Cultural Studies* 21: 155–167.

Milián, B, Grünberg, G, and Cho, BM (2002). *La Conflictividad Agraria en las Tierras Bajas del Norte de Guatemala: Petén y la Franja Transversal del Norte*. Ciudad de Guatemala: FLACSO, MINUGUA, CONTIERRA.

Mittermeier, RA, Myers, N, Thomsen, JB, et al. (1998). Biodiversity hotspots and major tropical wilderness areas: Approaches to setting conservation priorities. *Conservation Biology* 12: 516–520.

Mollett, S (2011). Racial narratives: Miskito and colono land struggles in the Honduran Mosquitia. *Cultural Geographies* 18: 43–62.

——— (2016). The power to plunder: Rethinking land grabbing in Latin America. *Antipode* 48: 412–432.

Mollett, S and Faria, C (2013). Messing with gender in feminist political ecology. *Geoforum* 45: 116–125.

Moodie, E (2010). *El Salvador in the aftermath of peace: Crime, uncertainty, and the transition to democracy*. Philadelphia: University of Pennsylvania Press.

Mora, AP (2011). *Border dilemmas: Racial and national uncertainties in New Mexico, 1848–1912*. Durham, NC: Duke University Press.

Morales, MR (2004). Esencialismo 'Maya', mestizaje ladino y nación intercultural: Los discursos en debate. In C Arenas Bianchi, CR Hale, and G Palma Murga (eds.), *Racismo en Guatemala? Abriendo el debate sobre el tema tabú* (pp. 279–360). Guatemala: Guatemala, Asociación para el Avance de las Ciencias Sociales en Guatemala.

Moraña, M, Dussel, E, and Jáuregui, CA (eds.) (2008). *Coloniality at large: Latin America and the postcolonial debate*. Durham, NC: Duke University Press.

Morgensen, SL (2011). *Spaces between us: Queer settler colonialism and indigenous decolonization*. Minneapolis: University of Minnesota Press.

Morrissey, JA (1978). A missionary directed resettlement project among the highland Maya of western Guatemala. PhD dissertation, Stanford University.

Movimiento Indio Tojil (1985). "Guatemala, de la republica burguesa centralista a la republica popular federal." Princeton University Digital Library, http://pudltest.princeton .edu/objects/145a5df4-3b82-46a6-b6ec-333b8ac052a6.

Mutimer, D (1999). Beyond strategy: Critical thinking and the new security studies. *Contemporary Security and Strategy*: 77–101.

Myers, N (1988). Threatened biotas: "Hot spots" in tropical forests. *The Environmentalist* 8: 187–208.

Nations, JD (2006). *The Maya Tropical Forest: People, parks and ancient cities.* Austin: University of Texas Press.

Nations, JD, and Nigh, RB (1978). Cattle, cash, food, and forest: The destruction of the American tropics and the Lacandon Maya Alternative. *Culture & Agriculture* 16: 1–6.

Nelson, DM (1988). *Guatemala, Polos de Desarrollo: El caso de desestructuración de las comunidades indígenas, Tomo II.* Mexico City: Editorial Praxis.

——— (1999). *A finger in the wound: Body politics in quincentennial Guatemala.* Berkeley: University of California Press.

——— (2003). "The more you kill the more you will live": The Maya, "race," and biopolitical hopes for peace in Guatemala. In DS Moore, A Pandian, and J Kosek (eds.), *Race, nature and the politics of difference* (pp. 122–146). Durham, NC: Duke University Press.

——— (2009). *Reckoning: The ends of war in Guatemala.* Durham, NC: Duke University Press.

Neumann, R (1998). *Imposing wilderness: Struggles over livelihood and nature preservation in Africa.* Berkeley: University of California Press.

Ng'weno, B (2007). *Turf wars: Territory and citizenship in the contemporary state.* Stanford, CA: Stanford University Press.

Nietschmann, B (1995). Defending the Miskito reefs with maps and GPS: Mapping with sail, scuba and satellite. *Cultural Survival Quarterly* 18: 34–37.

Nightingale, AJ (2003). A feminist in the forest: Situated knowledges and mixing methods in natural resource management. *ACME: An International E-Journal for Critical Geographies* 2: 77–90.

——— (2016). Adaptive scholarship and situated knowledges? Hybrid methodologies and plural epistemologies in climate change adaptation research. *Area* 48: 41–47.

Nordstrom, C (2004). *Shadows of War: Violence, power and international profiteering in the twenty-first century.* Berkeley: University of California Press.

Offen, KH (2003). The territorial turn: Making black territories in Pacific Colombia. *Journal of Latin American Geography* 2: 43–73.

Omi, M, and Winant, H (1994). *Racial formation in the United States from the 1960s to the 1990s* (2nd ed.). New York: Routledge.

Osorno, DE (2012). *La Guerra de los Zetas: Viaje por la frontera de la necropolítica.* Mexico City: Grijalbo.

Padilla, LA (ed.) (1990). *Guatemala: Polos de desarrollo: El caso de desestructuración de las comunidades indígenas, Tomo I.* México City: Centro de Estudios Integrados de Desarrollo Comunal.

Paley, D (2012). "Nueva Esperanza [New Hope]." Canadian Dimension, https://canadiandimension.com/articles/view/nueva-esperanza. Accessed December 30, 2014.

——— (2014). *Drug war capitalism.* Edinburgh, UK: AK Press.

Parenti, C (2011). *Tropic of chaos: Climate change and the new geography of violence.* New York: Nation Books.

Patterson, O (1982). *Slavery and social death: A comparative study.* Cambridge, MA: Harvard University Press.

Payeras, M (1980). *Los Días de la Selva.* La Habana: Casa de las Américas.

Peacock, SC, and Beltrán, A (2002). "Hidden powers in post-conflict Guatemala: Illegal armed groups and the forces behind them." Washington Office on Latin America, http://www.wola.org/media/Guatemala/HiddenPowersFull.pdf.

Peet, R, and Hartwick, E (2009). *Theories of development: Contentions, arguments, alternatives* (2nd ed.). New York: Guilford.

Pellow, DN (2016). Toward a critical environmental justice studies: Black lives matter as an environmental justice challenge. *Du Bois Review: Social Science Research on Race* 13(2): 221–236.

Peluso, NL (1992). *Rich forests, poor people: Resource control and resistance in Java.* Berkeley: University of California Press.

——— (1995). Whose woods are these? Counter-mapping forest territories in Kalimantan, Indonesia. *Antipode* 27: 383–406.

Peluso, NL, and Vandergeest, P (2001). Genealogies of the political forest and customary rights in Indonesia, Malaysia and Thailand. *Journal of Asian Studies* 60: 761–812.

——— (2011). Political ecologies of war and forests: Counterinsurgencies and the making of national natures. *Annals of the Association of American Geographers* 101: 587–608.

Perelman, M (2000). *The invention of capitalism: Classical political economy and the secret history of primitive accumulation.* Durham, NC: Duke University Press.

Ponciano, I (1998). Forestry policy and protected areas in the Petén, Guatemala. In RB Primack (ed.), *Timber, tourists, and temples: Conservation and development in the Maya Forest of Belize, Guatemala, and Mexico* (pp. 99–110). Washington, DC: Island Press.

Povinelli, EA (2002). *The cunning of recognition: Indigenous alterities and the making of Australian multiculturalism.* Durham, NC: Duke University Press.

Pulido, L (2015). Geographies of race and ethnicity 1: White supremacy vs white privilege in environmental racism research. *Progress in Human Geography* 39: 809–817.

——— (2016). Flint, environmental racism, and racial capitalism. *Capitalism Nature Socialism* 27(3): 1–16.

——— (2017). Geographies of race and ethnicity II: Environmental racism, racial capitalism and state-sanctioned violence. *Progress in Human Geography.* 41(4) 524–533.

Rabinow, P (1989). *French modern: Norms and forms of the social environment.* Cambridge, MA: MIT Press.

Ranganathan, M (2016). Thinking with Flint: Racial liberalism and the roots of an American water tragedy. *Capitalism Nature Socialism* 27(3): 17–33.

Razack, S (1998). *Looking white people in the eye: Gender, race, and culture in courtrooms and classrooms.* Toronto: University of Toronto Press.

Redford, K (1991). The ecologically noble savage. *Cultural Survival Quarterly* 15: 46–48.

REMHI (1998). *Guatemala: Nunca más.* Guatemala City: Recuperación de Memoria Histórica (REMHI), Oficina de Derechos Humanos del Arzobispado de Guatemala.

Remijnse, S (2002). *Memories of violence: Civil patrols and the legacy of conflict in Joyabaj, Guatemala.* Amsterdam: Rozenberg Publishers.

Rifkin, M (2009). *Manifesting America: The imperial construction of US national space.* Oxford: Oxford University Press.

Robbins, P (2012). *Political ecology: A critical introduction* (2nd ed.). Malden, MA: Wiley.

Robinson, CJ (2000). *Black Marxism: The making of the black radical tradition* (2nd ed.). Chapel Hill: University of North Carolina Press.

Rodríguez, D (2006). *Forced passages: Imprisoned radical intellectuals and the US prison regime.* Minneapolis: University of Minnesota Press.

Rodríguez, J, Taber, A, Daszak, P, et al. (2007). Globalization of conservation: a view from the south. *Science* 317: 755–756.

Rosset, P, Patel, R, and Courville, M (eds.) (2006). *Promised land: Competing visions of agrarian reform*. Oakland, CA: Food First Books.

SAA (2014). "Memoria de Labores, 2013–2014." Secretaría de Asuntos Agrarios (SAA), Gobierno de Guatemala, http://portal.saa.gob.gt/images/stories/PagInicio/2014/docs /MEMORIA 2014 SAA web.pdf. Accessed August 24, 2015.

Said, EW (1978). *Orientalism*. New York: Pantheon Books.

Saldaña-Portillo, MJ (2015). *Indian given: Racial geographies across Mexico and the United States*. Durham, NC: Duke University Press.

Samayoa Rivera, RO (n.d.). *Colonización de El Petén: Paralelo 17*. Gobierno de Guatemala, http://oskicat.berkeley.edu/record=b10961952~S1/.

Sanford, V (2013). El genocidio no es un enfrentamiento armado. *El Faro*, March 19, https://elfaro.net/es/201303/opinion/11448/El-genocidio-no-es-un-enfrentamiento-armado.htm, accessed August 18, 2017.

Sawyer, S (2004). *Crude chronicles: Indigenous politics, multinational oil, and neoliberalism in Ecuador*. Durham, NC: Duke University Press.

Schirmer, J (1998). *The Guatemalan military project: A violence called democracy*. Philadelphia: University of Pennsylvania Press.

Schlesinger, SC, and Kinzer, S (2005). *Bitter fruit: The story of the American coup in Guatemala* (2nd ed.). Cambridge, MA: Harvard University Press.

Schmitt, C (1985). *Political theology: Four chapters on the concept of sovereignty*. Chicago: University of Chicago Press.

Schwartz, NB (1990). *Forest society: A social history of Petén, Guatemala*. Philadelphia: University of Pennsylvania Press.

——— (2000). *Etnicidad, Regionalismo y el Estado: Las relaciones étnicas y sociales cambiantes en Petén, 1944–2000*. Antigua, Guatemala: Centro de Investigaciones Regionales de Mesoamérica.

Schwartz, NB, Corzo Márquez, AR, Calderón, E, et al. (1996). *Socioeconomic monitoring and evaluation of Conservation International/ProPeten Project in the Maya Biosphere Project, 1992–1996*. Guatemala: Conservation International and U.S. Agency for International Development.

Silva, DF (2007). *Toward a global idea of race*. Minneapolis: University of Minnesota Press.

Simpson, A (2011). On ethnographic refusal: Indigeneity, 'voice' and colonial citizenship. *Junctures: The Journal for Thematic Dialogue* 9: 67–80.

——— (2014). *Mohawk interruptus: Political life across the borders of settler states*. Durham, NC: Duke University Press.

Slater, C (2002). *Entangled Edens*. Berkeley: University of California Press.

Smith, A (2012). Indigeneity, settler colonialism, white supremacy. In D Martinez HoSang, O LaBennett, and L Pulido (eds.), *Racial formation in the twenty-first century* (pp. 66–93). Berkeley: University of California Press.

——— (2014). Native studies at the horizon of death: Theorizing ethnographic entrapment and settler self-reflexivity. In A Simpson and A Smith (eds.), *Theorizing native studies* (pp. 207–234). Durham, NC: Duke University Press.

Smith, CA (ed.) (1990). *Guatemalan Indians and the state, 1540–1988*. Austin: University of Texas Press.

Smith, N, and Katz, C (1993). Grounding metaphor: Towards a spatialized politics. In M Keith and S Pile (eds.), *Place and the politics of identity* (pp. 67–83). London: Routledge.

Smyth, F (2005). "The untouchable narco-state: Guatemala's army defies DEA." George Washington University, http://www.gwu.edu/~nsarchiv/NSAEBB/NSAEBB169/TO_11%5B1%5D.18.05_guatemala.pdf. Accessed January 10, 2012.

Solano Ponciano, L (2005). *Guatemala: Petróleo y minería en las entrañas del poder*. Ciudad de Guatemala: Inforpress Centroamérica.

——— (2013). Development and/as dispossession: Elite networks and extractive industry in the Franja Transversal del Norte. In C McAllister and DM Nelson (eds.), *War by other means: Aftermath in post-genocide Guatemala* (pp. 119–142). Durhman, NC: Duke University Press.

Spade, D (2015). *Normal life: Administrative violence, critical trans politics, and the limits of law*. Durham, NC: Duke University Press.

Speed S (in press). Structures of settler capitalism in Abya Yala. *American Quarterly* 69(4).

Stasiulis, D, and Yuval-Davis, N (eds.) (1995). *Unsettling settler societies: Articulations of gender, race, ethnicity and class*. London: Sage.

Stepan, NL (1991). *The hour of eugenics: Race, gender and nation in Latin America*. Ithaca, NY: Cornell University Press.

——— (2001). *Picturing tropical nature*. Ithaca, NY: Cornell University Press.

Stocks, A (2002). The struggle for Q'eqchi' community conservation and management of Mayan sacred (cave) sites: The case of the Caves of Candelaria and Bombil pek in Alta Verapaz, Guatemala. Paper presented at Protecting the Cultural and Natural Heritage in the Western Hemisphere: Lessons from the Past; Looking to the Future, Harvard University.

Stoler, AL (1995). *Race and the education of desire: Foucault's history of sexuality and the colonial order of things*. Durham, NC: Duke University Press.

——— (2002). *Carnal knowledge and imperial power: Race and the intimate in colonial rule*. Berkeley: University of California Press.

Stoll, D (ed.) (1990). *Is Latin America turning Protestant? The politics of evangelical growth*, Berkeley: University of California Press.

Sturm, C (2011). *Becoming Indian: The struggle over Cherokee identity in the twenty-first century*. Santa Fe, NM: School for Advanced Research Press.

Sundberg, J (1998a). NGO landscapes in the Maya Biosphere Reserve, Guatemala. *Geographical Review* 88: 388–412.

——— (1998b). Strategies for authenticity, space, and place in the Maya Biosphere Reserve, Petén, Guatemala. *Conference of Latin Americanist Geographers Yearbook 1998* 21: 85–96.

——— (1999). Conservation encounters: NGOs, local people, and changing cultural landscapes. PhD dissertation, University of Texas at Austin.

——— (2003a). Conservation and democratization: Constituting citizenship in the Maya Biosphere Reserve, Guatemala. *Political Geography* 22: 715–740.

——— (2003b). Masculinist epistemologies and the politics of fieldwork in Latin Americanist geography. *Professional Geographer* 55: 180–190.

——— (2004). Identities in the making: Conservation, gender and race in the Maya Biosphere Reserve, Guatemala. *Gender, Place & Culture* 11: 43–66.

———— (2005). Looking for the critical geographer, or why bodies and geographies matter to the emergence of critical geographies of Latin America. *Geoforum* 36: 17–28.

———— (2008). Placing race in environmental justice research in Latin America. *Society and Natural Resources* 21: 569–582.

———— (2014). Decolonizing posthumanist geographies. *Cultural Geographies* 21: 33–47.

Tallbear, K (2011). Why interspecies thinking needs indigenous standpoints. American Anthropological Association Meeting, Montreal, CA.

Taracena Arriola, A (2002). *Etnicidad, Estado y Nación en Guatemala, 1808–1944*. Antigua, Guatemala: Nawal Wuj.

———— (2004). Guatemala: El debate historiográfico en torno al *mestizaje*, 1970–2000. In DA Euraque, JL Gould, and CR Hale (eds.), *Memorias del mestizaje: Cultural política en Centroamérica de 1920 al presente* (pp. 79–110). Antigua, Guatemala: Centro de Investigaciones Regionales de Mesoamérica.

Taussig, M (1987). *Shamanism, colonialism, and the wild man: A study in terror and healing*. Chicago: University of Chicago Press.

Taylor, D (1997). *Disappearing acts: Spectacles of gender and nationalism in Argentina's "dirty war"*. Durham, NC: Duke University Press.

Thompson, EP (1975). *Whigs and hunters: The origin of the Black Act*. London: Allen Lane.

Todd, Z (2016). An indigenous feminist's take on the ontological turn: 'Ontology' is just another word for colonialism. *Journal of Historical Sociology* 29: 4–22.

Tuck, E (2009). Suspending damage: A letter to communities. *Harvard Educational Review* 79: 409–428.

Tuck, E, and McKenzie, M (2016). *Place in research: Theory, methodology and methods*. London: Routledge.

Tuck, E, and Yang, KW (2012). Decolonization is not a metaphor. *Decolonization: Indigeneity, Education & Society* 1: 1–40.

Tuhiwai Smith, L (2012). *Decolonizing methodologies: Research and indigenous peoples* (2nd ed.). New York: Zed Books.

UNODC (2013). "Global study on homicide." United Nations Office on Drugs and Crime, http://www.unodc.org/documents/gsh/pdfs/2014_GLOBAL_HOMICIDE_BOOK_web.pdf. Accessed May 22, 2015.

USAID (1990). Guatemala project paper: Maya Biosphere Project. In *Project 520-0395*, P (ed). Guatemala City: USAID Mission to Guatemala.

———— (1995). Project paper supplement: Maya Biosphere Project Petén activities. In *Project 520-0395*, DP (ed). Guatemala City: USAID Mission to Guatemala.

Van Ausdal, SK (2002). Development and discourse among the Maya of southern Belize. *Development and Change* 32: 577–606.

Vandergeest, P, and Peluso, NL (1995). Territorialization and state power in Thailand. *Theory and Society* 24: 385–426.

Velázquez Nimatuj, IA (2008). *Pueblos indígenas, Estado y Lucha por Tierra en Guatemala: Estrategias de sobrevivencia y negociación ante la desigualdad globalizada*. Guatemala: Asociación para el Avance de las Ciencias Sociales en Guatemala.

———— (2012). Desafío Maya: ¿"objetos de estudio" o sujetos intelectuales? *Latin American Research Review*: 21–23.

Viaene, L (2010). The internal logic of the cosmos as 'justice' and 'reconciliation': Micro-level Perceptions in post-conflict Guatemala. *Critique of Anthropology* 30: 287–312.

Vidal, J (2008). "The great green land grab." The Guardian, http://www.theguardian.com /environment/2008/feb/13/conservation. Accessed August 26, 2014.

Vizenor, G, Tuck, E, and Yang, KW (2014). Resistance in the blood. *Youth resistance research and theories of change:* 107–117.

Vizenor, GR (1994). *Manifest manners: Postindian warriors of survivance.* Middleton, CT: Wesleyan University Press.

Wagner, R (2001). *The history of coffee in Guatemala.* Bogotá, Colombia: Villegas Editores.

Wainwright, J (2008). *Decolonizing Development: Colonial power and the Maya.* Malden, MA: Blackwell.

Wainwright, J, and Bryan, J (2009). Cartography, territory, property: Postcolonial reflections on indigenous counter-mapping in Nicaragua and Belize. *Cultural Geographies* 16: 153–178.

Wakild, E (2011). *Revolutionary parks: Conservation, social justice, and Mexico's national parks, 1910–1940.* Tucson: University of Arizona Press.

Warren, KB (1998a). *Indigenous movements and their critics: Pan-Mayanism and ethnic resurgence in Guatemala.* Princeton, NJ: Princeton University Press.

——— (1998b). Indigenous movements as a challenge to the unified social movement paradigm for Guatemala. In S Alvarez, E Dagnino, and A Escobar (eds.), *Cultures of politics, politics of cultures: Re-visioning Latin American social movements* (pp. 165–195). Boulder, CO: Westview.

Watts, M (1992). Space for everything (a commentary). *Cultural Anthropology* 7: 115–129.

Weld, KA (2014). *Paper cadavers: The archives of dictatorship in Guatemala.* Durham, NC: Duke University Press.

West, P (2006). *Conservation is our government now: The politics of ecology in Papua New Guinea.* Durham, NC: Duke University Press.

Wilson, R (1995). *Maya resurgence in Guatemala: Q'eqchi' experiences.* Norman: University of Oklahoma Press.

Wolfe, P (2006). Settler colonialism and the elimination of the native. *Journal of Genocide Research* 8: 387–409.

——— (2008). Structure and event: Settler colonialism and the question of genocide. In AD Moses (ed.), *Empire, colony, genocide: Settler colonialism and the question of genocide* (pp. 102–132). Oxford, UK: Berghahn Books.

Wolford, W (2010). *This land is ours now: Social mobilization and the meanings of land in Brazil.* Durham, NC: Duke University Press.

Wright, MW (2011). Necropolitics, narcopolitics, and femicide: Gendered violence on the Mexico-U.S. border. *Signs* 36: 707–731.

——— (2012). Wars of interpretations. *Antipode* 44: 564–580.

Ybarra, M (2011a). Privatizing the Tzuultaq'a? Private property and spiritual reproduction in post-war Guatemala. *Journal of Peasant Studies* 38: 793–810.

——— (2011b). Slashed and burned: The debate over privatization of Q'eqchi' lands in northern Guatemala. *Society & Natural Resources* 24: 1027–1041.

———— (2012). Taming the jungle, saving the Maya Forest: Sedimented counterinsurgency practices in contemporary Guatemalan conservation. *Journal of Peasant Studies* 39: 479–502.

———— (2013). "You cannot measure a tzuultaq'a": Cultural politics at the limits of liberal legibility. *Antipode* 45: 584–601.

———— (2014). "Don't just pay it back, pay it forward: From accountability to reciprocity in research relationships." *Journal of Research Practice,* http://jrp.icaap.org/index.php/jrp/article/view/407/358. Accessed July 10, 2014.

———— (2016). "Blind passes" and the production of green security through violence on the Guatemalan border. *Geoforum* 69: 194–206.

Ybarra, M, Obando Samos, O, Grandia, L, et al. (2012). *Tierra, migración y vida en Petén, 1999–2009.* Guatemala City: CONGCOOP-IDEAR.

Zilberg, E (2011). *Space of detention: The making of a transnational gang crisis between Los Angeles and San Salvador.* Durham, NC: Duke University Press.

INDEX

www.ingramcontent.com/pod-product-compliance
Lightning Source LLC
Chambersburg PA
CBHW030329270326
41926CB00010B/1558